D1596757

CHINA

AND

KOREA

Northeast Asia

CHINA
AND
KOREA

DYNAMIC RELATIONS

Chae-Jin Lee
in collaboration with Doo-Bok Park

The Hoover Institution gratefully acknowledges the generous support of the Korea Foundation.

Hoover Press Publication No. 434

First printing, 1996

02 01 00 99 98 97 96   9 8 7 6 5 4 3 2 1

First paperback printing, 1996

02 01 00 99 98 97 96   9 8 7 6 5 4 3 2 1

Manufactured in the United States of America
The paper used in this publication meets the minimum requirements of American National Standard for Information Services—Permanence of Paper for Printed Library Materials, ANSI Z39.48-1984.

Library of Congress Cataloging-in-Publication Data

Lee, Chae-Jin, 1936–
    China and Korea: dynamic relations / Chae-Jin Lee, in collaboration with Doo-Bok Park.
        p.   cm.
    Includes bibliographical references and index.
    ISBN 0-8179-9421-1 (acid-free). — ISBN 0-8179-9422-X (acid-free)
        1. China—Relations Korea. 2. Korea—Relations China. I. Park, Doo-Bok II. Title.
K740.5.K6L44 1996
327.510519—dc20   96–3792
                                                       CIP

To

GEORGE M. BECKMANN

AND

KIM JUN-YOP,

WHO HAVE BEEN

EXTRAORDINARILY

SUPPORTIVE OF MY

ACADEMIC AND

PROFESSIONAL PURSUITS

CONTENTS

Preface ix

Chapter 1 INTRODUCTION 1

Chapter 2 CHINA AND THE KOREAN WAR 7

China's Decision to Enter the War 7

Military Campaigns 23

Armistice Negotiations 37

Chapter 3 MILITARY POLICY 59

Military Alliance 59

China's Détente Policy 65

Sino-Soviet Competition 70

Policy Cleavages 78

Sino-Soviet Reconciliation 84

The End of the Cold War 89

Chapter 4 DIPLOMATIC ISSUES 99

Relations with Pyongyang 99

The United Nations and Korea 102

Relations with Seoul 105

Seoul's Northern Diplomacy 112

China's Two-Korea Policy 122

Chapter 5 ECONOMIC RELATIONS 133

China and North Korea 134

China and South Korea 142

New Modes of Trade and Investment 151

Chapter 6 CONCLUSION 169

Notes 177

Bibliography 201

Index 211

PREFACE

• •

While studying political science at Seoul National University after the Korean War, I became aware of China's growing importance in the Korean Peninsula and therefore resolved to understand China's domestic politics and foreign policies. Over the years I have published a number of studies dealing with China's contemporary international relations. In this volume I have tried to bring the insights acquired in those studies to my earlier intellectual concern—the unfolding dynamic relations between China and Korea.

Much of the information was gathered during frequent research trips to China and South Korea. I learned a great deal from a variety of friends, scholars, diplomats, politicians, and businesspeople in both countries, as well as from my travel to North Korea. I am indebted to many individuals but particularly appreciate the contributions of Cui Longhao, Ding Min, Ge Zhenjia, Han Xu, Huang Hua, Li Changhuan, Pu Shan, Shi Min, Tao Bingwei, Yang Tongfang, Yu Xinchun, and Zhou Erliu in China; Chung Chong Wook, Hwang Byung Tai, Lee Sang Ock, Park Yong Doh, Roh Jae Won, and Yoo Chong Ha in South Korea; Ogawa Heishiro, Okonogi Masao, and Sato Hideo in Japan; Alexander Panov and Boris Zanegin in the former Soviet Union; and Daniel Bays, Thomas Bernstein, Charles Freeman, Norman Hastings, Ilpyong Kim, Chong-Sik Lee, Hong Yung Lee, Jonathan Pollack, Kenneth Quinones, Robert A. Scalapino, Dae-Sook Suh, and Philip West in the United States. I wish to thank Son Chu Whan and Choi Chang Yoon for a research grant from the Korea Foundation;

Jack Stark, Donald A. Henriksen, Anthony Fucaloro, and Kyung S. Lee for their encouragement; Mary Anderson, Patrick Coaty, Gabrielle Giner, Gwendolyn Hoyt, William Ing, June Kim, Theodore J. Lee, Therese Mahoney, and Wang Li for their assistance; and Patricia A. Baker, Jennifer E. Billstrom, Elizabeth Ann Wood, and other staff members of the Hoover Institution Press for editorial guidance. The Keck Center for International and Strategic Studies at Claremont McKenna College provided a favorable environment for my research.

The surnames have been written first for all Chinese, Korean, and Japanese individuals mentioned in the text (except Syngman Rhee). I have used the pinyin system to transliterate Chinese terms (except Chiang Kai-shek, Chiang Yen-shih, Kuomintang, Lee Teng-hui, and Li Hung-chang).

I was fortunate to be able to collaborate with Doo-Bok Park, an outstanding Korean specialist of Chinese affairs, in writing the chapter on economic relations. His thoughtful comments and suggestions on other chapters were also valuable.

None of the persons or organizations mentioned here should be held responsible for any part of my interpretations or for any omissions I may have made.

CHINA

AND

KOREA

The Korean Peninsula

CHINA

RUSSIA

Tumen River

Chonji Lake

Sonbong

Najin

Chongjin

Yalu River

Dandong

Taeyudong
Onjong

Sinuiju

Unsan

Chongchon R.

Hamhung

Pidan Island

NORTH KOREA

Pyongyang

Nampo

Wonsan

Tongchon

DMZ

Panmunjom

Kaesong

Haeju

38th Parallel

Munsan

Chunchon

Seoul

Chipyongli

Inchon

Han River

SOUTH KOREA

Kunsan

Nakdong R.

Pohang

Taegu

Masan

Pusan

Mokpo

Cheju Island

JAPAN

Chapter 1
INTRODUCTION

• •

The East Asian countries of China and Korea share a long history of complex, intimate relations. Bound together by geography, they are also linked by cultural affinities. For centuries their relationship was symbolized by a hierarchical tributary system in which China, the "Middle Kingdom," invoking its heavenly mandate (*tianming*), required neighboring "barbarians" such as the Koreans to pay homage to it as the center of the cosmic universe and to send tributary missions to the Chinese courts.[1] Korea's tributary relations with China began as early as the fifth century, were regularized during the Koryo dynasty (918–1392), and became fully institutionalized during the Yi dynasty (1392–1910).[2]

The Sinocentric tributary system differed from naked territorial absorption or outright political domination because it was based less on force than on persuasion and emulation and was as much cultural as political. This system also promoted commercial and cultural exchanges. John K. Fairbank and Ssu-yu Teng suggest that

> Since all foreign relations in the Chinese view were ipso facto tributary relations, it followed that all types of international intercourse, if they occurred at all in the experience in China, had to be fitted into the tributary system.[3]

China thus regarded Korea as a small vassal state populated by its younger brothers, reflecting the significant asymmetry between them in terms of size, population, and power. As long as the Korean governments faithfully fulfilled their tributary obligations, however, China did not interfere in their day-to-day internal affairs.

At times of great upheaval, however, the rulers of China or the dominant forces in Manchuria did not hesitate to invade or occupy Korea, notably during the Khitan and Jurchen invasions in the tenth and eleventh centuries and the Mongol invasions in the thirteenth century:

> The most severe suffering and destruction resulted from the invasion of 1254, when the Mongols took back with them more than 200,000 captives, left countless dead, and reduced the entire region through which they passed to ashes. It was also during this time that many irreplaceable cultural treasures were lost, outstanding among them the woodblocks for the Tripitaka produced two hundred years earlier.[4]

Likewise, the Manchus invaded Korea in 1627 and 1636 and extracted the promise of allegiance and tributary missions from the Korean king. Moreover, the Chinese, during the Hideyoshi invasions of Korea (1592–98) and the first Sino-Japanese War (1894–95), recognized that the Korean Peninsula could serve as a convenient "invasion corridor" to and from Japan.

Even though Korea maintained frequent and extensive tributary relations with the Middle Kingdom, there were deep policy cleavages among Korean leaders in their attitudes toward China. On the one hand, the kings of the Yi dynasty gained political legitimacy from China's recognition, which helped assure their dynastic stability for five centuries. The Koreans also eagerly borrowed from the Confucian civilization, accommodated China's hegemonic status, and relied on China's advice and protection. On the other hand, however, they resented China's condescension, resisted its military pressures, suffered from the exorbitant financial burden of tributary relations, and desired to seek independence from China. During the period of imperialism toward the end of the nineteenth century, disillusionment came when China not only failed to protect Korea from Japan and Russia but pursued a highhanded interventionist policy toward Korea. In 1888, for example, O. N. Denny, who, as foreign adviser, vented the Korean king's frustrations, asserted that in view of the "long train of cruel, unjust and tyrannical conduct" committed by Chinese officials, "China's professions of friendship for Korea, under the claim of suzerainty, become simply monstrous in their sincerity."[5]

The first Sino-Japanese War terminated China's claim of suzerainty over Korea. Strengthened by the successful Meiji reforms, Japan had decisively defeated the huge but weak China and, in the process, inflicted intense human suffering and widespread destruction on Korea. In the treaty of peace signed by Ito Hirobumi and Li Hung-chang on April 17, 1895, in Shimonoseki, Article One stated:

> China recognizes definitively the full and complete independence and autonomy of Corea [*sic*], and in consequence, the payment of tribute and the performance of ceremonies and formalities by Corea to China in derogation of such independence and autonomy, shall wholly cease for the future.[6]

China's lack of a direct role in Korea lasted for more than half a century.

The "independence" of Korea was short lived, however. The Russo-Japanese War (1904–5) demonstrated Japan's preeminent military power in East Asia and destroyed Korean sovereignty. In the Treaty of Portsmouth, concluded on September 5, 1905, under President Theodore Roosevelt's mediation, Russia acknowledged Japan's paramount political, military, and economic interests in Korea.[7] In the secret Taft-Katsura agreement (1905), the United States also recognized Japan's control over Korea in exchange for Japanese acceptance of U.S. hegemony over the Philippines. The same year Ito Hirobumi imposed a protectorate treaty on the weakened Yi dynasty and single-handedly dictated Korea's foreign and domestic affairs. Five years later, Japan annexed Korea outright.

The Japanese Empire brutally colonized Korea and made it a strategic and economic base for its aggressive campaigns against Manchuria and China proper during the 1930s and early 1940s. A large number of Chinese and Korean patriots collaborated both at home and abroad against Japan's imperialist designs for a "Greater East Asia Co-prosperity Sphere." The seeds for Korea's eventual partition were sown during the second Sino-Japanese War (1937–45), when the Kuomintang government at Chongqing embraced the Korean provisional government (which Syngman Rhee had led as president in the early 1920s) and the Korean Restoration Army; the Chinese Communist Party at Yanan supported the North China Korean Volunteer Army (led by Mu Chong) and the Northeast Anti-Japanese United Army (in which Kim Il Sung served as a division commander).[8]

After Japan's defeat in World War II, the United States and the Soviet

Union carved up Korea along the 38th parallel and for three years were an occupation force in their respective areas. When the United States and the Soviet Union failed to achieve a negotiated unification of Korea in 1948, each power sponsored the inauguration of its own client state—the Republic of Korea (South Korea), headed by President Syngman Rhee, and the Democratic People's Republic of Korea (North Korea), under Premier Kim Il Sung. Meanwhile, Mao Zedong triumphed in the Chinese civil war, driving Chiang Kai-shek to Taiwan and proclaiming the founding of the People's Republic of China on October 1, 1949, in Beijing. Hence both China and Korea suffered the tragedy of national division and became key players in the worldwide cold war.

Conceived as a socialist state with profound ideological commitments and international revolutionary fervor, China under Mao Zedong espoused a rigid "two-camp" outlook in world politics, dividing the globe into the socialist camp headed by the Soviet Union and the capitalist camp led by the United States. This perspective manifested itself in the Sino-Soviet military alliance and China's costly involvement in the Korean War. That war opened the door for China's return to the Korean Peninsula after a fifty-five-year hiatus and at the same time cemented the U.S. policy of containment and isolation against China.

Despite China's general posture of peaceful coexistence during the latter half of the 1950s and the first half of the 1960s, it engaged in an escalating dispute with Soviet "revisionism," threatened Taiwan by military means, and invaded India in 1962. At the height of the Great Proletarian Cultural Revolution, the Chinese zealously pursued a militant, revolutionary, and isolationist foreign policy, articulated the theory of the "three worlds," and championed Third World interests. The People's Republic of China (PRC) has thus sought to restore the grandeur of the Middle Kingdom, but it has also demonstrated a remarkable degree of flexibility, initiating both gradual and dramatic changes in its domestic policies and foreign affairs. In the 1970s it castigated the Soviet Union as the principal threat to its national security and world peace and wanted the United States, Japan, Western Europe, and China to form a united front against Soviet "hegemonism." In this connection the Chinese normalized their relations with the United States and Japan, joined the United Nations and other international organizations, and abrogated their thirty-year alliance with the Soviet Union.

Guided by Deng Xiaoping's pragmatic policies in the post-Mao era, the Chinese again modified their approach, declaring that "revolution is not exportable" and that "there is no such thing as world revolution in state relations."[9] They discarded the inefficient Maoist model of economic self-reliance and launched a bold open-door economic policy. Believing that the two superpowers—the United States and the Soviet Union—had reached a global strategic equilibrium, China did not want to align itself with either country but instead maintained a foreign policy of independence and peaceful cooperation. This evenhanded nonalignment policy led to President George Bush's China visit in February 1989 and President Mikhail Gorbachev's summit meeting with Deng Xiaoping in May 1989.

In the process of reconfiguring their policies, the Chinese have learned that there are neither permanent friends nor permanent enemies in international relations and that the hyperbolic rhetoric of socialist revolution and international solidarity is no longer crucial to fulfilling their national interests. After the demise of the Soviet Union and the end of the cold war, China has, almost by default, emerged as the guardian of the few remaining socialist states. Yet, in view of their four modernizations campaign, the Chinese have moved away from an ideologically inspired outlook on regional and global issues and have opted for diplomatic resolutions of international conflicts.

The foregoing generalizations about Chinese policy adaptations also apply to the Korean Peninsula. Although the Chinese continued to uphold the legacy of the Korean War—honoring their military alliance with North Korea and supporting its diplomatic and economic activities—they have transformed their overall relationship with South Korea. During the 1980s extreme hostility was replaced by functional cooperation in such areas as trade, sports, communications, and exchanges of delegates and relatives. Despite North Korea's disapproval, the Chinese responded favorably to South Korea's ambitious "northern diplomacy," which sought to improve relations with China, the Soviet Union, Eastern Europe, and, secondarily, North Korea. As long as South Korea did not undermine Chinese policy priorities or provoke North Korea, they accepted it as a constructive approach that was consistent with their posture toward Taiwan, the United States, and Japan. China attempted to exercise a moderating influence over North Korea and finally normalized diplomatic relations with South Korea in 1992. With its de jure two-Korea policy consummated, China's role has become an increasingly important in the management of Korean affairs.

In view of the dynamic nature of China's contemporary relations with the Korean Peninsula, this study begins with an examination of the PRC's participation in the Korean War. Then addressed is the subsequent evolution of Chinese military, diplomatic, and economic policies toward North and South Korea, which are viewed as having been largely determined by three considerations: (1) China's internal political developments and shifting policy priorities, especially in regard to ideology, security, and economy; (2) China's evolving perceptions of North Korean and South Korean intentions and capabilities; and (3) China's changing relations with the Soviet Union (Russia), the United States, and Japan.

Chapter Two

CHINA AND
THE KOREAN WAR

• •

CHINA'S DECISION TO ENTER THE WAR

On June 25, 1950, less than a year after its establishment, the People's Republic of China faced a major international crisis when war erupted on the neighboring Korean Peninsula. Still struggling to end their own civil war against the Kuomintang, Mao and his associates were also trying to rehabilitate China's war-torn economic system. New governmental machinery, both central and local, had yet to be constructed, and the leaders urgently needed to end the chaos and create a viable community in the sprawling country. Even though the Sino-Soviet Treaty of Friendship, Alliance and Mutual Assistance had been concluded on February 14 of that year, the young nation was struggling to become part of the world community.[1] Despite all these compelling demands, PRC leaders could not afford to underestimate the potentially dangerous spillover effect of the Korean War, which began when Premier Kim Il Sung of North Korea, in an attempt to unify the country militarily, initiated a large-scale attack against South Korea across the 38th parallel on June 25.

There has been little consensus about the roles played in the war by the major powers and North Korea.[2] Western scholars long assumed that Mao was surprised by Kim Il Sung's decision to invade South Korea and that the war forced him to postpone his plans to "liberate" Taiwan and Tibet. Most PRC documents, memoirs, and studies about the Korean War

are conspicuously silent on this question, although a few continue to maintain the fiction that U.S. "imperialists" and their South Korean "puppets" started the Korean War.

In a classic study on China's entry into the Korean War, Allen Whiting
states that "there is no clear evidence of Chinese participation in the planning and preparation of the Korean War." Pu Shan, who took part in the
Korean armistice negotiations, remembers that the Chinese were completely surprised by the outbreak of the war. Hao Yufan and Zhai Zhihai,
too, argue that "Beijing was not informed and thus not prepared for North
Korea's military action" because early in 1950 China decided to implement a large demobilization that would reduce its People's Liberation Army
(PLA) from 5.4 million to 3 million. Also China "paid very little attention
to the Korean Peninsula and knew very little about the North Korean
situation." The Chinese embassy in Pyongyang was not operative in June
1950, and Chinese ambassador Ni Zhiliang had not yet arrived in North
Korea. In addition China had a limited force (namely, the 42d army) stationed along the Yalu River, indicating that Mao was unaware of Kim's
military plan.[3]

The thesis of China's noninvolvement in Kim's decision sharply con-
trasts with the argument that focuses on the supposed rivalry and suspicion between Stalin and Mao. Marshall Shulman suggests that because
Stalin assumed that Mao was prepared to round out his victory by attacking the Western salient in Korea, the Nationalist stronghold on Taiwan,
and the Western colonial positions in Indochina, Stalin was compelled to
approve Kim's plan for military invasion so that he could preserve his
dominant position in North Korea and exercise his influence over China.
Adam Ulam goes so far as to conclude that Stalin instigated the Korean
imbroglio "for the specific purpose of discouraging the Chinese Communists from breaking away from Soviet tutelage."[4]

On the basis of archival materials newly available in Russia, Kathryn
Weathersby contends that Stalin initially preferred the traditional czarist
policy of maintaining a balance of power on the Korean Peninsula but
that he finally, after repeated requests, agreed in April 1950 to support
Kim's plan.[5] Citing Stalin's relationship with Mao as a major factor, she
explains that if Stalin refused to support Kim Il Sung's goal of reunifying
his country, Stalin would again be open to the charge of hindering the
cause of revolution in the East. Added to this contest for the leadership of
Asian revolutionary movements was Stalin's calculation that, after war
began, the United States would protect Chiang Kai-shek on Taiwan, thus

blocking Mao's possible rapprochement with the United States and necessitating Mao's dependency on the Soviet Union. Stalin, then, shrewdly regarded the Korean War, coupled with the Sino-Soviet treaty, as a device to prevent Mao from becoming another Tito. This conspiracy theory, though not without merit, underestimates Mao's strategies and actions in regard to the Korean War.

New evidence suggests that Mao was fully aware of the general scenario, if not the precise timing and manner, of Kim's invasion plan and that Mao encouraged and assisted in the military preparations. Even though Mao was less involved in planning the Korean War than was Stalin, the Chinese connections with Kim were substantial even before June 25, 1950. According to newly released Russian diplomatic documents, Kim Il Sung reported to Soviet ambassador Terentii Shtykov that in Beijing in May 1949 Mao promised Kim Il (director of the Bureau of Political Affairs, Korean People's Army) that two Chinese divisions composed of ethnic Koreans stationed in Manchuria would be immediately transferred to North Korea and that another division of ethnic Koreans committed to a battle against the Kuomintang forces in southern China would be sent to North Korea at a later date. Mao advised Kim Il that North Korea should be prepared to launch either a surprise attack or a protracted war against South Korea at any time. In the event of a protracted war, Japan might intervene, Mao cautioned, but he told Kim Il that, if this were to happen, it should not be a cause for alarm because the Soviet Union and China were nearby. He also promised that, if it became absolutely necessary, China could send its forces to Korea. Yet Mao advised Kim Il that North Korea should not attack South Korea in the near future because the general international situation was not favorable and because the Chinese Communist Party was still tied down in the continuing civil war against Chiang Kai-shek. Kim Il Sung's report to Shtykov may have exaggerated or distorted Mao's statements to enhance the North Korean case for war, but Mao did indeed transfer the two Chinese divisions—the 164th and the 166th—to North Korea in 1949 as promised.[6]

It is probable that, during their treaty negotiations in Moscow, Stalin and Mao discussed Kim Il Sung's plan to invade South Korea. According to a Chinese source, Stalin informed Mao that "Kim Il Sung came. He wants to move against the South. Kim is young and brave; however, he overestimates the favorable factors and underestimates the unfavorable ones." Nikita Khrushchev remembers that, when Stalin asked Mao about Kim's plan, Mao approved and expressed the opinion that the United States would not intervene in an internal Korean matter. Mao told Stalin that "we still should help Xiao Kim [little Kim]. Korea now faces a complicated situation." This discussion indicates that, although Stalin was ambivalent about Kim's ambitious plan, Mao was sympathetic and paternalistic.[7]

At about the same time Lin Biao (vice chairman of the Central Military Commission) reported to Mao in Moscow that some of the Korean soldiers in the PLA (who numbered approximately sixteen thousand), after they crossed the Yangzi River, had begun creating a disturbance because they wanted to return home. A three-member North Korean military delegation led by Kim Kwang Hyop (commander of the Second Army Corps) came to Beijing in January 1950 and requested that those Korean soldiers and their military equipment be transferred to North Korea; on January 21 Nie Rongzhen (acting chief of the PLA General Staff) recommended to the Central Military Commission that the North Korean request be granted. The following day the Central Military Commission approved the Nie recommendation. This speedy decision was consistent with Mao's promise to Kim Il in May 1949. Kim Kwang Hyop asked Nie, however, to keep the Korean soldiers in China until April because it was difficult to accommodate and deploy them in North Korea.[8]

On May 13, Kim Il Sung and Pak Hon Yong (vice premier and minister of foreign affairs), who had visited Moscow in April, arrived at Beijing and met with Mao and other Chinese leaders. Kim told Mao that Stalin had approved his invasion plan but had suggested a discussion between China and North Korea. Not fully satisfied with Kim's message, Zhou Enlai asked Soviet ambassador to China N. V. Roshchin to ascertain Stalin's "personal clarifications" directly. On the following day Stalin sent a telegram to Mao in which he stated:

> In a conversation with the Korean comrades Filippov [Stalin] and his friends expressed the opinion that, in light of the changed international situation, they agree with the proposal of the Koreans to move toward reunification. In this regard a qualification was made that the question should be decided finally by the Chinese and Korean comrades together, and in case of disagreement by the Chinese comrades the decision on the question should be postponed until a new discussion. The Korean comrades can tell you the details of the conversation.[9]

On May 15 Mao questioned the soundness of Kim's plan. Kim explained that he had devised a three-stage plan that would (1) strengthen

North Korean military forces; (2) offer a proposal for peaceful unification to South Korea; and (3) start military action as soon as South Korea rejected the peace proposal. After having waged a successful revolutionary war against the Kuomintang in China, Mao was not in a position to deny Kim the same opportunity. Mao recommended that North Korea swiftly encircle major South Korean cities and concentrate its forces against the enemy. When Mao asked whether Japan might intervene in Korea, Kim replied that such a possibility was remote but that the United States might send twenty or thirty thousand Japanese troops to Korea. Mao promised Kim that, if the United States intervened, China would send forces to assist North Korea. He added that the Soviet Union's agreement with the United States in regard to the 38th parallel would make it inconvenient for the Russians to participate in the war but that China had no such constraints. Mao asked if Kim wanted an additional Chinese force deployed along the Sino-Korean border and weapons and ammunition from China. Kim expressed appreciation but declined the offer, for he was confident that, with sufficient Soviet military supplies at hand, he could win the war in a month. Mao apparently considered this response "arrogant."[10] Mao proposed that, after unification, Korea conclude a treaty of friendship, alliance, and mutual assistance with China, provided it was approved by Stalin. Informed of Mao's proposal, Stalin promptly agreed.

Evidently Stalin recognized Mao's expertise in the Asian revolutionary theater and the importance of the geostrategic relationship between China and Korea. Seasoned strategists such as Stalin and Mao would realize that, if China were opposed to the Korean War, Kim would face great difficulties, even if his initial military attack were successful. It is also conceivable that, by ensuring Mao's involvement in drawing up Kim's invasion plans, Stalin intended to share the responsibility for Kim's military adventures. As Goncharov, Lewis, and Xue suggest, Kim recognized signs of the incipient Stalin-Mao rivalry and adroitly manipulated the situation to obtain their support for his military ambitions. In view of his "uncertain partnership" with Stalin, Mao was perhaps more inclined to support Kim's designs than China's own national interests and policy priorities dictated at that time. It remains controversial, however, whether Mao made any speculations to Kim (and Stalin) about possible United States intervention in the war.[11]

Contrary to Kim's confident prediction, the Truman administration swiftly responded to the Korean War because it assumed that this was no civil war but an integral part of a Stalin-led international communist conspiracy to test U.S. resolve and that if the United States did not stand up against the North Korean attack, a devastating chain reaction might ensue, particularly in Europe.[12] On June 25 the United States requested an emergency meeting of the United Nations Security Council, which passed a resolution calling for the immediate cessation of hostilities and the withdrawal of North Korean forces to the 38th parallel. On June 27 the Security Council adopted a resolution recommending that "the Members of the United Nations furnish such assistance to the Republic of Korea as may be necessary to repel the armed attack and to restore international peace and security in the area." This resolution laid the legal basis for U.S. military intervention in Korea. On the same day President Harry Truman decided to provide U.S. air and naval support for South Korea and to send the Seventh Fleet to the Taiwan Straits to "neutralize" the area.

The Chinese viewed Truman's Taiwan decision as a belligerent attempt to intervene in China's internal affairs and denounced what they regarded as America's armed aggression in violation of the United Nations Charter. They also sensed that the United States might launch an attack against China from Korea, Taiwan, or Indochina. On June 28 Mao declared:

> The U.S. invasion of Asia can only touch off the broad and resolute opposition of Asian people. On January 5, Truman said in an announcement that the United States would not intervene in Taiwan. Now his conduct proves that what he said was false. Moreover, he shredded all international agreements related to the American commitment not to intervene in China's internal affairs. The United States thus reveals its imperialist nature in its true colors. . . . The United States is unable to justify in any way its intervention in the internal affairs of Korea, the Philippines, and Vietnam. The sympathies of the Chinese people and the vast people of the world lie with the countries that have been invaded, and by no means with the American imperialism.[13]

While focusing on the relevance to China and Taiwan of U.S. military actions, Mao was careful not to make provocative statements on the Korean War itself. He offered moral support to North Korea but refrained from any promises of military assistance.

The Chinese were impressed by the rapidity with which North Korea captured Seoul—the successful three-day blitzkrieg—and the speed with which the United States committed its forces to defend South Korea. They recognized the promise of North Korean military advances as well as the potentially adverse consequences of U.S. determination shown in Truman's decisions. On June 30 Zhou Enlai dispatched a group of top Chinese military intelligence personnel led by Chai Chengwen to Pyongyang. These "diplomats" set up the Chinese embassy in North Korea and collected firsthand information about the changing Korean situation.[14] The embassy linked up with the Representative Office of the Northeast Administrative Council that had existed in North Korea for some time. A Chinese antiaircraft artillery unit was ordered to move to Sinuiju to defend the Yalu River bridges.

In his meeting with Roshchin on July 2 (only a week after the Korean War began), Zhou Enlai said that, if the United States crossed the 38th parallel, Chinese troops would enter the war disguised as North Korean soldiers and that, for this purpose, China had already assembled three armies (120,000 troops) near Shenyang. Zhou asked whether the Soviet Union could provide air cover for Chinese operations in Korea. He counseled that 60,000 out of 120,000 U.S. forces stationed in Japan could land at Pusan, Mokpo, Masan, and other ports and move northward on the railways and recommended that North Korean forces move quickly south toward those ports. He also advised strengthening the North Korean defenses at Inchon to prevent a U.S. amphibious landing. This conversation indicates that Mao and Zhou had anticipated the possibility of Chinese military intervention in Korea and were paying close attention to the progress of the war. In his response to Zhou on July 5, Stalin said that it was appropriate for China to assemble nine divisions along the Sino-Korean border so that they could enter Korea as "volunteers" in the event that the enemy crossed the 38th parallel. Stalin promised Zhou that the Soviet air force would protect Chinese "volunteers" in Korea. More specifically, Stalin informed Zhou on July 7 that the Soviet Union was willing to send an air force division with 124 Z-fighters to China.[15]

On the same day, Zhou chaired a meeting of the Central Military Commission. At the meeting it was decided to move the 13th Army Corps of the Fourth Field Army, three artillery divisions, and a military hospital (with a capacity for sixty thousand patients) to Manchuria, to set up a Northeast Frontier Force (NFF) at Andong (now Dandong), and to appoint Su Yu as NFF commander. (Later Deng Hua, former commander of the 15th Army Corps, replaced Su Yu because of Su's illness; Gao Gang, commander of the Northeast Military Region, was in charge of the NFF's logistic affairs.) This meeting coincided with the U.N. Security Council's decision to establish the United Nations Command (UNC) for Korea under a U.S. general (to be filled by General Douglas MacArthur). The NFF

with 255,000 troops was clearly created with China's possible intervention in Korea in mind. While this military contingency plan was under
way in Manchuria, Zhou Enlai emphasized in his meeting with the Indian
ambassador to China K. M. Panikkar on July 21 that China had no intention of becoming involved in the Korean War and had no desire to see the
war extended beyond Korea.[16]

On August 4 the Political Bureau of the Chinese Communist Party
met to discuss the Korean situation. Mao stated: "If U.S. imperialists won
the war, they would become more arrogant and would threaten us. We
should not fail to assist the Koreans. We must lend them our hands in the
form of sending our military volunteers there. The timing could be further
decided, but we have to prepare for this."[17] Zhou added that "in order to
win the war, China's strength must be added to the struggle." The next
day Mao sent a telegram to Gao Gang:

> Various units of the Frontier Force have been assembled. It is unlikely
> that they will have any operational tasks before the end of the month.
> However, we should prepare these units for battle by the first 10 days of
> September. Comrade Gao Gang is assigned to be in overall charge. Please
> convene a meeting of the cadres at the corps and division levels in the
> second 10 days of the month and there instruct them on the purpose and
> significance of the operation and its general direction. By the end of the
> month, various units should make full preparations and await orders to
> set off.[18]

At the same time Nie Rongzhen, acting chief of the PLA General Staff,
instructed the NFF to be ready for battle by the end of August. On August
18, Mao, who recognized that more time was needed for sufficient military preparedness, instructed Gao: "The deadline for the Frontier Force
to complete its training and other preparatory work can be extended up
to the end of September. Please supervise and speed up the preparations
so that everything is wrapped up by September 30." On the following day
Mao had a three-hour discussion with P. F. Yudin (an eminent Marxist
scholar from the Soviet Union) and observed that the Korean War might
take one of two possible courses. If the United States continued to use the
current level of forces in Korea, Mao said, it would certainly be defeated;
this would be the most desirable course. If, however, the United States
intended to win the war and decided to deploy thirty to forty divisions in
Korea, North Korea would require China's assistance. He said that joint
military action between China and North Korea could defeat the United

States and that there would then be an opportunity for the Soviet Union and China to start a third world war. About this time Mao became convinced that the United States would attempt an amphibious landing to the rear of North Korean forces. Chai Chengwen reported that the United States would land at Nampo (formerly Chinnampo), Wonsan, Inchon, or Kunsan, and Deng Hua predicted a U.S. landing near Seoul or Pyongyang. The Operations Bureau of the PLA's General Staff correctly predicted that MacArthur would land his forces at Inchon. These assessments and warnings were apparently ignored by Kim. Mao also suggested a number of other military and tactical maneuvers to North Korea (such as a temporary retreat from the Pusan-Taegu perimeter and a concentrated attack against South Korean forces) but to no avail.[19]

At the Central Military Commission (CMC) meetings held by Zhou on August 26 and 31, it was determined that the NFF, which consisted of eleven armies (thirty-six divisions with 700,000 troops), would participate in a three-tier deployment. The CMC designated another 100,000 troops of the Fourth Field Army as reinforcements and estimated that there would be 200,000 Chinese casualties during the first year of battle. On August 28 Mao told Yudin that the Korean War would be protracted and that the United States would increase its troops in Korea. The Soviet Union agreed to send thirty-eight air force and antiaircraft specialists to China. If Mao had committed a significant portion of his NFF forces along the Pusan-Taegu perimeter before MacArthur landed at Inchon, the war could have been reversed dramatically. Kim was, however, a confident and proud nationalist and wanted to achieve national liberation without relying on foreign troops. Stalin probably felt that, if China intervened in the war at this time, it would widen the scope of the war and might lead to World War III. Mao's approach was to be well prepared but to wait and see—he did not wish to commit his forces to Korea prematurely. He was mollified by assurances from U.N. secretary-general Trygve Lie that the United States had inadvertently strayed into Chinese territory and had mistakenly bombed Chinese border towns and by the news that the UNC had issued an order to prohibit further military operations in Manchuria.[20]

The stunning success of MacArthur's Inchon landing fundamentally altered the strategic calculations and policy choices of Stalin, Mao, and Kim. The Chinese were deeply concerned about the sudden collapse of North Korean forces and the triumphant northward rush of UNC forces close to the 38th parallel. Yet Zhou Enlai led Panikkar, the Indian ambassador, to conclude that China showed "no undue interest [in the Korean development] beyond [an] expression of sympathy" and that the "direct participation of China in Korean fighting seems beyond [the] range of possibility unless of course a world war starts as a result of UN forces passing beyond [the] 38th parallel and [the] Soviet Union deciding directly to intervene." He reported to New Delhi, London, and Washington that "China by herself will not interfere in the conflict and [will] try to pull others' chestnuts out of the fire." A few days later, however, Panikkar reported to Indian prime minister Jawaharlal Nehru that Nie, speaking of the U.S. aircraft bombings in Manchuria, had bitterly said that "China would not take such provocations lying down." Panikkar also made the assessment that China had now decided on a more aggressive policy of indirect intervention in Korea. When Hubert Graves (counselor of the British embassy in Washington) conveyed Panikkar's report to Livingston T. Merchant (deputy assistant secretary of state for Far Eastern affairs) on September 27, Graves said that he did not take Panikkar's fears seriously because he was a volatile and unreliable reporter.[21]

On September 30, about the time when the Joint Chiefs of Staff (JCS) approved General MacArthur's plan for U.N. military operations north of the 38th parallel and when the Third Division of the South Korean army crossed the 38th parallel, Zhou Enlai issued a public warning: "The Chinese people enthusiastically love peace, but in order to defend peace, they never have been and never will be afraid to oppose aggressive war. The Chinese people absolutely will not tolerate foreign aggression, nor will they supinely tolerate seeing their neighbors being savagely invaded by imperialists." As this warning was widely reported in the Western press, the United States was not sure whether it was a bluff or not.[22]

Meanwhile, the desperate Kim and Pak cabled a special appeal to Stalin on September 29 in which they said that "when the enemy crosses the 38th parallel, it will be absolutely necessary for the Soviet armed forces to directly participate [in the war]." If the Soviet Union were unable to do so, they implored Stalin to at least "organize and send the international volunteer armies of China and other democratic countries to help our struggles." Kim gave the same message to Shtykov in person. On receiving the North Korean appeal, Stalin promptly asked Roshchin to tell Mao or Zhou that the Korean situation was very critical and that five to six divisions of Chinese volunteers should be sent to the 38th parallel as soon as possible.[23]

On October 1 Mao received a similar message from Kim and Pak. It stated:

The present military situation is extremely serious. Our people's army is courageously resisting the enemy that landed [at Inchon]. But the people's army on the front has already encountered a very unfavorable condition. Since the war started, the enemy has used about one thousand aircraft of all kinds every day to wantonly bomb our front and rear during day and night. As we cannot resist the enemy air force at all, the enemy has fully demonstrated its power. At every battlefield the enemy operates a large-scale mechanized army under air cover, and we face a very serious loss of troops and matériel. Our traffic, transportation, communications, and other facilities in the rear are destroyed in large quantities. The enemy forces that landed [at Inchon] are linked up with their forces moving from the south; they cut up our troops between the south and the north. As a result, our people's army on the southern front which is separated and divided up by the enemy is in unfavorable conditions. It cannot receive weapons and ammunition. Some of our forces are dispersed and encircled by the enemy. We believe that it is possible that the enemy continue to attack and move toward the northern area of the 38th parallel. If our various unfavorable conditions are not improved, the enemy will be able to accomplish its attempt.

We are determined to overcome all difficulties and to smash the enemy's plan to turn Korea into their colony and military bases. We are determined not to spare even the last drop of our blood in our struggle to gain the Korean people's independence, liberation, and democracy. We must assemble our forces, organize and train new divisions, regroup about 100,000 troops in the south, move them to a militarily advantageous area, mobilize all the people, and prepare for a protracted war.

If the enemy capitalizes on our grave crisis, gives no respite to us, and continues to advance to the north of the 38th parallel, it is impossible to overcome this crisis by our own capabilities. Hence we have no choice but to ask for your special assistance: if the enemy attacks the north of the 38th parallel, we urgently request that you directly dispatch the Chinese People's Liberation Army to assist our military operations.[24]

On the same day MacArthur issued an ultimatum for the unconditional surrender of the North Korean forces.

Even though Mao had anticipated this turn of military events in Korea since early July and had made the necessary preparations, reaching a final decision was tortuous. He would need to bring about a policy consensus in the Political Bureau, formulate a plan for military cooperation with the Soviet Union, and make an accurate assessment of U.S. policy. At the Political Bureau, which continued to meet from October 2 on, the debate as to whether China should enter the Korean War was intense. Many top leaders, including Zhou Enlai, Chen Yun, Lin Biao, and Ren Bishi, expressed reservations about China's direct military participation in Korea. Supported by other key leaders, including Nie Rongzhen, Gao Gang, and Peng Dehuai, Mao played a decisive role in swaying the Political Bureau in favor of China's entering the Korean War.[25]

On October 2 Mao sent a telegram to Stalin:

> We have decided to send some of our troops to Korea under the name of [Chinese People's] Volunteers to fight the United States and its lackey Syngman Rhee and to aid our Korean comrades. From the following considerations, we think it necessary to do so: the Korean revolutionary force will meet with a fundamental defeat, and the American aggressors will rampage unchecked once they occupy the whole of Korea. This will be unfavorable to the entire East. Since we have decided to send Chinese troops to fight the Americans in Korea, we hold that, first, we should be able to solve the problem; that is [we are] ready to annihilate and drive out the invading armies of the United States and other countries. Second, since Chinese troops are to fight American troops in Korea (although we will use the name Volunteers), we must be prepared for a declaration of war by the United States and for the subsequent use of the U.S. air force to bomb many of China's main cities and industrial bases, as well as an attack by the U.S. navy on [our] coastal areas. . . . Under the current situation, we have reached a decision to order the 12 divisions stationed in advance in South Manchuria to set off on October 15.[26]

In an attempt to prevent the United States from crossing the 38th parallel, Zhou Enlai met with Panikkar in the early morning of October 3 to transmit an urgent message to the United States. If UNC forces crossed the 38th parallel, Zhou said, China would have no option but to send its troops across the Yalu River to defend North Korea; the Chinese would not send troops if only South Korean forces crossed the parallel. Zhou also said, in an effort to advance China's international status, that China would accept no settlement of the Korean question to which China was not a party. There was considerable debate in the U.S. bureaucracies about the seriousness of China's démarche, but Dean Acheson did not take it as "an authoritative statement of policy." The United States thus ignored Zhou's warning and allowed the First Cavalry Division to cross the parallel on October 7. Thomas Christensen contends that, on the one hand, if the United States had recognized China and had received a direct message from Zhou Enlai, the Sino-American military confrontation in Korea might have been avoided. In this sense it was a "lost chance."[27]

On the other hand, the Chinese dismissed U.S. assurances (transmitted by the Indian government) that the United States had no desire to engage in hostilities with China, threaten Korea's neighbors, or establish military bases in Korea. The United States argued that the U.N. Security Council resolution of June 27, 1950, authorized the UNC forces to cross the parallel and that the parallel was an "artificial barrier" having no basis for existence in law or reason. For all practical purposes, the Truman administration had radically changed its war policy from that of repelling North Korean aggression to realizing the goal of a unified, democratic, and independent government in Korea under U.N. auspices.

On October 8 Mao decided to send the Chinese People's Volunteers (CPV) to Korea and appointed Peng Dehuai (commander of the First Field Army and of the Northwest Military Region) as CPV commander in chief. Chinese ambassador Ni Zhiliang and Counselor Chai Chengwen went to an underground bunker in Moranbong to convey Mao's decision to Kim, who was in the middle of a heated debate with Pak. Pleased with the message from Beijing, Kim thanked Mao and the Chinese Communist Party and made a toast to victory by the Chinese army. While Peng flew to Shenyang to assume his new responsibilities and to meet with Pak Il U (minister of home affairs and one of the returnees from Yanan) on the same day, Zhou Enlai and Lin Biao left China for discussions with Stalin. At his meeting with Zhou in a resort village on the Black Sea on October 10, Stalin reneged on his promise to provide air cover for Chinese military operations in Korea because he feared a war with the United States. Stalin was pessimistic about the prospect of rescuing Kim's regime and explored the possibility of Kim's setting up a government in exile in China.[28]

On the same day the Chinese Ministry of Foreign Affairs issued a stern warning:

The American war of invasion in Korea has been a serious menace to the security of China from its very start. . . . The Chinese people cannot stand idly by with regard to such a serious situation created by the invasion of Korea by the United States and its accomplice countries and to the dangerous trend toward extending the war. . . . The Chinese people firmly advocate a peaceful solution to the Korean problem and are firmly opposed to the extension of the Korean war by America and its accomplice countries. And they are even more firm in holding that aggressors must be answerable for all consequences resulting from their frantic acts in extending aggression.[29]

As soon as Mao received the negative report from Zhou, he ordered Peng to halt the military movement and asked him to return to Beijing for further deliberations.[30] On October 13 Mao, despite his disappointment over Stalin's desertion, reaffirmed his earlier decision to enter the war even without the Soviet air umbrella in Korea. His telegram to Zhou in Moscow read as follows:

> After discussion with comrades on the Politburo, we have reached a consensus that the entry of our army into Korea continues to be to our advantage. In the first phase, we can only fight the puppet [Republic of Korea] army. With a certainty of success in dealing with the puppet army, we can establish a base in the large mountain area to the north of the Wonsan-Pyongyang line and thus encourage the Korean people. The Korean situation would change to our advantage if we could wipe out several divisions of the puppet army in the first phase. The adoption of our active policy mentioned above is favorable to China, Korea, the East, and the world. If we do not send troops [to Korea], the reactionaries at home and abroad would be swollen with arrogance when the enemy troops press on toward the Yalu River. Consequently, it would be unfavorable to various parties and especially unfavorable to Northeast China. [In such a situation], the entire Northeast Frontier Force would be tied down and the power supplies in South Manchuria would be controlled [by hostile parties]. In short, we hold that we should enter the war. We must enter the war. Entering the war is greatly to our advantage; conversely, it is greatly to our disadvantage if we do not enter the war.[31]

Apparently moved by Mao's courage and determination, Stalin promised on October 14 to extend the Soviet air umbrella to Chinese territory but not to Korea. He also agreed to provide substantial military supplies and fighter planes to China. Zhou Enlai returned to Beijing and reaffirmed Stalin's commitment of military assistance and air cover in China; on October 18 Mao issued the final order for the CPV to enter Korea the next day.[32]

As illustrated in Mao's telegrams to Stalin and Zhou, the Chinese decision to enter the Korean War was based on a number of factors, but the geostrategic reality was probably paramount. To protect the Sino-Korean border, which was crucial to the strategic and industrial security of Manchuria, and to deny an opportunity for the United States to threaten China on both fronts (Korea and Taiwan), Mao felt it necessary to deliver a decisive blow to U.S. military advances in Asia once and for all. He believed that, just as Japan had used its annexation of Korea as a bridgehead to invade China, U.S. control of the Korean Peninsula would pose a similar threat to China.[33] Mao was also bound to Kim by a strong revolutionary and ideological solidarity and a zeal for anti-imperialist struggles. (He was also grateful to Kim for assisting the CCP during a critical phase of the Chinese civil war in Manchuria.) Had China not intervened in the Korean War, Mao would have lost an opportunity to assume a leadership role in Asian revolutionary movements as well as damaged China's international status, encouraged counterrevolutionary elements in China, and undermined the viability of the newly formed Sino-Soviet alliance system. Despite Stalin's reluctance, Mao was certain that the Sino-Soviet treaty and the Soviet possession of atomic weapons would limit the range of U.S. strategic options against China. He did not underestimate the growing importance of American atomic bombs but assumed that it was unlikely that the United States would launch a nuclear attack against China.

An important but subtle factor that is often neglected in Western accounts of the Korean War is the influence of China's traditional and cultural relationship with Korea on Mao's decision-making process. Mao's pursuit of revolutionary leadership in Asia can be viewed as a continuation of China's traditional world outlook and a reassertion of its historical hegemony over Korea. As discussed in chapter 1, the tributary relations between China and Korea were unequal and hierarchical. Viewed in this historical perspective, Mao's paternalistic attitude toward North Korea (referring to Kim as "Xiao Kim") is not surprising. As an "older brother" Mao may have felt that he had an obligation to respond to his younger brother's urgent appeal. This sense of brotherly ties, which was largely absent in Stalin's conceptualization of the Korean question, may explain the extraordinary degree of support and patience that Mao showed to Kim during the war. The CPV's entry into the Korean War was reminiscent of that of General Li Rusong of the Ming dynasty, who, toward the end of the sixteenth century, had led an expeditionary force of fifty thousand across the Yalu River to defend Korea against Hideyoshi's invasion.[34]

Meanwhile, General MacArthur assumed an increasingly arrogant posture in Korea after Inchon, summarily dismissing the likelihood of direct Chinese military intervention and promising that the war would be over by Thanksgiving and U.S. soldiers back home by Christmas. In their meeting at Wake Island on October 15, when President Truman asked about the possibility of Chinese or Soviet interference in Korea, MacArthur confidently responded:

> Very little. Had they interfered in the first or second months it would have been decisive. We are no longer fearful of their intervention. We no longer stand hat in hand. The Chinese have 300,000 men in Manchuria. Of these probably not more than 100/125,000 are distributed along the Yalu River. Only 50/60,000 could be gotten across the Yalu River. They have no Air Force. Now that we have bases for our Air Force in Korea, if the Chinese tried to get down to Pyongyang there would be the greatest slaughter.[35]

He explained that the Russians had an air force in Siberia and excellent pilots but no ground troops readily available for the Korean War.

As to possible Russian air support for Chinese ground troops in Korea—a topic that Stalin and Zhou had discussed four days earlier—MacArthur said:

> Russian air is deployed in a semicircle through Mukden and Harbin, but the coordination between the Russian air and the Chinese ground would be so flimsy that I believe Russian air would bomb the Chinese as often as they would bomb us. Ground support is a very difficult thing to do. Our Marines do it perfectly. They have been trained for it. Our own Air and Ground Forces are not as good as the Marines but they are effective. Between untrained Air and Ground Forces an air umbrella is impossible without a lot of joint training. I believe it just wouldn't work with Chinese Communist ground and Russian air. We are the best.[36]

MacArthur staunchly refused to believe that the Chinese forces assembled in Manchuria intended to enter Korea and held all Chinese troops—both Nationalist and Communist—in contempt. A day before the Wake Island conference, the Far East Command's daily intelligence summary (under General Charles A. Willoughby) reported that "a total of 24 divisions are disposed along the Yalu River at crossing points" but advised that China's recent warnings "are probably in a category of diplomatic blackmail." It also concluded that the Soviet Union and China "have decided against further expensive investment in support of a lost cause [in Korea]." The Central Intelligence Agency, too, reported that, despite Zhou's threats and troop movements in Manchuria, "there are no convincing indications of an actual Chinese Communist intention to resort to full-scale intervention in Korea." The Truman administration shared this ill-advised consensus assessment and tragically miscalculated Mao's intentions and capabilities.[37]

MILITARY CAMPAIGNS

To avoid the complications of a direct Chinese military confrontation with the United Nations and the United States, Mao sent the PLA to Korea disguised as volunteers; all insignia and other identifying signs of the PLA were removed before entering Korea, and PLA officers wore North Korean uniforms. The rallying cry "resist America, aid Korea, protect the home [homeland], and defend the country" (*kangmeiyuanchao baojiaweiguo*) combined three incendiary political slogans—anti-imperialism, internationalism, and patriotism. The emphasis on family and country stirred enthusiasm among the weary soldiers who had just served in the Chinese civil war. Lin Biao, who had extensive military experience in Manchuria, was Mao's first choice to lead the Chinese People's Volunteers (CPV) in Korea, but the position eventually fell to Peng Dehuai, an outstanding strategist and courageous leader.[38]

On October 20, Peng, accompanied by Pak Hon Yong, traveled from Sinuiju to Taeyudong, a small gold mining village in northern Pyongan Province, to meet with Kim Il Sung.[39] Kim warmly welcomed Peng and profusely thanked Mao and the CCP. Peng responded:

> It was not easy for Chairman Mao and the CCP Central Committee to make this decision. The mainland of China has just been liberated and we are confronted by many difficulties. Now that we have sent out our troops we must be prepared for what may happen next. First, we'll see if we can be helpful to a fair and rational solution of the Korean problem, of which the key lies in defeating invading US troops. Second, we must be prepared for the United States to declare that a state of belligerency exists between it and China. At least we should be prepared in case it bombs our northeast and industrial cities, as well as our coastal areas.[40]

Peng listed three possibilities for the future of the CPV and the Korean War: (1) the enemy would be wiped out and the Korean problem solved rationally; (2) the Chinese volunteers could hold on but not defeat the enemy and both parties refuse to budge; and (3) the volunteers would be pushed back. He pledged that "we will do our best to realize the first possibility." He also explained Mao's plan of having the CPV advance, set up a defense perimeter north of the line linking Pyongyang with Wonsan, and attack Pyongyang and Wonsan in six months. For this purpose the CPV initially had 340,000 troops, with plans to increase to 600,000 troops. Mao appointed Deng Hua, Hong Xuezhi, and Han Xianchu as deputy commanders and Xie Fang as chief of staff for Peng (commander in chief and political commissar) at the CPV headquarters in Taeyudong; for the liaison with North Korea, Pak Il U was appointed deputy commander and deputy political commissar of the CPV. The Chinese Communist Party at Taeyudong was led by Peng as secretary and Deng and Pak as deputy secretaries.[41]

On October 21, Peng sent a telegram to Mao in which he recommended abandoning the idea of perimeter defense because the U.N. forces, which had captured Pyongyang on October 19, were advancing toward the Yalu River at an unexpectedly swift pace. Peng now wanted to destroy the advancing U.N. forces by mobile warfare tactics, a recommendation quickly approved by Mao. The critical weaknesses in the UNC were its failure to detect the presence of massive Chinese troops in Korea and its reliance on roads, which made it impossible for U.N. forces to be tightly or closely formed. The South Korean forces moved so quickly that they became vulnerable; and there was a huge gap (about 80 km) between the Eighth Army (commanded by General Walton H. Walker) in the west and the X Corps (commanded by General Edward N. Almond) in the east. It is not clear whether Mao understood that it was unusual to separate the U.S. command structures between two fronts or that there was a lack of personal and operational cooperation between Walker and Almond. In any case, Mao ordered Peng Dehuai on October 21 to keep the U.S. forces on the two fronts isolated by occupying the mountainous areas between them.[42]

To capitalize on the UNC's weaknesses, Mao and Peng employed a classic Chinese stratagem: disguising the troops, luring the enemy deep into a trap, and encircling and attacking from the rear and the flanks. The first major military clash took place on October 25 in the Unsan-Onjong area. The 118th Division of the Fortieth Army launched a surprise attack against the Third Battalion, Second Regiment, South Korea's Sixth Division.[43] Roy B. Appleman describes the engagement:

Eight miles west of Onjong the 3rd Battalion came under enemy fire. The troops dismounted from their vehicles to disperse what they thought was a small force of North Koreans. But the roadblock turned out to be a Chinese trap. In the action that followed the Chinese destroyed the battalion as an organized force. Approximately 400 of 750 ROK's in the battalion escaped, however, and in the afternoon infiltrated back to Onjong. Among those captured in this action was Lt. Glen C. Jones, KMAG adviser to the battalion, who later died in a prison camp.[44]

On the following day the CPV occupied Onjong. For the next few days fierce fighting ensued in a wide range of battlefields on the western and eastern fronts. By November 3, the overwhelming power of the CPV had forced the UNC forces to retreat south of the Chongchon River. As Hong Xuezhi recalls, the CPV soldiers, who were on foot, were unable to catch up with the U.N. forces, who rapidly escaped by motor vehicles. The CPV committed a number of mistakes, however, including the Thirty-eighth Army's failure to capture Hoechon on time: it mistook South Korean troops for U.S. forces, and its advance was blocked by retreating North Korean troops and refugees. Peng was so angry that he threatened to have the Thirty-eighth Army's commander (Yang Xingchao) court-martialed. The CPV halted its first offensive campaign on November 5 because Chinese soldiers were exhausted from thirteen days of continuous fighting under heavy air strikes and because their rations and ammunition had run out.[45]

Elated by the CPV's achievements, Mao congratulated Peng on the first victory in Korea and told him that the enemy had grossly underestimated the CPV's strength (setting it at forty to sixty thousand as of October 30). Already speaking of the importance of advancing toward Pyongyang, he ordered the Ninth Army Corps (commanded by Song Shilun) to move from Shandong Province to the eastern front in Korea. On November 13 he sent a report to Stalin explaining the current military situation in Korea.[46]

Despite devastating setbacks, MacArthur continued to misjudge the intentions and capabilities of the CPV. In response to an inquiry from the JCS concerning China's "overt intervention" in Korea, on November 4 MacArthur stated that although China's intervention was a distinct possibility, "there are many fundamental logical reasons against it and sufficient evidence has not yet come to hand to warrant its immediate acceptance." The Far East Command (FEC) and the Eighth Army believed that the motive for China's military action in late October and early November was to protect the Supung hydroelectric power plants on the Yalu River and that the Chinese forces would dig in on a defensive line to do this. MacArthur thought that the Chinese forces stopped fighting because they were badly beaten and frightened.[47]

On November 7 the FEC estimated that there were 34,500 Chinese troops in Korea—27,000 in the Eighth Army zone and 7,500 in the X Corps zone. Two days later it raised the number of Chinese troops to 76,800—about one-fifth of the actual Chinese forces (380,000) deployed in Korea at that time.[48] Such blunders in the UNC's intelligence estimates were made in part because the CPV moved at night, thus escaping aerial observation, and "remained hidden in the hills under perfect camouflage discipline." MacArthur declared:

> I believe that with my air power, now unrestricted so far as Korea is concerned except as to hydroelectric installations, I can deny reinforcements coming across the Yalu in sufficient strength to prevent the destruction of those forces now arrayed against me in North Korea.[49]

On November 16 he told U.S. ambassador John Muccio that China had sent no more than thirty thousand soldiers across the border and that the area still in the hands of North Koreans and Chinese Communists would be cleared within ten days of an all-out offensive. (It was two days later that Mao informed Peng that the enemy estimated the CPV troops at sixty to seventy thousand.) In response to a request from Zhou Enlai, Stalin agreed to deliver five hundred Soviet trucks to China.[50]

On November 24, MacArthur flew to Eighth Army Headquarters on the Chongchon River and directed the UNC to end the war by Christmas. The U.N. Air Force conducted large-scale bombing attacks against bridges, roads, and military facilities on the Yalu River. Yet Peng, correctly anticipating MacArthur's military plans and maneuvers, launched his second campaign with 230,000 Chinese forces against 130,000 U.N. troops on the west and 150,000 Chinese troops against 90,000 U.N. forces on the east. Stunned by the CPV's overwhelming onslaught, MacArthur finally realized that he had a major crisis on his hands. On November 28 he reported to the JCS: "The Chinese military forces are committed in North Korea in great and ever increasing strength. No pretext of minor support under the guise of volunteerism or other subterfuge now has the slightest validity. We face an entirely new war."[51]

On December 3, MacArthur sent another pessimistic report to the

JCS: it was impossible to defend the waist of Korea; Walker could not hold the Pyongyang area but would be forced to withdraw to the Seoul area. MacArthur concluded that, "unless some positive and immediate action is taken, hope for success cannot be justified and steady attrition leading to final destruction [of the U.N. forces] can reasonably be contemplated." He proposed to incorporate the Kuomintang armies into the UNC because they represented "the only source of potential trained reinforcements available for early commitment to the war in Korea." The JCS rejected this suggestion on the grounds that using the Kuomintang forces would disrupt the unity of the U.N. forces, isolate the United States diplomatically, and extend hostilities to Formosa and other areas. Contrary to his earlier contempt for Chinese military capabilities, MacArthur now reported: "The Chinese troops are fresh, completely organized, splendidly trained and equipped and apparently in peak condition for actual operations."[52]

On December 7 MacArthur issued instructions for a withdrawal of the U.N. forces in successive positions, if necessary, to the Pusan area. He ordered the Eighth Army to hold the Seoul area as long as possible without risking envelopment and the X Corps to withdraw from the Hungnam area and rejoin the Eighth Army. The consensus between Secretary of State Dean Acheson and Secretary of Defense George Marshall was that the Chinese military intervention in Korea was a Stalinist conspiracy to pin down U.S. forces in Asia so that the Soviets would have a free hand in Europe. To them, Korea was not an important arena but Europe was of prime concern. Acheson stated that the United States was fighting "the wrong nation" and "the second team" and that the real enemy was the Soviet Union. In this context General J. Lawton Collins (army chief of staff) argued that "Korea was not worth a nickel" and that the only chance to save the United States in Korea was to threaten to use atomic bombs. It was agreed that a cease-fire would be highly desirable and that abandoning Korea and evacuating South Korean forces to Japan should be considered. The JCS told MacArthur on December 29 that "Korea is not the place to fight a major war" and instructed him to inflict costly damage to the Chinese forces but to prepare for an orderly evacuation to Japan.[53]

After their military success at the end of November, the CPV commanders, uncertain as to why the UNC forces had retreated so rapidly, did not engage in hot pursuit. They were surprised when the Eighth Army abandoned Pyongyang without a fight on December 5; by December 16 it had withdrawn south of the 38th parallel. General Walker's death in an automobile accident on December 23 completed the rout. In only two months the CPV had restored the status quo antebellum in Korea and rescued Kim's regime from territorial extinction. General MacArthur's promise of victory by Christmas was irreparably shattered. Acheson characterized MacArthur's retreat as "the greatest defeat suffered by American arms since the Battle of Manassas."[54] It was feared that the Chinese "hordes" would rely on human wave tactics and the shrill sounding of bugles and whistles. However, the CPV's real strength was identified as a "first-rate army" equipped with the tactics of deception and surprise.[55]

Amid China's second offensive campaign, Mao, Zhou, and Gao met Kim Il Sung in Beijing on December 3. When Kim expressed his appreciation to Mao for China's selfless assistance, Mao modestly replied that China and North Korea were involved in a mutually supportive campaign. Gao reported that it was difficult, however, to coordinate Chinese and North Korean forces and cited an episode of a North Korean tank unit accidently attacking the Thirty-ninth Army. Mao proposed a unified command to avoid such accidents, and Kim readily accepted, saying that Stalin had made a similar suggestion. Mao and Kim agreed to set up a Sino-Korean Joint Military Command at Taeyudong and to appoint Peng Dehuai as commander in chief and political commissar, Deng Hua and Kim Ung (commander of the KPA's First Army Corps) as deputy commanders, and Pak Il U as deputy political commissar. Taking into consideration Kim's pride and sensitivity, Zhou proposed that all important documents be jointly signed by Peng, Kim Ung, and Pak, and Mao emphasized that the joint command be kept secret. Yet this integrated command structure was only a facade. For all practical purposes the CPV headquarters was in charge; only a small North Korean liaison office was attached to Taeyudong.[56]

In an attempt to maintain a smooth triangular military relationship in the face of the formidable common enemy, Mao solicited Stalin's advice throughout the war, kept Stalin informed of China's military campaigns, and shared Peng's battle reports with him. In a message on December 1, Stalin congratulated Mao on the CPV's success in Korea. Zhou said that when Stalin received a report detailing the Chinese soldiers' heroic struggles, he was moved to tears. Stalin told Mao that just as the Soviet Union had obtained experience in modern warfare by fighting Nazi Germany, the Chinese forces would experience modern warfare in fighting against the U.S. forces and become a powerful army as a result.[57]

While intense fighting continued in Korea, the Chinese were actively engaged in diplomacy at the United Nations. At the U.N. Security Council toward the end of November, Wu Xiuquan (director of the Soviet and East European Department of the Ministry of Foreign Affairs) delivered a lengthy speech condemning U.S. policies in Formosa and Korea and submitted a draft resolution, which was subsequently sponsored by the Soviet Union. The draft resolution condemned the United States for "its criminal acts of armed aggression against the Chinese territory of Taiwan and armed intervention in Korea" and demanded the complete U.S. withdrawal from both areas.[58]

The U.S. ambassador to the United Nations, Warren R. Austin, interpreted Wu's behavior either as an indication of China's political immaturity or as evidence of its "planned terror tactics" but did not believe that China was a Soviet satellite.[59] The Chinese showed no willingness to seek a diplomatic compromise at the Security Council and used the international forum to defy the United States. On November 30 the Security Council rejected the Chinese-inspired draft resolution by a vote of nine to one (the dissenting vote cast by the Soviet Union), with the Indian representative abstaining. In turn the Soviet Union vetoed the six-power resolution, which held the Chinese frontier with Korea "inviolate," but called on China to immediately withdraw its forces from Korea.

In response to U.N. secretary-general Trygve Lie's proposal that a cease-fire be established along the 38th parallel, on December 3 Wu presented three demands: (1) withdrawal of U.N. troops from Korea, (2) withdrawal of the U.S. Seventh Fleet from the Taiwan Straits, and (3) China's representation in the United Nations.[60] From their strong position on the battlefield, the Chinese were relying on Korea to achieve their non-Korean policy objectives, for by demanding such a high price for a cease-fire, they showed no true interest in an armistice. Thus it was still Mao's ambition to drive U.N. forces out of Korea by military means.

For the same reason, the Chinese rejected the thirteen-power resolution adopted by the General Assembly on December 14 by a vote of fifty-two to five, with one abstention (the Republic of China). That resolution asked the president of the General Assembly to constitute a group of three persons that would make recommendations for a satisfactory cease-fire in Korea. In his meeting with Lie, Wu called the resolution "illegal and not in any way binding on the Chinese People's Government" and refused to meet with the three-member Cease-Fire Group.[61] On December 22, Zhou Enlai said that the Cease-Fire Group was illegal because the resolution was adopted without the participation and concurrence of the People's

Republic of China and because the proposal for a cease-fire first and negotiations afterward would allow the United States to "gain a breathing
space and prepare to attack again." After reminding the United States of
the trick used by General George Marshall in 1946 to assist Chiang Kai-
shek's military preparations, Zhou declared:

> We firmly insist that, as a basis for negotiating for a peaceful settlement
> of the Korean problem, all foreign troops must be withdrawn from Ko-
> rea, and Korea's domestic affairs must be settled by the Korean people
> themselves. The American aggression forces must be withdrawn from
> Taiwan, and the representatives of the People's Republic of China must
> obtain a legitimate status in the United Nations.[62]

Despite China's effective military campaign in December, Mao disagreed with Peng about what the next military operation should be and
whether to cross the 38th parallel.[63] Peng and other CPV leaders felt that
the CPV needed time to recuperate before launching another major offensive effort in the spring of 1951. The Chinese soldiers were exhausted and
weakened by arduous nighttime battles, constant air strikes, a bitter winter climate, and poor food. The supply lines were overextended and vulnerable to enemy air attacks at a time when the UNC's essential military
capabilities were intact and thus enjoyed a distinct advantage in military
technology and air power. The CPV command, sharing the view that the
United States would not easily give up Korea and that crossing the 38th
parallel had no particular strategic or political significance, wanted to
cross the parallel in February or March 1951, when its Nineteenth Army
Corps would be ready for combat in Korea. It was also aware of
MacArthur's threat to bomb Manchuria, blockade the Chinese coastal
area, and mobilize the Kuomintang troops against China.

Mao's more optimistic position was dictated by political considerations. At a time when India and other Asian countries in the United Nations were maneuvering to bring about a cease-fire along the 38th parallel, Mao wanted to cross the parallel immediately and thus establish a
superior position on the battlefield. Zhou told Panikkar that, because
MacArthur had already breached the 38th parallel, China had no further
obligation to honor that dividing line. In his telegram to Peng on December 13, Mao said that the CPV would suffer great political disadvantages
if it stopped north of the 38th parallel and instructed the CPV to cross the
parallel and advance toward Kaesong and Seoul. He firmly believed that
the proposed cease-fire was designed merely to buy time for U.S. counter-

attacks. On December 21, Mao asked Peng to concentrate his attacks on South Korean forces because their destruction would leave U.S. forces isolated and compel their departure from Korea.[64]

On December 29 Mao told Peng and Gao:

> This fighting will remove the old impression of the so-called 38th Parallel from the people's brains. It does not matter whether our forces rest and recuperate on the north or the south of the 38th Parallel. If we do not fight now, continue to rest during the winter since early December, and make no move, it will necessarily arouse an idle speculation among capitalist countries and a lot of questions and discussions among democratic countries. If our forces follow the plan to wage a successful campaign in the first half of January, destroy several [South Korean] puppet divisions and a portion of U.S. forces, and then rest for a couple of months to prepare for the spring offensive, it will have a very good effect on the democratic camp and the masses in capitalist countries, will give a new blow to imperialists, and will increase their feeling of pessimism and failure.[65]

Mao reported that Stalin understood the difficulties of China's war efforts in Korea and promised to provide an additional two thousand automobiles for the CPV. He also said that General Matthew Ridgway (who had replaced Walker as commander of the Eighth Army) had ordered the UNC forces not to retreat again.

Peng had no choice but to implement what he regarded as an unwise and untimely military operation ordered by Mao. The CPV commanders chose December 31 as the launching date for their third offensive campaign—a few days before the full moon that would be ideal for nighttime fighting. Knowing that U.S. soldiers would be lax on New Year's Eve, they quickly pushed through the 38th parallel, captured Chunchon on January 2 and Seoul on January 4, and crossed the Han River on January 5. On that day the North Korean troops held a victory celebration in Seoul, and there was a jubilant mass party at Tiananmen Square in Beijing. The Dutch chargé d'affaires in Beijing reported that the elated Chinese thought anything was possible for them.[66]

To the surprise of the Chinese, however, the U.N. forces retreated to the Suwon area, moving close to the 37th parallel. Peng, concerned about logistic problems and a possible counterattack by U.N. forces and not wanting to repeat the mistake made by North Korea in the summer of 1950, halted his southern advance. This decision evidently angered Kim Il

Sung, and Soviet ambassador to North Korea G. R. Lazarev, perhaps with
Stalin's and Kim's blessing, openly complained about Peng's decision to
stop before the 37th parallel and pressured him to move toward Pusan
and force the U.N. forces out of Korea. Pu Shan remembers that Peng
rejected this Soviet "order" and told the Soviets to fight the Americans
themselves. This issue was finally settled by Mao and Stalin: Stalin praised
Peng as a military genius and recalled Lazarev to Moscow; Mao continued to emphasize that the CPV observe a strict military and political discipline in Korea, treat Korean comrades as brothers, and protect the environment and conditions of life in Korea.[67]

On January 17, after the First Committee of the U.N. General Assembly had adopted some of the principles developed by the Cease-Fire Group
in regard to the Korean and other Far Eastern questions, Zhou Enlai proposed that a seven-nation conference be held in China to discuss the withdrawal of all foreign troops from Korea and the removal of U.S. armed
forces from Taiwan and the Taiwan Straits. Zhou also suggested that the
People's Republic of China take its rightful place in the United Nations at
the beginning of the conference. (Note that Zhou did not include either
North Korea or South Korea in the conference.) Acheson called Zhou's
counterproposal "nothing less than an outright rejection" of the U.N.
cease-fire proposal and "further evidence of their contemptuous disregard of a world-wide demand for peace." The United States accelerated
its efforts to adopt a U.N. resolution to condemn China as an aggressor in
Korea.[68]

Mao paid little attention to America's anti-Chinese diplomacy in the
United Nations and persisted in his design to achieve total military victory in Korea. On January 14 he told Peng that the UNC might take one
of two possible actions. One, if the UNC realized that the CPV was well
prepared with a great military capacity the UNC could offer token resistance and then withdraw from Korea. Two, the UNC might put up stiff
resistance in the Taegu-Pusan area. In that case, Mao said, the CPV should
resume an all-out attack to drive the U.N. forces out of Korea. Mao and
Peng had discussed and planned another major Chinese offensive campaign in February or March, after a sufficient period of rest and preparation. On January 25 General Matthew Ridgway, believing that offense
was the best defense, launched a large-scale offensive operation on both
fronts, taking the unprepared CPV leadership by surprise. The CPV commanders were impressed by Ridgway's effective and well-coordinated plan
and were hard-pressed to meet the UNC attack. On January 27, Peng

recommended to Mao that China consider a cease-fire and retreat 15 to 30 kilometers or give up the territory south of the Han River. As a frontline commander who knew the battlefield, Peng, because the CPV still controlled a large area in South Korea, argued that a cease-fire would be advantageous because it would reduce the sacrifices of Chinese soldiers. On the following day Mao rejected Peng's recommendation and ordered him to mount an immediate counterattack. To Mao, a CPV retreat was unacceptable, and he believed that the United States was not interested in a genuine cease-fire and that the only way for China to win was to score another big military success. Peng, reluctant to follow Mao's order, modified it by maintaining a defensive position in the west and counterattacking in the east.[69]

However, faced with a devastating assault by the UNC and by a shortage of supplies and reinforcements, Peng stopped the fourth offensive campaign at Chipyongli, evacuated Inchon on February 10, and ordered the CPV to retreat on February 16. This first major defeat for the CPV was the result, according to Du Ping (director of the CPV political department), of poor military planning, underestimating enemy strength, and insufficient troops and artillery. Hong Xuezhi added that ground troops and artillery units were poorly coordinated and that Chinese mobility was constrained by the small and narrow terrain in Korea. To counter the UNC's superior air power, Stalin promised to bolster the CPV's air force and to send Soviet air force advisers to China.[70]

At the end of February, Mao felt that the UNC, following its arrival at the 38th parallel, would choose one of three scenarios: (1) make a further northern advance, capitalizing on the Chinese soldiers' fatigue, (2) stop at the parallel for ten to twenty days, or (3) stay at the parallel for two to three months, construct long-term fortifications, and then resume its attack. He felt that the United States would choose one of the first two plans and was also concerned about a possible U.N. amphibious landing on Tongchon or Wonsan on the east coast or on Nampo on the west coast. In his detailed report to Stalin on March 1, Mao said that the CPV had suffered heavy casualties and faced a protracted war in Korea (at least another two years) because the UNC, now fighting a war of attrition, had destroyed about 30 to 40 percent of Chinese supplies. He also explained that the CPV had adopted a system of rotating Chinese troops on the battlefield. On March 3, Stalin informed Mao that the Soviet Union would send two air force divisions to provide air cover for Chinese and North Korean ground troops and offered to construct two airfields for the CPV.

On March 15, Stalin promised Mao that another Soviet air force division would be dispatched to Korea to assist in the forthcoming major battles and urged Mao to deploy a Chinese air force division to the front.[71]

It was Acheson's view that, for political and military reasons, the UNC should cross the 38th parallel again, if this could be accomplished without heavy losses. He argued that a general advance across the parallel would "(a) greatly increase the cost of aggression for the Moscow-Peiping axis, (b) explode the myth of Chinese military power, (c) render less likely Chinese adventures in other areas, and (d) produce strains within the Peiping regime and between Peiping and Moscow." Although the JCS's preferred policy was "aggressive defensive operations" to stabilize the military situation in Korea (in part because the U.N. forces were close to the limits of their capabilities), the CPV leaders gave up Seoul on March 14 and retreated to the north of the 38th parallel by early April.[72]

Now that the tide of the war had reversed in his favor, MacArthur began examining the weakness of the Chinese military. On March 24 he stated:

> This weakness is being brilliantly exploited by our ground forces. The enemy's human wave tactics definitely failed him as our own forces become seasoned to this form of warfare; his tactics of infiltration are but contributing to his piecemeal losses, and he is showing less stamina than our own troops under rigors of climate, terrain and battle. Of even greater significance than our tactical success has been the clear revelation that this new enemy, Red China, of such exaggerated and vaunted military power, lacks the industrial capacity to provide adequately many critical items essential to the conduct of modern war.

He then said that the United Nations might change its policy of limiting the war to Korea and expand its military operations to Chinese coastal areas and interior bases, which "would doom Red China to the risk of imminent military collapse." He went on to say, however, that he stood ready at any time to confer with "the commander in chief of the enemy forces." This unauthorized and unexpected statement created consternation and embarrassment in the Truman administration and in the United Nations. The Department of State issued a statement dissociating the U.S. government from MacArthur's position and explaining that the political issues raised by him were far beyond his responsibilities as a field commander. The JCS reminded MacArthur of those restrictions, and President Truman was on the verge of dismissing MacArthur for his insubordination.[73]

Adding to the uproar was the disclosure of an earlier letter of MacArthur's (written to Congressman Joseph Martin Jr. on March 20), which indirectly criticized the Truman administration's Korea policy and declared that "there is no substitute for victory" in war. On April 11, on the unanimous recommendation of the JCS, Acheson, Marshall, and Bradley, President Truman announced that he was relieving MacArthur of all his commands in the Far East and appointing Ridgway as his replacement. Truman made it clear that U.S. policy had not changed: The war was limited to Korea and a peace would be negotiated, but these goals were not to be achieved through appeasement of the aggressors. Because MacArthur was viewed as opposing a settlement, his dismissal increased speculation that there would be a negotiated settlement of the Korean War. The Chinese did not believe, however, that the change from MacArthur to Ridgway improved the prospects for peace in Korea because it did not signify any substantive change in U.S. policy.[74]

To preempt a possible UNC amphibious landing in North Korea and recover lost territory, Mao began a fifth offensive campaign on April 22 with the objective of crossing the 38th parallel and advancing to the southern Han River. Equipped with T-34 tanks, the CPV moved with what a U.S. military officer called "the heaviest Communist artillery fire of the war."[75]

For the next few weeks the CPV launched a series of large-scale attacks against U.N. forces on both fronts, recaptured Kaesong, Munsan, and Chunchon, and reached the northern outskirts of Seoul. General Van Fleet, Eighth Army commander, assumed that the aim of a powerful Chinese strike was to capture Seoul and present it as a gift to Mao on May Day. Unlike Ridgway, Van Fleet—determined not to give up Seoul because it would "ruin the spirit of the nation"—risked fighting with the Han River at his back. Because the JCS felt that the CPV might combine a significant air attack against U.N. forces with an attack by the largest number of Chinese ground troops ever committed during the war, they authorized Ridgway to conduct an air reconnaissance of the air bases in Manchuria and the Shandong Peninsula and to attack those bases in the event of a major enemy air attack from outside Korea. The JCS did not, however, authorize Ridgway to conduct air or naval action against Manchuria, the Soviet territory, or North Korean power complexes including the Yalu River installations or to undertake any operations within fifteen miles of Russian territory. In the second half of May the UNC carried out an ambitious counterattack with mechanized forces, under extensive air cover, and recovered a considerable amount of territory north of the 38th parallel.[76]

The chaotic and costly Chinese retreat was described by Hong Xuezhi as involving "great confusion and damage." Nie Rongzhen admitted that China suffered particularly significant losses in the east. According to a Chinese account, the panic-stricken 180th Division of the Sixtieth Army (with fourteen thousand troops) was encircled and almost completely annihilated.[77]

The Chinese admitted to suffering 85,000 casualties during the entire period of the fifth offensive campaign (from April 24 to June 10), but the UNC estimated Chinese casualties at 105,000 during the second half of May alone, including 11,526 prisoners. On May 30, Ridgway reported to the JCS that "the enemy has suffered a severe major defeat. Estimates of enemy killed in action submitted by field commanders come to total so high that I cannot accept it." He also noted "a noticeable deterioration in the fighting spirit of CCF forces." Although intending to inflict the maximum casualties on "a defeated and retiring enemy," he overruled Van Fleet's plan of an amphibious landing at Wonsan or Tongchon because he followed Truman's policy: seeking a negotiated settlement of the war rather than its expansion deep into North Korea.[78]

After the failure of his fifth offensive campaign, Mao ordered a defensive strategy to stabilize the battle lines more or less along the 38th parallel and seriously considered a cease-fire rather than a total military victory. In a telegram to Peng on May 26, the frustrated Mao admitted that it was impossible to encircle and completely destroy an enemy division or even a battalion because there was an imbalance in military equipment and combat aircraft. He ordered Peng not to let the UNC cross the Pyongyang-Wonsan line. Warning him about a possible UNC amphibious landing at Wonsan, Mao realized that his "man-over-weapons" doctrine had a limited applicability to the technologically superior U.S. forces and that his tactics of "people's war" and "united front" were less than effective in an alien territory. Unlike China, Korea presented a number of problems to Chinese forces—the language barrier, unfamiliar terrain, small peninsular territory, and limited popular support. At the end of May, Mao sent Xu Xiangqian (chief of the PLA General Staff) to Moscow to obtain enough additional Soviet military assistance for sixty Chinese divisions.[79]

ARMISTICE NEGOTIATIONS

On May 17, 1951, the Truman administration adopted the important document NSC 48/5, which specified that the "ultimate objective [was] to seek by political, as distinguished from military means, a solution of the Korean problem." It stated:

The intervention of the Chinese Communist forces in Korea has so changed the situation that it appears militarily impossible now to bring about a situation under which a unified, non-communist Korea could be achieved by political means. Therefore, while in no way renouncing the ultimate political objective which we hold for Korea, the present task should be to bring about a settlement of the Korean problem which at the minimum will deny to communist control that part of Korea south of the 38th Parallel and will provide for the phased withdrawal from Korea of non-Korean forces as militarily practical.

The document confirmed the U.S. policy of not extending hostilities to China or into a general war with the Soviet Union but emphasized that a political settlement should not "jeopardize the United States position with respect to the USSR, to Formosa, or to seating Communist China in the UN." It was clear from the outset of negotiations that the United States intended to decouple an armistice in Korea from China's interest in non-Korean issues.[80]

On the following day the U.N. General Assembly adopted a resolution to impose an embargo on the exports of arms, ammunition, and other strategically relevant materials to China and North Korea. At the same time, however, Acheson met with George F. Kennan, who was on leave of absence from the Department of State, and asked him to have a secret dialogue with Soviet ambassador to the United Nations Jacob Malik. On May 31 and June 5, Kennan and Malik met at Malik's villa on Long Island and explored a possible cease-fire in Korea. Malik asked a number of questions (such as the U.S. attitude toward China, whether all foreign troops would withdraw from Korea, where the demarcation line would be, and who would be on a control commission) and expressed the Soviet desire to see a peaceful solution "at the earliest possible moment." Kennan noticed an important omission in Malik's response—no reference to the status of Formosa or Chinese seating in the United Nations. Kennan assumed that the Soviet Union had influenced China and North Korea to become amenable to proposals for a cease-fire. On the basis of his conversation with Malik, Kennan advised Acheson that "we will not hesitate to grasp at once the nettle of action directed toward achieving a cease-fire" because "the dangers of inaction far exceed those of action." At this sensitive moment Acheson restrained Rhee's well-known propensity to make flagrant, irresponsible, and damaging public statements.[81]

As Kennan had assumed, on receiving a Soviet report on the first Malik-Kennan meeting, Mao and Kim met in Beijing on June 3 and agreed that, in view of the military situation in Korea, it was an advantageous time to begin cease-fire negotiations. They also agreed not to conduct a major offensive during the two months of negotiations. Accompanied by Gao a few days later, Kim flew to Moscow to meet Stalin. On June 22, however, when U.S. ambassador Alan G. Kirk attempted to discuss the Korean question with Chinese ambassador Wang Jiaxiang in Moscow, a member of the Chinese embassy declined to receive an informal note from Kirk on the grounds that "no diplomatic relations exist."[82]

On the following day Malik delivered a radio broadcast on the U.N.-sponsored "The Price of Peace" program in which he proposed that, as a first step toward a peaceful settlement of the Korean question, "discussions should be started between the belligerents for a cease-fire and an armistice providing for the mutual withdrawal of forces from the thirty-eighth parallel."[83] He failed to support Zhou's earlier demands for discussing the U.S. Seventh Fleet in the Taiwan Straits and Chinese representation in the United Nations. At this time the Soviet Union and the United States reached the same conclusion: the negotiations for a cease-fire in Korea should not address other extraneous political issues.

The Department of State immediately issued a positive response: "We are ready to play our part in bringing an end to hostilities and in assuring against their resumption." Two days later, Truman said that "we are ready to join in a peaceful settlement in Korea now" but cautioned that the settlement would not reward aggression. There was an appreciable change in China's public pronouncements. In *Renmin Ribao* editorials (June 25 and July 3), China welcomed Malik's proposal as "fair and reasonable." Instead of repeating the goal of driving the invaders to the sea, the Chinese now argued that it would be a great victory to push them to the 38th parallel. And they refrained from mentioning their political demands in discussing the armistice negotiations in Korea.[84]

On June 30 Ridgway made the following broadcast:

Message to the Commander in Chief, Communist Forces in Korea.

As Commander in Chief of the United Nations Command I have been instructed to communicate to you the following: "I am informed that you may wish a meeting to discuss an armistice providing for the cessation of hostilities and all acts of armed force in Korea, with adequate guarantees for the maintenance of such armistice.

Upon the receipt of word from you that such a meeting is desired I shall be prepared to name my representative. I would also at that time suggest a date at which he could meet with your representative. I propose that such a meeting could take place aboard a Danish hospital ship [jutlandia] in Wonsan Harbor."[85]

The message was ambiguously addressed to a person (Commander in Chief, Communist Forces in Korea) who did not exist in a strict sense. The JCS had rejected Ridgway's original plan to specifically address his message to Commander in Chief, Chinese Communist Forces in Korea, and Supreme Commander, North Korean Forces, because they did not wish to enhance China's prestige and importance.

On the same day Mao sent a telegram to Stalin in which he explained the contents of Ridgway's message and expressed his opinion that the armistice negotiations should begin on July 15 and that the location of the meeting should not be Wonsan Harbor, where U.S. forces were concentrated, but Kaesong near the 38th parallel. Stalin urged Mao to insist on Kaesong, to begin the meeting between July 10 and 15, and to send representatives of North Korean and Chinese forces to the meeting. Asked for advice on the armistice negotiations, Stalin told Mao that China should assume a role of leadership concerning the negotiations. On July 1, Kim sent Stalin a detailed list of North Korea's delegates and an outline of proposals for his approval. On the following day Stalin told Kim that he must consult with China in regard to the negotiating positions. Stalin wished to make sure that Mao would be primarily responsible for the success or failure of the negotiations but decided to send five Soviet military advisers to CPV headquarters. On July 2, Kim Il Sung as commander in chief of the Korean People's Army and Peng Dehuai as commander in chief of the Chinese People's Volunteers sent a joint response to Ridgway in which they agreed to suspend military activities and to hold peace negotiations. They proposed to begin the talks "at Kaesong, on the 38th parallel" between July 10 and 15, and Ridgway accepted a meeting at Kaesong.[86]

Mao issued a series of instructions to Peng and Kim on logistic and procedural aspects of the forthcoming conference.[87] He gave an exact itinerary for the joint Sino-Korean delegation so that they could arrive at Kaesong by July 6 and ordered Peng to sweep the mines in the Kaesong area, to guarantee the security of UNC delegates, and to prevent any disturbance. He reminded Peng and Kim that "we are the hosts for the conference." He also warned them that the UNC might initiate a major offensive under air cover or an amphibious landing at Wonsan or elsewhere in the rear.

Whereas the five-member UNC delegation, led by Vice Admiral C. Turner Joy, included a South Korean general (Paek Sun Yop), the communist delegation, headed by General Nam Il (KPA chief of staff and vice premier), included Li Sang Cho (director of the KPA Bureau of Intelligence), Chang Chun San (director of the KPA Bureau of Military Mobilization), Deng Hua (CPV deputy commander), and Xie Fang (CPV chief of staff). Mao, however, sent a top-level civilian team led by Li Kenong (vice minister of foreign affairs) and Qiao Guanhua (director of the Bureau of Press, Ministry of Foreign Affairs). Mao also assigned the best possible interpreters: Pu Shan (a graduate of Harvard University) for English translations and Ding Min (a graduate of Qinghua University) for Korean translations. The JCS, in contrast, rejected the idea of designating Ambassador John Muccio and William J. Sebald (political adviser to SCAP) as political advisers to the UNC delegation because they wanted to confine the negotiations to military matters.[88]

In his telegram—jointly addressed to Li Kenong, Kim, and Peng on July 9—Mao instructed that a reference to Malik's proposal be stricken from Nam Il's opening statement because the proposal was not mentioned in Ridgway's message of June 30. It is conceivable that, from the very beginning of the conference, Mao did not intend to give much credit or importance to the Soviet Union. On the following day Nam Il presented three specific demands in his opening statement:

1. Cease all hostile military actions

2. Establish the 38th parallel as the military demarcation line, withdraw the armed forces of both sides to 10 kilometers from the parallel, and discuss the exchange of prisoners

3. Withdraw all foreign troops from Korea as early as possible

In response to Joy's statement that the armistice talks should not include discussion of political or economic matters of any kind, Deng Hua argued that the military and political aspects of the Korean question were so interrelated that it would be impossible to completely separate them. Yet Deng did not bring up the U.S. Seventh Fleet or China's representation in the United Nations.[89]

After intense debate, both sides finally agreed on the following items on July 26.

1. Adopting an agenda

2. Determining a military demarcation line, a demilitarized zone, and a cessation of hostilities

3. Arranging a cease-fire, an armistice, and a supervising organization

4. Making arrangements for prisoners of war

5. Making recommendations to the government of the countries concerned on both sides.

The communist side attached high priority to the withdrawal of foreign troops from Korea and wanted to adopt a separate agenda item on this question, but the UNC argued that this was a political matter that should not be discussed at the armistice talks. Mao instructed Li to develop the following argument: "Each nation sent its troops to Korea to fight war, not to enjoy tourism. Why can the armistice conference have a right to discuss a cease-fire, but cannot have a right to discuss the withdrawal of foreign troops?" As a compromise, both sides agreed to address this issue in the item "Recommendations to the governments." Because the UNC found that meeting in the communist-controlled city of Kaesong presented them with a number of logistic and psychological problems, in October it extracted an agreement from the communist delegation to move the site of the conference to Panmunjom, which neither side controlled.[90]

At the initial stage of the negotiations, the UNC delegates regarded Nam Il as the "dominant figure" who had "the final say" and the Chinese delegates as "junior and silent partners." As the negotiations progressed, however, the UNC noticed that Nam invariably read prepared texts and constantly sought a nodding sign or messages from his Chinese colleagues. At this point, the UNC negotiators recognized that the Chinese delegates were the "superiors" and the North Koreans were the "inferiors." In the end Joy concluded that Nam was just "merely the figurehead" and that Xie exercised "the actual power."[91]

Joy described the nervous, slender, and chain-smoking Nam as "a cat on a hot tin roof." In contrast, Joy said that "[Xie's] saturnine yellow face was a set mask, revealing nothing, expressing nothing." Joy assessed the thin, angular, and graceless Xie as follows:

> He gave me the impression of Shakespeare's "Yond Cassius has a lean and hungry look . . . such men are dangerous." Hsieh [Xie] was indeed dangerous. He possessed a bitterly sharp mind, and used it effectively. His head was radically close-cropped, giving the impression of a high forehead. Sharp eyes flicked restlessly as he watched proceedings. . . . His remarks were extemporaneous and fluent. Hsieh Fang was markedly the mental superior among the Communist delegation. He conducted himself in a self-assured manner at all times.

The UNC delegates noticed that, compared with the North Koreans, Chinese delegates appeared to be less doctrinaire, more confident, and more eager to strike a compromise. When tempers flared, however, both sides exchanged harsh invectives. William K. Harrison, who replaced Joy in May 1952, went as far as to call his communist counterparts "common criminals."[92]

At the time of the negotiations the UNC did not know that Xie was following a carefully prepared scenario prepared by Li Kenong (or Wu Xiuquan during Li's absence) and Qiao Guanhua. The Western accounts made much of an episode on August 10, 1951, when, after Joy's statement, Nam refused to respond, and neither side spoke for two hours and eleven minutes. This tense psychological maneuver was coordinated behind the scenes by Li.[93] (Joy at last broke the silence.) At the beginning of the negotiations Nam Il had accepted a UNC proposal concerning the press but quickly reversed himself after a recess, probably because of Li's instructions. In most cases Li wrote the draft or multiple drafts of a delegate's statement and submitted them to Mao and Zhou for revision and approval. Via Li and Qiao, Mao and Zhou closely monitored the negotiations at Panmunjom and directed every important proposal and maneuver made by the communist delegates.

Throughout the cease-fire negotiations, Mao was in frequent communication with Stalin and Kim but maintained the fiction that Nam Il was a "spokesman" because the CPV did not represent the PRC government in a technical sense and were "guests" in Korea and to save face for Kim.

Undoubtedly Mao took into account Kim's interests and aspirations and was able to iron out whatever policy differences they may have had in private. A Chinese participant in the Panmunjom talks remembers that Kim played a minor role in the negotiations and that there was not much substantive discussion between Chinese and North Korean delegates. The Chinese delegates kept a low profile in the plenary sessions but were active in the meetings of subdelegates, liaison officers, and staff members, where the actual negotiations and compromises often took place. Mao expected that bringing about a negotiated cease-fire in Korea would take a relatively short period of time, but he underestimated the complexity of the agenda items—especially the establishment of a military demarcation line and prisoners of war issues. (Qiao Guanhua had predicted to Wilfred Burchett, a procommunist Australian journalist, that the talks would last about three weeks.)[94]

To Mao's surprise, an intense, prolonged discussion arose over determining a military demarcation line. As Nam Il stated on July 10, the communist side assumed that the 38th parallel would be readily acceptable to the United States because Acheson, Marshall, and JCS chairman Omar Bradley had already testified at the "MacArthur Hearings" in favor of a cease-fire and military settlement at or near the 38th parallel and Malik had specifically mentioned the 38th parallel in his proposal of June 23. They argued that this parallel was consistent with historical facts and well known in the world and that the war had occurred because one belligerent had violated the parallel. Moreover, they contended that no other stable line could be established before an armistice was agreed on and implemented. In his report written on the twenty-fourth anniversary of the PLA's founding on August 1, 1951, Peng Dehuai made it clear that a demilitarized zone should be set up along the 38th parallel.[95]

The UNC rejected the 38th parallel as a *military* demarcation line and insisted that the line should be determined on the basis of a careful assessment of comparative military capabilities and current exigencies in Korea. Joy pointed out that the UNC maintained air superiority over all Korea and controlled the entire coastal area. On this basis Ridgway believed that the line should be "somewhere between the Yalu and Tumen Rivers on the north and the line of contact on the ground." Likewise, Joy insisted on the Pyongyang-Wonsan line as a military demarcation line. He stated:

> Considering only ground forces, a cease-fire arrangement with all forces remaining in place would appear reasonable. This, however, would stop

only a part of the hostile action. Our Navy would still be free to blockade and bombard along both coasts of North Korea. Our Air Force would
still be able to reconnoiter and inflict military damage over all of North
Korea. If, then, we are to agree on a military armistice whereby our
ground, air, and naval forces cease operations against your forces, we
contend that the location of the demilitarized zone in all fairness, must
be appropriately influenced by all of these factors.

The Communists called Joy's argument "naive and illogical" and continued to insist that the 38th parallel was "just, reasonable, realistic, and
practicable."[96]
    The United States rejected the 38th parallel for several reasons: First,
it felt that the parallel was a symbol of political division in Korea and that
its acceptance could be seen as a "reward" for North Korean and Chinese
aggression. The domestic critics of Truman's Korea policy—such as Sena-
tors Robert A. Taft and Richard M. Nixon—proclaimed that a truce at
the 38th parallel would be an "appeasement peace."[97] Second, it believed
that the actual battle line—north of the parallel on the east and south of
the parallel on the west—meant a net territorial gain for the UNC and
presented a more defensible position than did the 38th parallel. Third, the
United States was sensitive to Rhee's outspoken opposition to the 38th
parallel. Fourth, the United States was reluctant to agree on the parallel
because this definite line would create a sanctuary for defensive fortifications and be an obstacle to exercising military pressure against the communist forces.
    In August, Joy detected that the Chinese were more flexible toward
the question of a military demarcation than their North Korean partners.
Toward the end of October the communist side offered to accept the actual line of ground contact as a demarcation line and to fix it immediately
and irrevocably. The UNC did not wish to do so, however, until the armistice agreement was signed. Ridgway, who was adamantly opposed to
establishing a de facto cease-fire without the settlement of other issues,
reported to the JCS on November 13, 1950: "We have much to gain by
standing firm [on this issue]. We have everything to lose through conces-
sion. With all my conscience I urge we stand firm." He was quite certain
that the communist forces were "badly hurt" and desired the earliest possible suspension of hostilities.[98]
    The JCS, however, overruled Ridgway's position. On November 27
the two sides accepted the military demarcation line based on the actual

line of ground contact as well as the four-kilometer-wide demilitarized zone, provided the military armistice was signed within thirty days. The communist side proposed twenty days, but Mao ordered Li to accept the UNC proposal for thirty days. (Mao told his delegates not to look too eager to complete the cease-fire negotiations.) If the armistice were not signed within thirty days, the two sides agreed to revise the line so that "the revised military demarcation line will coincide exactly with the line of contact between both sides immediately prior to the signing of the military armistice agreement."[99]

For political and psychological reasons the UNC attempted to include Kaesong (the ancient capital south of the 38th parallel) in the demilitarized zone but faced stiff resistance from the communist negotiators. Again the JCS ordered Ridgway to give up Kaesong lest the negotiations break down or reach a stalemate.[100] The de facto cease-fire allowed China and North Korea to solidify their defensive positions, at least for thirty days.

To implement and administer the cease-fire agreements, the two sides settled on the composition and functions of the bilateral Military Armistice Commission without much disagreement. The UNC nominated Sweden, Switzerland, and Norway as members of the Neutral Nations Supervisory Commission (NNSC), but the communist side nominated Poland, Czechoslovakia, and the Soviet Union. The nomination of the Soviet Union startled the UNC and aroused an acrimonious discussion at Panmunjom. The UNC rejected the neutral status of the Soviet Union, but Nam Il argued that

> The Soviet Union is one [member] of the United Nations which is not only most strictly opposed to interventions in the Korean war, but it also is most strongly in favor of a peaceful settlement of the Korean question. If the Soviet Union could not be nominated as a neutral nation, there would be no neutral nation at all existing in the world.[101]

The Soviet Union may have designated itself as a neutral state in an attempt to demonstrate Stalin's blamelessness concerning the Korean War or to secure a direct role in the NNSC's supervisory activities. The Communists may have suggested the Soviet Union, knowing that it would be unacceptable, so that they could then trade off Norway from the commission (Norway had supported the U.N. action in Korea). The discussion continued for months before the two delegations settled on two nominees from each side—Sweden, Switzerland, Poland, and Czechoslovakia—as NNSC members.

In the beginning the UNC proposed that the Neutral Nations Inspection Teams (NNIT) under the NNSC have the right of unlimited access throughout Korea to inspect violations of the armistice agreement, but the communist side wanted to limit the ports of entry for the NNIT. Whereas the UNC reduced the proposed number of ports of entry on each side from twelve to eight and then to seven, the communist side increased its proposed number from three to four. As a compromise, the two delegations accepted five ports of entry on each side. They also struck a compromise on the monthly rotation of military personnel on both sides. In view of the communist opposition, however, the United States, to Joy's chagrin, abandoned the right of aerial reconnaissance and the proposed prohibition on construction and repair of airfields.

On February 6, 1952, the communist delegation proposed that, within three months after the armistice agreement had been signed and become effective, the two sides hold a political conference to settle several issues: (1) the withdrawal of all foreign troops from Korea, (2) the peaceful settlement of the Korean question, and (3) other questions related to peace in Korea. Because the Communists identified "other questions" as "a series of warlike measures in the East" taken by the United States, it opened the door to a discussion of the presence of the U.S. Seventh Fleet in the Taiwan Straits and of Japan's peace treaty and security treaty with the United States. Hence the UNC proposed to substitute "other Korean questions related to peace" for "other questions related to peace in Korea." On February 17 the two sides agreed to hold a political conference to discuss "the withdrawal of all foreign forces from Korea, the peaceful settlement of the Korean question, etc." As William H. Vatcher reports, the rapidity of this agreement caught the Communists completely off balance, but the United States was not interested in withdrawing its troops from Korea in the near future, believing that any precipitous withdrawal would expose South Korea to "the savage retaliation of a brutal Communist occupation." Ridgway told the JCS that "no promises, no assurances, no international agreements, nothing but the barrier of superior forces will guarantee against such occupation." Mutual distrust between the United States and China/North Korea was profound.[102]

In July 1951, Mao did not expect that the prisoner of war (POW) issue would become the most intractable and complex stumbling block to a negotiated cease-fire in Korea because he assumed that the United States would honor a provision (Article 118) of the 1947 Geneva Convention, which mandated the repatriation of all prisoners of war without delay after active hostilities ceased. In fact, Acheson, Ridgway, and Joy preferred to exchange all the prisoners of war, but they were forced to follow Truman's strong belief in voluntary repatriation.[103] As soon as the issue came to the floor at Panmunjom, the UNC sought to exchange POWs on a one-for-one basis because it held more POWs than did the Communists. More important, it categorically repudiated the concept of total repatriation as incorporated in the Geneva Convention and advocated the principle of "nonforcible repatriation."

In addition to the moral and humanitarian justification for voluntary repatriation, the United States was concerned that a large number of communist repatriates would increase the enemy's military strength. It also felt guilty about automatically repatriating all the POWs at the end of World War II, for some of them, especially in the Soviet Union and other socialist states, had been persecuted. The United States thus had a distinct political and ideological imperative in dealing with the POW issue. On May 1, 1951 (seventy days before the beginning of the truce talks), for example, the JCS issued explicit instructions to Ridgway: "You should initiate and maintain a comprehensive program for interrogation, indoctrination, and reorientation of POWs with a view toward their eventual utilization as avowed anti-Communists."[104]

The communist delegates maintained that returning all POWs to their homes was an internationally recognized principle that was nonnegotiable. Said Li Sang Cho, "It is clearly revealed that by force and cruel mistreatment you wanted to deliver them to a certain friend of yours in South Korea and a part of them to a certain friend of yours in Formosa. This is the so-called voluntary repatriation." In view of their political contest with Chiang, the Chinese were determined not to let any prisoners of war go to Formosa. Chai Chengwen claimed that the UNC used Kuomintang agents to indoctrinate and threaten Chinese prisoners of war and that a majority of them were uneducated and thus vulnerable to coercion. As early as February 1952 both Acheson and Marshall were aware of "the unwillingness of any Communist regime to recognize in any way that an inhabitant of its territory voluntarily could choose to escape from its control." They were skeptical about China and North Korea accepting the voluntary repatriation of POWs.[105]

On December 18, 1951, the POW lists were exchanged. The UNC held 132,474 prisoners of war (95,531 North Koreans, 20,700 Chinese, and 16,243 South Koreans), and the communist side reported 11,559 prisoners of war (7,142 South Koreans, 3,198 Americans, and 1,219 other nationals). (The two sides accused each other of concealing the actual number of POWs.) After screening the POWs, the UNC reported on April 19, 1952, that about 70,000 prisoners of war (53,900 North Koreans, 5,100 Chinese, 3,800 South Koreans, and 7,200 civilian internees) expressed their desire to be repatriated; the communist side said that about 12,000 South Korean and other UNC prisoners of war opted for repatriation.[106]

The Chinese were particularly upset by the high percentage of their POWs who, despite their "volunteer" status, did not want to come home; the North Korean percentage was much lower. On April 22, Mao instructed Li Kenong to take a "hard-line position" on the POW issue. In May 1952 Zhou Enlai assured Madam Pandit (Indian ambassador to the United Nations and Nehru's sister) in Beijing that China was eager to see a truce in Korea but that China could not accept the repatriation of only 70,000 communist prisoners of war. He hinted that if 100,000 were returned, a compromise might be reached. This message was promptly delivered to Nehru and the Department of State. The United States, however, balked at returning any POWs against their will.[107]

On June 15, 1952, Zhou Enlai apparently told Panikkar that the nonrepatriates could be brought to Panmunjom, not under military escort, and that they could be interviewed by "neutral personnel" from the four neutral states and the Red Cross. The United States expressed interest but questioned the suggestion's authenticity because of Panikkar's reputation as an unreliable messenger. It is possible that the United States' bombing of North Korean power plants, including the Supung stations on the Yalu River on June 23, may have dampened Zhou's conciliatory overtures. In any case, on July 14 he notified the Indian embassy in Beijing that he was withdrawing his earlier proposal.[108]

The Truman administration considered soliciting Soviet assistance in regard to the POW stalemate but was opposed by U.S. ambassador to the Soviet Union George F. Kennan, who argued that it was to the Soviet Union's advantage to tie down and drain U.S. forces in Korea. Kennan also thought that the Soviet Union did not favor voluntary repatriation because its soldiers might then be unreliable in the event of war. The continuing military confrontation between the United States and China served Stalin's interests as long as it did not spread beyond Korea. Kennan suggested that the United States attempt to frighten China before Zhou Enlai's scheduled visit to Moscow in August 1952 so that China would make "panicky demands" on Russia. The United States proceeded to conduct saturation bombings over North Korea, tighten its economic embargo against China, and build up Nationalist Chinese forces. It also spread rumors that an amphibious landing was planned for September 1952. In response, the CPV doubled its size from July 1951 (277,000) to July 1952 (680,000), increased its air force activities, and expanded its airfields in Manchuria and North Korea. It also constructed an extensive system of underground fortifications dubbed the "underground great walls." Mao continued to provide North Korea with military supplies and economic assistance.[109]

On August 17, 1952, Zhou Enlai led a sixty-member Chinese delegation to Moscow for two main purposes: to obtain Stalin's assistance for China's First Five-Year Economic Plan and to discuss the Korean question.[110] The delegation included top-level economic specialists (such as Vice Premier Chen Yun) and military leaders (such as Deputy Chief of the General Staff Su Yu and Air Force Commander Liu Yalou). At their first meeting on August 20, Stalin supported China's position at Panmunjom and reaffirmed the Soviet promise to provide military assistance for sixty divisions. Stalin suggested three steps to solve the POW question: First, that the repatriation of POWs be based on the formula that the UNC detain 30 percent of the communist POWs and the communist side detain 13 percent of UNC POWs, or this ratio could be reduced by half. If this step were not successful, the second step was to conclude the cease-fire first and then resolve the POW issue. If neither step was effective, the third step would be to transfer the nonrepatriates to the custody of neutral states so that representatives of each side could visit them and persuade them to return home.

Stalin said, however, that China should maintain a firm position toward the United States as the only way to resolve the Taiwan and Korean questions and urged Zhou not to let Chinese aircraft cross the 38th parallel. If they did, Stalin contended, it would mean a formal state of war between China and the United States because the Chinese aircraft did not belong to the "volunteers" but to the Chinese state. He was likely afraid that were China in a formal state of war with the United States, it would drag the Soviet Union in in accordance with Article 1 of the Sino-Soviet treaty. At Moscow the two governments signed a number of agreements on economic issues and one on extending the joint use of the naval base at Port Arthur. The last agreement demonstrated their continuing naval cooperation and the importance of the Soviet defense commitment for China.

On Zhou's suggestion, Stalin invited Peng Dehuai, Kim Il Sung, and

Pak Hon Yong to Moscow on September 1. At their meeting on September 4, Stalin said that the Chinese and Korean people were heroes. He repeated his admonition that Chinese aircraft should not cross the 38th parallel and promised to provide jet fighters to China and North Korea, to equip three North Korean air force divisions, and to offer five antiaircraft artillery units and two thousand automobiles. Again he suggested that the exchange of POWs be based on a ratio, which neither Zhou nor Kim accepted. On Mao's instruction Zhou consulted with Stalin in regard to a strategy at the United Nations and to India's and Burma's proposals for nonaggression treaties with China.[111]

In the aftermath of Zhou's and Kim's meetings with Stalin, the communist side changed its position, suggesting that all Chinese POWs, not necessarily all North Korean POWs, should be repatriated. Yet the United States was not amenable to this suggestion either. The Panmunjom talks remained in recess from October 1952 to March 1953, and fighting intensified in Korea, especially in the "Iron Triangle" area. Mao continued to be obsessed with the idea of a U.S. amphibious landing at the Yalu River, Chongchon River, Wonsan, Tongchon, or Nampo.[112] And the United States was absorbed in the presidential elections and the transfer of power from Truman to Dwight D. Eisenhower.

Meanwhile, the United Nations began debating the POW issue. Speaking before the General Assembly on October 24, Acheson reaffirmed America's uncompromising adherence to the principle of nonforcible repatriation of POWs. A few days later Andrey Vyshinsky proposed that the cease-fire be immediately implemented in Korea and that an eleven-member committee on Korea decide the disposition of the POW issue by a two-thirds majority. The Chinese and North Korean governments endorsed this proposal, but the First Committee turned it down. Encouraged by Britain, Canada, and France, Indian ambassador Krishna Menon introduced a draft resolution on November 17 that was designed to move all POWs to demilitarized zones, to set up a repatriation commission (composed of Sweden, Switzerland, Poland, and Canada, which would choose another member as an umpire with a deciding vote), and to stipulate that the commission settle the POW issue under the principle of nonforcible repatriation. The disposition of any remaining nonrepatriates would be referred to a political conference or to the United Nations. After Vyshinsky harshly criticized the Indian resolution on November 24, Acheson praised Menon for his statesmanship and supported the Indian proposal with a few revisions. On December 1 the First Committee passed it by a vote of fifty-three to five, with one abstention, as did the General Assembly by a vote of fifty-four to five two days later. It took nine days for Zhou to decide to reject the Indian resolution. He argued that the resolution had been adopted without the participation of China or North Korea and that there were no legitimate Chinese or North Korean prisoners of war who refused to return home. He said that the role of the United Nations envisaged in the resolution was a ploy by the United States to force the retention of prisoners of war. Acheson speculated that Vyshinsky's harsh words were intended to "head off incipient Chinese softening" toward the Indian formula. Nehru made every diplomatic effort to gain China's acceptance of the Indian resolution and felt that China had been inclined to do so. After his discussions with Nehru and other Indian leaders in New Delhi, U.S. ambassador Chester B. Bowles concluded that China had "everything to gain from a truce" but that the Soviet Union had "everything to gain from continued fighting." The extent to which China and the Soviet Union coordinated their reactions to the Indian proposal remains unclear.[113]

A series of meetings, statements, and proposals in February and March 1953, however, paved the way for a break in the deadlock over the POW issue. On February 7, Mao stated at the National Committee of the Chinese People's Political Consultative Conference that China desired peace but that U.S. imperialists made unreasonable demands and intended to expand the aggression. As Stalin had suggested to Zhou in August 1952, Mao proposed a cease-fire first and settling other issues afterward, the same proposal that he had flatly rejected in December 1950. Yet in his report prepared on February 19, Zhou Enlai argued that China should not initiate any move at Panmunjom because the United States might interpret it as a sign of Chinese weakness. Mao predicted that the United States would turn to the Soviet Union for assistance.[114]

By taking advantage of the resolution adopted by the League of Red Cross Societies, General Mark W. Clark, UNC commander in chief, proposed on February 22, 1953, to discuss the exchange of seriously sick and wounded POWs at Panmunjom. This initiative was taken to resume the deadlocked negotiations, but the Communists did not immediately respond. On March 5, Stalin died. After representing China as one of the four principal pallbearers in Moscow at the Stalin obsequies, Zhou Enlai had extensive discussions with Premier Georgy Malenkov, Foreign Minister Vyacheslav Molotov, and other Soviet leaders between March 8 and 17. On March 19 the Soviet Council of Ministers decided to support

Clark's proposal and recommend that the Panmunjom negotiations be resumed. It also stressed that Peng and Kim send a joint response to Clark that would make a positive contribution toward resolving the POW issue and realizing a cease-fire in Korea. Moreover, the council suggested that the POWs should not be repatriated against their will and that Poland, Czechoslovakia, Switzerland, and Sweden should handle POW matters. The post-Stalin leadership quickly transcended the hard line articulated by Vyshinsky in the United Nations a few months earlier and took an important step to bring about a negotiated settlement of the Korean War as part of their "peace offensive" and "new look."[115]

On March 23, after Zhou returned from Moscow, Mao told Ding Guoyu, a Chinese negotiator at Panmunjom, that President Eisenhower might abandon Truman's self-constraint, using the issue of sick and wounded POWs. Mao added that the UNC might even refuse to accept "our documents" or to hold the meetings of liaison officers. He instructed Ding to make fewer protests to the UNC and to agree to the Clark proposal. A few days thereafter, Peng and Kim sent a joint reply to Clark expressing the hope that exchanging the seriously sick and wounded would lead to the smooth settlement of the entire POW issue, thereby achieving an armistice in Korea.[116]

On March 30 Zhou Enlai announced a major proposal to untangle the POW conundrum:

> The Government of the People's Republic of China and the Government of the Democratic People's Republic of Korea, in pursuance of their consistently maintained peace policy and their position of consistently working for the speedy realization of an armistice in Korea and striving for a peaceful settlement of the Korean question thus to preserve and consolidate world peace, are prepared to take steps to eliminate the differences on this question so as to bring about an armistice in Korea. To this end, the Government of the People's Republic of China and the Government of the Democratic People's Republic of Korea propose that both parties to the negotiations should undertake to repatriate immediately after the cessation of hostilities all those prisoners of war in their custody who insist upon repatriation and to hand over the remaining prisoners of war to a neutral state so as to ensure a just solution to the question of their repatriation.

This was the first time that Zhou Enlai publicly modified the principle of total repatriation and conceded to the mechanism for nonforcible repatriation. The following day Kim endorsed Zhou's proposal, as did Molotov. At the United Nations General Assembly Vyshinsky expressed his "full solidarity with this noble act" of China and North Korea.[117]

That the Chinese were aware that the Eisenhower administration might use the atomic bomb against China may have played a role in Zhou's conciliatory posture. There were a number of other important reasons, however, for his concessions on the POW issue. First, the Chinese felt that it was time to stop the expensive war efforts in Korea and concentrate on China's First Five-Year Plan beginning in 1953. Second, there are indications that they wished to transcend the two-camp international outlook and pursue a policy of peaceful coexistence. Third, they recognized the serious morale problem among Chinese troops who were caught in the stalemate. Fourth, they believed that North Korea was undergoing serious economic difficulties and required a period for reconstruction. Most important, Zhou presumably agreed with Malenkov in Moscow that the communist side should take the initiative to bring about a negotiated end to the Korean War. Adam Ulam says, "The evidence that it was Stalin's death that removed obstacles to a cease-fire is well-nigh overwhelming."[118]

The Zhou proposal created the momentum for Operation Little Switch, an exchange of seriously sick and wounded POWs that took place from April 20 to April 26. The UNC sent 5,194 North Koreans, 1,030 Chinese, and 446 civilian internees in exchange for 149 Americans, 471 South Koreans, and 64 other POWs. Encouraged by this operation, the communist side presented a revised version of the Zhou proposal, but it still did not fully satisfy the UNC. Unlike its predecessor, the Eisenhower administration decided to solicit assistance from the post-Stalin Soviet leadership. In meetings with Voroshilov on April 20 and Molotov on May 28, Ambassador Charles E. Bohlen said that the success or failure of negotiations at Panmunjom would affect the future of U.S.-Soviet relations and that a failure of the negotiations might lead to an undesirable situation. On June 3 Molotov informed Bohlen: "The Soviet Government has taken note of the information you gave me on May 28, concerning the armistice talks at Panmunjom; as you know the outcome of these talks does not depend on us, but it has been noted with satisfaction that the path to the successful conclusion of these armistice talks has been mapped out." Even though this message was carefully phrased and deliberately vague, it demonstrated that the Soviet Union was able to secure or learn of a commitment from China and North Korea for "the successful conclusion" of the talks. Molotov wanted to get credit for the breakthrough and improve relations with the United States. On the following day communist negotiators at Panmunjom offered a conciliatory proposal to the UNC. After a few minor adjustments, on June 8 the two senior delegates initialed the "Terms of Reference for Neutral Nations Repatriation Commission." Pleased with the final settlement of the thorny POW issue, Zhou Enlai called Li Kenong to express his appreciation to Li and the other Chinese delegates, who were all in tears.[119]

The terms for POW repatriation were as follows:

1. The Neutral Nations Repatriation Commission (NNRC) consists of India, Sweden, Switzerland, Poland, and Czechoslovakia.

2. India serves as the umpire, chairman, and executive agent of the commission and provides sufficient armed forces for its operations.

3. The commission takes custody of all prisoners of war who do not exercise their right of repatriation.

4. Representatives of the nations to which prisoners of war belong have an opportunity to explain to all prisoners of war their rights in the presence of the commission members.

5. Any prisoner of war who decides to exercise the right of repatriation shall be repatriated.

6. The disposition of all prisoners of war who still do not exercise their right of repatriation shall be determined by the Political Conference.

On June 10 Vice Minister of Foreign Affairs Zhang Hanfu met representatives of the five neutral nations and invited them to participate in the NNRC; by June 13 each nation had delivered an affirmative answer to Zhang.[120] After eighteen months of grueling negotiations, the POW issue had finally been settled. The two delegations then moved rapidly to wrap up other remaining issues such as the final determination of a military demarcation line.

On June 18, however, Rhee, who had been vociferously criticizing what he deemed to be appeasement at Panmunjom and demanding the simultaneous withdrawal of Chinese and U.N. forces from Korea, unilaterally released about twenty-seven thousand anticommunist North Korean POWs and about fifty Chinese POWs. Clark said, "All hell broke loose at Rhee's order." The United States denied its involvement in the incident and gave assurances that a similar situation would not occur. The Eisenhower administration considered invoking the secret Eveready plan to remove Rhee from power but instead offered a mutual security treaty and economic and military assistance programs to secure Rhee's compliance with the armistice agreement. The communist side attacked the "Syngman Rhee clique's criminal act" and U.S. complicity and demanded the return of the released prisoners. On June 20, Peng received Mao's permission to delay the scheduled signing of the armistice agreement. During the week beginning July 13, the CPV conducted the largest offensive against South Korean forces since the beginning of the truce negotiations, inflicting heavy casualties (about seventy-eight thousand according to a Chinese source) and capturing a new territory of 178 square kilometers in the Iron Triangle area. The offensive was intended to punish Rhee and show what might happen were he to violate the cease-fire arrangement. The Chinese, however, did not use Rhee's action as an excuse to abort the accomplishments at Panmunjom.[121]

On July 27, 1953, two senior delegates—William K. Harrison Jr. and Nam Il—signed the armistice documents at Panmunjom. Afterward they departed without uttering a word to each other. The documents were delivered to the supreme commanders—Peng at Kaesong, Kim at Pyongyang, and Clark at Munsan—for their signatures. At 10:00 P.M. the armistice went into effect throughout Korea. On August 5, Operation Big Switch to repatriate POWs began. Altogether, the UNC returned 75,801 prisoners of war, including 5,640 Chinese, and received 12,773 prisoners of war, including 3,326 Americans.[122]

On September 23 the NNRC took custody of all nonrepatriates— 22,604 Chinese and North Koreans and 359 members of the U.N. forces— and began the tense and chaotic process of interviews and explanations with them. Of these, only 638 prisoners of war were repatriated; 88 Chinese and Koreans applied to go to India. On December 23 the commission concluded its mission, and Chairman K. S. Thimayya of India decided that, since the Political Conference had not met, he would return all the remaining nonrepatriates to their previous custodians on January 20, 1954. The commission transferred 347 nonrepatriates (including 21 Americans) to the communist side, and 21,820 prisoners of war (including 14,227 Chinese) to the UNC. The UNC released all Korean nonrepatriates in South Korea, and the Chinese, whom Chiang Kai-shek's agents had diligently cajoled and indoctrinated in the camps, left Inchon to go to

Formosa—the last thing the PRC wanted. This was carried out despite Zhou Enlai's "violent" and "furious" opposition. At the National Security Council meeting on January 21, CIA director Allen Dulles exclaimed that the release of nonrepatriates "constituted one of the greatest psychological victories so far achieved by the free world against Communism."[123]

The Political Conference that was envisaged in the "Recommendations to the governments" failed to materialize. Beginning on October 25, 1953, Arthur Dean had intermittent meetings with Huang Hua and Ki Sok Pok at Panmunjom, but they disagreed on the conference's composition, time, and place. Dean insisted on a two-sided conference, with the Soviet Union as a voting participant on the communist side, but Huang wanted to invite neutral states, including the Soviet Union, which he defined as a nonvoting neutral state, to a "round table" meeting. Dean accused the Chinese of being "stooges" of the Soviet Union, and Huang assailed American "perfidy." Neither was prepared to expunge the accusations from the record. The bitter and angry talks completely nullified the provisions for the Political Conference and the withdrawal of foreign forces from Korea and eventually led to the Geneva Conference on Korea, which was convened on April 26, 1954.

The Chinese hailed their intervention in the Korean War as a "great victory" and held a mass celebration for Peng in Beijing on August 11, 1953. Despite the enormous human sacrifices and economic costs, they were proud of the fact that the CPV fought well against the most powerful and richest nation in the world and brought about a military stalemate in Korea. Mao, although unable to achieve a total military victory, eventually opted for a negotiated settlement because he accepted the military realities in Korea and wished, among other things, to focus on China's economic reconstruction. He was by and large satisfied with the restoration of Kim's regime and the status quo antebellum in Korea. The combination of the armistice and a buffer zone set up in the Korean Peninsula lessened his national security concerns vis-à-vis the United States. He said that, if the 38th parallel had not been restored, the front line might have reached the Yalu and Tumen Rivers and threatened the people in Shenyang, Anshan, and other northeastern areas. This was indeed the first time that China had effectively stood up against the West since the Opium War. In the process, Mao enhanced China's prestige in the international community and its role as a leader of anti-imperialist revolutionary movements in Asia. Even Joy admitted that "the Korean armistice was a victory for Red China: her prestige has continued to rise." Philip West suggests that, by the end of the Korean War, China had become Goliath-like in its restoration of Chinese pride as the Middle Kingdom and that "within five years China's voice has carried more weight throughout the Western and Asian worlds, from Geneva to Bandung, than it had at any other point in modern times."[124]

The Resist-America and Aid Korea movement aroused strong patriotic sentiments as well as internationalism among the Chinese and bolstered popular support for Mao amid external adversity. The heroic struggles and international solidarity displayed in the Korean War were immortalized in Chinese novels (such as Ba Jin's *Tuanyuan* [Reunion]), poems, movies, textbooks, and other popular media. Yet the war deprived Mao of the opportunity to "liberate" Taiwan and achieve China's representation in the United Nations. If he had accepted a cease-fire in December 1950 or January 1951, he might have bargained for the removal of the U.S. Seventh Fleet from the Taiwan Straits or China's entrance to the United Nations Security Council. The Chinese military grew in number during the war and gained invaluable experience in Korea, but it also came to recognize the limits of Mao's "man-over-weapons" doctrine and the importance of advanced military technology. In this sense, Nie Rongzhen said that the Korean War was a "university for modern warfare." The Chinese also learned how difficult and costly it was for China to confront the United States and use military ventures as a means of foreign policy.[125]

The Korean War solidified and institutionalized the American policies of military containment, diplomatic isolation, and economic sanctions toward China and North Korea. To stop the spread of Chinese influence, the United States erected a chain of defensive walls around China, ranging from the bilateral security treaties with Japan, South Korea, the Philippines, and Taiwan to multilateral systems, including the Southeast Asia Treaty Organization. The Eisenhower administration viewed communist rule in China as a "passing phenomenon" and intensified its worldwide anti-Beijing crusade. Even though the Soviet Union and China had been united in a common struggle against the United States during the war, and the Sino-Soviet military alliance had served as an effective deterrent, preventing a U.S. attack against Manchuria, Mao had mixed feelings about Stalin and the Soviet Union—he appreciated Soviet assistance and advice but was disillusioned by the Soviet Union's less than full support for Sino–North Korean war efforts. The war planted a poisonous seed in the evolution of Sino-Soviet relations and prompted competition and rivalry with respect to the Korean Peninsula.

After having devoted much energy and commitment to the Korean War, it was natural for the Chinese to develop a strong vested interest in Korean affairs and to cherish the revolutionary solidarity with North Korea that had been cemented in blood. Thus the Chinese emerged as legitimate and influential players in managing the Korean question. They embraced Kim as a younger brother and generously provided him with military protection and economic and diplomatic support. Kim, however, transcended his earlier dependency on the Soviet Union and began manipulating the growing Sino-Soviet competition for his own interests. Just as Kim regarded the United States as a principal spoiler of his goal of national liberation, Rhee felt that Chinese military intervention had shattered his lifelong dream of Korean independence and unification. He vigorously carried out anti-Beijing measures in South Korea (one popular song included the phrase "smash the [Chinese] barbarians"), but there had been no record of intentional atrocities committed by the CPV during the war. The Chinese praised Kim as a hero and denounced Rhee as a villain and a puppet. The war crystalized China's unabashedly pro-Pyongyang and anti-Seoul attitudes, which colored China's Korea policy for many years to come.

Chapter Three
MILITARY POLICY

• •

MILITARY ALLIANCE

T he Chinese completed the last phase of the CPV's withdrawal from North Korea in October 1958, but they retained a strategic interest in the Korean Peninsula as guarantors of North Korean security. As a manifestation of this interest, Zhou Enlai and Kim Il Sung signed a Treaty of Friendship, Cooperation and Mutual Assistance at Beijing on July 11, 1961—five days after Kim had signed a similar treaty with Nikita Khrushchev at Moscow. The Soviet Union and North Korea took the initiative in formulating the treaties, but the Chinese also had a number of reasons for accepting the treaty with North Korea.[1] First, the United States had revised its security treaty with Japan in 1960 to further solidify its anticommunist military containment system in the Asian-Pacific region; in April 1961, the new John F. Kennedy administration had attempted to overthrow Fidel Castro's rule in Cuba through the abortive Bay of Pigs invasion. Second, a series of disruptive events in South Korea, especially the student uprising in April 1960 and the military coup d'état in May 1961, increased the atmosphere of instability and uncertainty in the Korean Peninsula. A third and more important impetus was the growing Sino-Soviet conflict, which Kim Il Sung manipulated for his security. Hence the Chinese regarded this new treaty as an important instrument to counterbalance not only the assertive U.S. military presence in South Korea but also the Soviet Union's potential military ambitions in North Korea.

Article Two of the Sino–North Korean treaty, which took effect September 10, 1961, declared:

> The two Contracting Parties shall collectively take all measures to prevent either Contracting Party from being attacked by any other country. If either of the Contracting Parties should suffer armed attack by any country or coalition of countries and thus find itself in a state of war, the other Contracting Party shall immediately extend military and other assistance with all means at its disposal.

This provision, a more direct and categorical commitment than that of the U.S.–South Korean security treaty, is identical to Article One of the Soviet–North Korean treaty and a carbon copy of Article One of the Sino-Soviet treaty, which Zhou Enlai extracted from Soviet foreign minister Vyshinsky in 1950. There are a few notable differences, however, between the two treaties signed by Kim Il Sung. Whereas the Soviet–North Korean document refers to the goals and principles of the United Nations, that reference is conspicuously absent from the Sino–North Korean treaty. Both China and North Korea had fought against the United Nations Command and were excluded from the world organization, unlike the Soviet Union. The U.N. General Assembly had branded both China and North Korea as aggressors during the Korean War. In contrast to the Soviet–North Korean treaty, the Sino–North Korean treaty emphasized the importance of Marxism-Leninism, proletarian internationalism, and brotherly relations. Compared with their Soviet counterparts, the Chinese espoused a greater sense of permanency and stability in their military relations with North Korea. The Soviet–North Korean treaty stipulates that either party can abrogate the treaty after the initial ten-year period (by giving a one-year advance notice every five years to the other party), but neither China nor North Korea can amend or terminate their treaty without mutual agreement. By the early 1960s the two Korean governments were fully and formally integrated with the opposing cold war alliance systems.[2]

In the context of Sino-Soviet conflicts, the Chinese particularly valued the symbolic and substantive importance of North Korea and actively accommodated North Korea's aspirations and requests, as exemplified by their boundary negotiations, diplomatic cooperation, and economic assistance programs. In the early 1960s the Chinese successfully implemented the treaty, preventing North Korea from drifting into Moscow's embrace and developing a common ideological and strategic perspective with North Korea. In the joint statement issued by Liu Shaoqi (chairman of the People's

Republic of China) and Choe Yong Kun (president of the Supreme People's Assembly) on June 23, 1963, both sides agreed to fight against imperialism and modern revisionism and expressed their firm resolve to "uphold the comradeship in arms and great unity between the two Parties and the two peoples which were cemented with blood in the protracted common struggles against imperialist aggressors and further consolidated through the Treaty of Friendship, Cooperation and Mutual Assistance."[3]
They also stated:

> In order to foster the forces of Japanese militarism and turn them into a "shock brigade" for its aggression in Asia, U.S. imperialism is pressing for an early conclusion of the "ROK-Japan talks" and knocking together an aggressive Northeast Asia military alliance. . . . The U.S. imperialists are incessantly carrying out criminal schemes in southern Korea to provoke a new war and thereby aggravate the tension, and are intensifying their barbarous fascist suppression of the people there.

The two countries in effect formed a united front against Soviet "revisonists," U.S. "imperialists," Japanese "militarists," and South Korean "fascists." The Chinese rhetoric against South Korea was fundamental and ferocious; indeed, to support the North Korean arguments, it was more critical of South Korea than of Taiwan. At a mass rally at Pyongyang in September 1963, Liu Shaoqi stated:

> In contravention of the Korean armistice agreement, it [U.S. imperialism] is constantly introducing into south Korea various kinds of new-type weapons including atomic weapons and constantly committing armed provocations along the military demarcation line. . . . South Korea under the occupation of U.S. imperialism is a hell on earth. The south Korean people living under intolerable conditions have time and again courageously launched a just struggle against U.S. imperialism and for national salvation. The U.S. puppet Syngman Rhee has been overthrown by the south Korean people. Another U.S. puppet Park Chung Hee will be overthrown too by the south Korean people sooner or later. The scheme of U.S. imperialism to perpetuate the division of Korea is doomed to failure. The day will surely come when the U.S. aggressors will have to get off the sacred soil of Korea.[4]

When the Soviet Union, the United States, and Britain signed the Limited Nuclear Test Ban Treaty at Moscow in July 1963, both China and North Korea denounced it as a Soviet sellout and part of the U.S. strategic conspiracy. The treaty was denounced as a hoax designed to perpetuate the nuclear monopoly by the three nuclear powers and to deny the sovereign right of national self-defense to nonnuclear countries. When China detonated its first successful nuclear weapon in October 1964, Kim Il Sung, not unexpectedly, extended his "warmest congratulations" to Mao Zedong and said:

> The success of the nuclear test by the Chinese People's Republic is a great victory for the Chinese people and a tremendous victory for the socialist camp and the peace-loving peoples of the whole world. This is not only an inspiration to all the revolutionary peoples in struggle but also a great contribution to the cause of peace in Asia and the world, and is a telling blow to the U.S. imperialists who are stubbornly pushing ahead their policy of nuclear blackmail.[5]

The Sino–North Korean militant friendship reached a high point when they jointly opposed diplomatic normalization between Japan and South Korea. They assailed the rapprochement as an anticommunist military alliance among the United States, Japan, and South Korea and reaffirmed their own mutual security arrangements. In 1969, once the extremely xenophobic and chaotic phase of the Cultural Revolution was over, Mao invited Choe Yong Kun to attend the twentieth anniversary of China's founding. In discussions with Choe, Mao Zedong expressed a desire to normalize diplomatic and political relations with North Korea, and Zhou Enlai stressed the "continuous growth and consolidation of the military friendship between the peoples of China and Korea."[6]

The Chinese were eager to mend fences with North Korea, in part because a military confrontation with the Soviet Union over Zhenbao (Damansky) Island in the Ussuri River and other disputed areas in the Xinjiang region during 1969 made it imperative that China stabilize its relationship with other neighboring countries. Moreover, there was a growing concern about the potentially explosive military situation in Korea, especially with respect to the seizure of the USS *Pueblo* in January 1968 and the destruction of the U.S. reconnaissance plane EC-121 (with a crew of thirty-one) over North Korea in April 1969. The Chinese accused the U.S. military of provocations against North Korea and the Soviet Union of searching for and picking up the EC-121 plane and the "American spies."[7]

The Chinese also sought military solidarity with North Korea because they were disturbed by the joint communiqué issued by President Richard M. Nixon and Prime Minister Sato Eisaku on November 21, 1969.[8] In the communiqué Sato acknowledged that the security of the Republic of Korea was essential to Japan's own security and that maintaining peace and security in the Taiwan area was most important for the security of Japan. At the National Press Club in Washington, Sato added that, if South Korea or Taiwan came under armed attack, Japan would consider the peace and security of the Far East, including Japan, threatened and would take measures to ensure that the United States would use its military bases and facilities in Japan to counter such an attack. He pledged to make "active contributions" to the peace and security of Asia, especially in economic areas.

The communiqué linking Japan's security with that of South Korea and Taiwan provoked scathing attacks from China and North Korea. Zhou Enlai asserted that, "abetted by U.S. imperialism and drunk with rabid ambition," the Sato government was attempting to "step up the revival of militarism and realize its old dream of a Greater East Asia Co-Prosperity Sphere." It was also claimed that, in U.S. imperialism's counterrevolutionary global strategy, "the Japanese reactionaries have been used to act as a gendarme in Asia and the fugleman in opposition to the Chinese, Korean, Vietnamese and all other peoples of Asia."[9]

A few months after the Nixon-Sato communiqué, Zhou Enlai made a three-day visit to Pyongyang to strengthen bilateral military ties. At a state banquet hosted by Kim Il Sung, Zhou called the Nixon-Sato communiqué a "new U.S.-Japanese military alliance spearheaded against the peoples of Asia" and unequivocally stated:

China and Korea are neighbors linked by mountains and rivers. There exists a traditional militant friendship between the Chinese and Korean peoples. This friendship cemented with blood was forged and has grown in the course of the protracted struggle against our common enemies, U.S. and Japanese imperialism. The militant friendship between the Chinese and Korean peoples is the embodiment of the intimate relationship of our two peoples who share weal and woe and are as closely linked as lips and teeth. Common interests and common problems of security have bound and united our two peoples together. In the face of new threats of aggression and war by the U.S. and Japanese reactionaries, the Chinese and Korean peoples must unite closely and enhance preparedness against war in our common fight against the enemies. The Chinese Government and people will, as always, work for the consolidation and development of the militant friendship and unity between China and Korea.[10]

In a joint communiqué issued on April 7, 1970, Zhou and Kim agreed that "U.S. imperialism is the main force of aggression and war and the most ferocious common enemy of the peoples of the world. . . . Resolute and uncompromising struggles must be waged against U.S. imperialism through to the very end."[11] In addition to attacking Japanese "reactionaries" for their aggressive policy in Asia, they said:

> The Chinese side firmly condemns U.S. imperialism and its lackey the Park Chung Hee puppet clique for their frantic new war provocations against the Democratic People's Republic of Korea and their barbarous massacre and unprecedented fascist violent repression of the revolutionaries and patriotic people in south Korea. . . . The Chinese side fully supports the correct policy of the Government of the Democratic People's Republic of Korea for the reunification of the fatherland, the policy of making the U.S. aggressor troops withdraw from south Korea and realizing the reunification of the country by the Koreans themselves independently and free from interference by any foreign force.

Although the Chinese repaired their military alliance with North Korea, which had been disrupted by the Cultural Revolution, the militant overtones of the Zhou-Kim communiqué, coupled with the Sino-Soviet border clashes, the Nixon-Sato communiqué, and South Korea's participation in the Vietnam War, heightened tension and animosity in East Asia. The situation was aggravated by a potential revival of the Sino-Japanese rivalry in the Korean Peninsula. Then, a few Chinese diplomats assigned to Pyongyang expressed reservations about China's accommodation with Kim Il Sung's extreme policy lines and were either reprimanded or demoted. In the aftermath of Zhou's visit, China and North Korea signed several agreements on Chinese aid to North Korea, economic and technical cooperation, long-term commercial transactions in support of North Korea's Six-Year Plan (1971–1976), and protocols on a border railway and the mutual supply of goods. China presumably also agreed to bolster North Korea's military preparedness.[12]

CHINA'S DÉTENTE POLICY

Despite Zhou Enlai's unconditional promise to wage "resolute and uncompromising struggles" against U.S. imperialism and Japanese militarism, the Chinese were ready to welcome and reciprocate Richard Nixon's peaceful overtures. After their large-scale border clashes with the Soviet Union in 1969, they were keenly aware of the technological and strategic superiority of the Soviet forces deployed in Siberia and Outer Mongolia. The Chinese felt that any cooperation with the United States would help them in their security dilemma with the Soviet Union. Like Nixon, they practiced the classic policy of balancing one power against another. Added to the evolving triangular strategic relationship were China's other policy objectives: to enhance its diplomatic status after the disastrous Cultural Revolution, contain Japanese militarism and rearmament, seek trade with the United States, weaken Taiwan's diplomatic and military capabilities, and mitigate tensions in the Korean Peninsula. The convergence of Sino-American strategic interests led to Henry A. Kissinger's secret mission to Beijing in July 1971 and Richard Nixon's visit to China in February 1972. These were followed by diplomatic normalization between China and Japan in September 1972. As a result, the Chinese, ending the legacy of the Korean War in their relations with the United States, broke down the traditional American policies of diplomatic isolation, military containment, and economic sanctions against China.

The rapidity with which China pursued détente with the United States and Japan graphically illustrated the different strategic interests of Beijing and Pyongyang and had an unsettling effect on the Korean Peninsula. The Chinese sent a high-level delegation led by Li Xiannian (vice premier) and Li Desheng (a Korean War veteran and director of the PLA's General Political Department) to Pyongyang the day before Nixon announced Kissinger's secret mission to China. While Kissinger was still in Beijing, Mao Zedong, Lin Biao, and Zhou Enlai sent a joint message to Kim Il Sung to commemorate the tenth anniversary of the Sino–North Korean security treaty. The Chinese recognized the treaty's "extremely important role" in developing friendship and cooperation between the two countries and opposing aggression by the United States and Japan. Criticizing the "even more sinister and cunning tactics" of the U.S. imperialist aggressive polic, the Chinese pledged:

Should the U.S. and Japanese reactionaries dare to launch a war of aggression against the Chinese and Korean peoples, the Chinese people will, as always, firmly unite with the Korean people and fight shoulder to shoulder with them to thoroughly defeat the aggressors.

Although Kim Il Sung publicly acknowledged that Nixon was going to visit China with a "white flag," thus implying the defeat of U.S. policy toward Asia, Kim was undoubtedly disappointed by China's reconciliation with the United States, which he continued to regard as North Korea's archenemy.[13]

At their summit meetings in February 1972, Zhou and Nixon had "extensive, earnest, and frank discussions" on a wide range of global and regional issues and agreed that "neither should seek hegemony in the Asia-Pacific region and each is opposed to efforts by any other country or group of countries to establish such hegemony." In their joint communiqué, issued in Shanghai on February 27, 1972, Zhou endorsed North Korean proposals for achieving peaceful reunification and for abolishing the United Nations Commission for the Unification and Rehabilitation of Korea (UNCURK). Nixon made it clear, however, that the United States would maintain close ties with South Korea and support South Korea's efforts "to seek a relaxation of tension and increased communication in the Korean Peninsula." According to Kissinger's report, Mao and Zhou specifically disavowed China's threatening Japan or South Korea and refrained from asking Nixon to withdraw U.S. forces from South Korea. There is no evidence that Zhou told Nixon or Kissinger what he had stated or promised during his Pyongyang visit in 1970.[14]

The sudden Sino-American détente shocked both North and South Korea and compelled them to open a dialogue, reorganize their political systems, and adjust their policies to the changing environment, in that both countries were apprehensive of big-power diplomacy. In a historic joint communiqué issued on July 4, 1972, the two Korean sides agreed to seek peaceful and independent unification of Korea "without being subject to external imposition and interference" and to fulfill national unity by transcending "differences in ideas, ideologies, and systems."[15] They promised to refrain from armed provocations and to promote various exchange programs. Moreover, they installed a direct hot line linking the two capitals and pledged to stop making propaganda broadcasts and slanderous reports against each other. Implementing these and other related matters was entrusted to a new North-South Coordinating Committee.

Coming after more than a quarter century of divisiveness, this major political breakthrough was widely acclaimed at home and abroad.

Closely associated with the new inter-Korean accommodation were efforts by Seoul and Pyongyang to solidify their respective political structures, for both felt that having a strong internal position would be conducive to effective external relations. In South Korea President Park Chung Hee declared a national emergency and enacted a constitutional amendment. In October 1972, Park proclaimed martial law and suspended elements of the constitution, on the grounds that South Korea needed sweeping structural reform to carry on the dialogue with North Korea and to cope with the rapidly changing international situation. To justify these extraordinary steps, Park argued:

> There is now taking place a significant change in the balance of power among the big powers around the Korean Peninsula. I think that this change may, directly or indirectly, bring forth a dangerous effect on the security of our country, because it might result in transforming the existing order in Asia as a whole and also threaten to affect adversely the security systems which have so far served as the effective backbone for maintaining the peace in this region. No one can guarantee that there will never be a resumption of war in the area.[16]

The subsequent constitutional referendum in November 1972 made it possible for Park to prolong his presidency indefinitely and to institute a highly authoritarian system (*yushin*) in Korea.

The constitutional revision in North Korea, which among other things changed Kim Il Sung's formal status from premier to head of state, a title comparable to Park's, may also have been precipitated by external stimuli.[17] Moreover, North Korea, as part of its external adaptation, cultivated informal contacts with Seoul's two principal allies—the United States and Japan. Kim even expressed a willingness to establish diplomatic relations with Japan without an abrogation of the Japanese–South Korean treaty.

The Chinese welcomed the dialogue between Pyongyang and Seoul and endorsed the inter-Korean joint communiqué as "a good beginning for the cause of the independent peaceful reunification of Korea" with a "positive impact on the development of the situation in Asia and the world."[18] Although reiterating their commitment to North Korean defense and expressing concern about South Korean military modernization, the Chinese hoped that the inter-Korean communiqué would serve as a framework for institutionalizing peaceful cooperation and military stability in the Korean

Peninsula. They were concerned that an escalation of tension in Korea might disturb China's fragile new relationship with the United States and Japan or that the Soviet Union might take advantage of the unstable situation to further its own long-standing strategic interests in Korea.

The same logic probably applied to China's efforts to discourage Kim Il Sung from considering military action at the time of the communist victories in Indochina in 1975. In their meeting in Wuhan, Mao apparently rejected Kim's proposal that China and North Korea undertake joint military action to expel U.S. forces from South Korea and Taiwan. The joint communiqué signed by Kim Il Sung and Deng Xiaoping on April 26, 1975, noted that "the new victories the Indochinese peoples have won in their liberation struggles greatly inspire the people of all countries." It is most likely, however, that Mao and Deng urged Kim to follow a peaceful road to Korean reunification. Mao Zedong's and Zhou Enlai's health was deteriorating, and a power struggle had emerged in China between the hard-liners, led by Mao's wife (Jiang Qing), and the moderates, headed by Deng Xiaoping. Exhausted by factional infighting and ideological debates, the Chinese were not interested in supporting a risky armed adventure in the Korean Peninsula.[19]

After the successive deaths of China's top leaders—Zhou Enlai, Zhu De, and Mao Zedong—and the arrest of the radical "gang of four" led by Jiang Qing in 1976, Premier Hua Guofeng adopted the pragmatic four modernizations policy and agreed to reinstate Deng Xiaoping, who had been purged in a bloody riot at Tiananmen Square in April 1976. A coalition of moderate Chinese leaders transcended ideologically inspired domestic policy in the post-Mao era and gradually realigned China's foreign policy to accommodate shifting global and regional developments. The coalition was particularly successful in concluding a Treaty of Peace and Friendship with Japan in September 1978 and in normalizing diplomatic relations with the United States in December 1978. Hence China's détente policy toward the United States and Japan was fully realized.

As an integral part of China's pragmatic foreign policy, Hua Guofeng visited North Korea in May 1978 and Deng Xiaoping visited in September of the same year.[20] Hua's five-day visit to Pyongyang was intended to explain China's domestic political situation and new policy priorities to the uneasy Kim Il Sung and to renew China's traditional support for North Korea. When Kim visited Beijing in 1975, Hua had not participated in high-level meetings, but he had attended various social functions, including Kim's farewell banquet. The Hua mission included Geng Biao (vice premier), Huang Hua (foreign minister), and Chen Muhua (minister of economic relations with foreign countries).

As had been the case in the Sino–North Korean joint communiqué of 1975, Hua supported North Korea's "just struggle for the independent and peaceful reunification" of Korea, recognized North Korea as the "sole legitimate sovereign state" of Korea, opposed any form of a two-Korea solution, and demanded the complete withdrawal of U.S. forces from South Korea as well as the dissolution of the United Nations Command. Hua specifically ruled out cross-recognition of North and South Korea and their simultaneous admission to the United Nations, declaring categorically that "we do not recognize the South Korean authorities."

Hua devoted special attention to the discussions of China's four modernizations program and North Korea's Second Seven-Year Plan (1978-1984), which envisaged more than a doubling of gross industrial output and an average annual growth rate of 12.1 percent. Hua offered a package of economic and military assistance to ease North Korea's foreign debt problems, which had grown after the international oil crisis; among other matters, he agreed to increase the amount of Chinese oil supplied to North Korea.

There was a clear cleavage in China's and North Korea's perceptions of Moscow's military threat and hegemonic behavior. Thus, in deference to Kim's wishes, Hua did not launch a frontal attack against Soviet "social-imperialism" and "hegemonism" but praised the expansion of an "international anti-hegemonist united front." Hua refused, however, to echo Kim's staunch opposition to Japan's "militaristic ambitions" and "economic exploitation" in South Korea and may have urged Kim to moderate his anti-Japan rhetoric and to improve relations with Japan. The theme of Japanese militarism, which was central to the Zhou-Kim joint communiqué of 1970, was abandoned by Hua. Although China opposed the United States' reinforcing South Korea's "potentiality for war," Hua did not refer to U.S. military aid to South Korea during his North Korea journey. His characterization of the Park government was less provocative and militant than before: he did not use such expressions as "fascist dictatorship," "suppression of democratic struggle," or "continual military provocations" against North Korea. In accord with North Korea's anti-American stance, he delivered the customary attack on U.S. "imperialist policy" in Korea but diminished the severity and vindictiveness of his remarks. Although Kim expressed hope and support for China's liberation of Taiwan, Hua remained silent on the Taiwan issue.

Hua and Kim agreed not to issue a joint communiqué despite references to their "successful conclusion" and "identical views," probably not wanting to publicize their policy differences, especially in regard to the Soviet Union, Japan, the United States, and Indochina. Or they may have felt that joint communiqués had a way of becoming more of a liability than an asset for foreign policy. The new Chinese leaders may have also recognized the diminishing utility of painstakingly compromised joint communiqués or perhaps did not wish to stir up domestic political controversy over sensitive external issues.

SINO-SOVIET COMPETITION

In the early 1980s the Chinese vigorously competed with the Soviet Union to woo Pyongyang by means of security guarantees, diplomatic patronage, and economic assistance, especially after the Sino-Vietnamese war and the Soviet invasion of Afghanistan. Whereas China publicly assailed the Soviet Union's aggressive policy in Afghanistan, North Korea privately viewed the Soviet action sympathetically. The Chinese could not afford to lose North Korea as a military ally or see it support the Soviet strategy in the Asian Pacific region: if North Korea allowed the Soviet Union to station divisions on the peninsula or to use Najin or Nampo as its naval bases, akin to Vietnam's Cam Ranh Bay, it would challenge China's security. As they had during the Korean War, the Chinese believed that any hostile foreign military force in North Korea would threaten their interests in the northeastern region and the Bohai Sea. Given China's deteriorating relations with other socialist countries, such as Vietnam, Cuba, Mongolia, and Albania, North Korea's relative importance loomed large. It was crucial to Chinese prestige and influence that Kim Il Sung not support the Soviet-sponsored campaign against Beijing or join the Soviet-dominant Council for Mutual Economic Assistance (as Vietnam did) and that he cooperate with China in the nonalignment movement. Nevertheless, the Chinese found it difficult to satisfy North Korea's requests for sophisticated weapons and advanced technology—an area in which the Soviet Union still enjoyed a distinct advantage.

In an attempt to counterbalance the Soviet ascendancy in North Korea, the Chinese reaffirmed their treaty obligations and accelerated a high-level exchange program with North Korea. Even though Kim Il Sung told a Liberal Democratic Party (LDP) delegation in August 1980 that he was willing to abrogate both treaties if the United States agreed to transform the armistice agreement into a peace treaty with North Korea, the Chinese never expressed reservations about their treaty relationship with North Korea. On the contrary, they made every effort to reaffirm that relationship during the 1980s. In a joint message to Kim Il Sung on the treaty's twentieth anniversary, Hu Yaobang, Ye Jianying, and Zhao Ziyang noted that the treaty had played an "important role" in strengthening the cooperative relationship between Beijing and Pyongyang and guaranteeing peace in Asia and the world for twenty years. They also pledged to solidify their "great unity" (weida tuanjie) with North Korea. A Renmin Ribao editorial (July 11, 1981) demanded "complete withdrawal" of U.S. troops from South Korea. The same theme was repeated during Premier Li Chong Ok's visit to China in January 1981 and during Premier Zhao Ziyang's visit to North Korea in December 1981.[21]

From April 26 to April 30, 1982 (shortly after a massive celebration of Kim Il Sung's seventieth birthday), Deng Xiaoping, accompanied by his newly designated heir apparent Hu Yaobang (CCP general secretary), made a secret visit to Pyongyang. Hu described this "internal visit" (neibu fangwen) as "rich and colorful inspections" and as the "most unforgettable experience" in his life. Wang Bingnan (president of the Chinese People's Association for Friendship with Foreign Countries) explained that, by keeping the visit secret, Deng and Hu were able to bypass ceremonial procedures and conduct substantive discussions without interruption. In addition, the secrecy avoided their appearing to participate in Kim's birthday celebration and allowed them to meet Kim's son and heir apparent, Kim Jong Il. Thus, a close working relationship between Kim Il Sung and Hu Yaobang was established.[22]

In June 1982, soon after the secret visit, Defense Minister Geng Biao, together with Liang Biye (a Korean War veteran and deputy director of the PLA's General Political Department), visited North Korea. They toured the demilitarized zone, inspected North Korea's army, navy, and air force, and observed military exercises. At a Pyongyang meeting, Geng, a Long March veteran, criticized America's "hegemonic" and "aggressive" policy in Korea and South Korea's "fascistic rule." He promised military support to North Korea until "final victory" is achieved. This promise became translated into considerable military assistance from China to North Korea. According to U.S. and Japanese intelligence sources, for example, China delivered forty F-7 fighter aircraft (the improved Chinese version of the MiG-21) from Xian to Sinuiju on March 31 and April 1, 1982, adding to North Korea's estimated stockpile of 120 Soviet-made MiG-21s and 180 Chinese-made MiG-19s. This delivery, however, did not upset the military balance in the Korean Peninsula because South Korea had 228 F-5 fighter aircraft and 54 F-4 Phantoms in addition to the U.S. Air Force unit stationed there.[23]

In September 1982, Deng and Hu rolled out the red carpet for Kim Il Sung's visit to China. Deng took Kim to Chengdu, and Hu accompanied Kim to Xian. At one of several lavish banquets, Hu declared:

> History shows that as the destinies of our two peoples were inseparably linked together, we were not separated in the past nor will we be separated in the future. . . . You may rest assured that no matter what may happen in the world in the future, the Chinese people will invariably stand foursquare behind the Korean people as in the past and support the Korean people's just cause of socialist construction and the independent and peaceful reunification of the country.[24]

Kim responded:

> We are very pleased with the invariable, continued development of great Korea-China friendship which has a historical tradition. Korea-China friendship is an invincible one which no force can ever break. It will further flourish down through generations. It will last as long as the mountains and rivers to the two countries exist.[25]

During his visit to Chengdu, Kim reportedly inspected a new Chinese nuclear facility and asked Deng to make nuclear technology and enriched uranium available to North Korea.[26]

The emphasis on friendship "down through generations" paved the way for Kim Jong Il's "internal visit" to China on June 2, 1983. Accompanied by Defense Minister O Chin U, the junior Kim, who had visited China on several occasions as a member of the advance party for Kim Il Sung's visit, met with most members of the CCP's Political Bureau and Secretariat and traveled some sixty-three hundred kilometers. Hu Yaobang was Kim's host during his tour of Qingdao and Nanjing, and Hu Qili (a member of the CCP Secretariat and former chairman of the All-China Youth Federation) guided Kim to Shanghai and Hangzhou. A documentary film made during Kim Jong Il's China visit was widely used in Japan to show his international acceptability. Kim Jong Il's visit was followed by his father's secret meeting with Deng Xiaoping at Dalian in August 1983.[27]

The Chinese had handled both Kims' visits with great care, and the North Koreans reciprocated by warmly welcoming Hu Yaobang and Yang Shangkun to Pyongyang in May 1984. About half a million people turned out to greet them, and Kim Il Sung escorted them to Wonsan, Hamhung, and Chongjin. On various public occasions, Hu and other Chinese leaders reiterated the immutability of China's "brotherly affection" (*xiongdi qingyi*) and "militant friendship" (*zhandou youyi*) with North Korea.[28]

Unlike the Soviet Union, China was able to draw on a shared legacy of struggle—namely, the Korean War—to reinforce its ties with North Korea. The Chinese, taking great pains to keep alive the memory of that shared past, have created special ceremonies for October 25 (the day of the CPV's official entry into the Korean War) and July 27 (Armistice Day). On these days and at the spring festival (*qingming*), Chinese military personnel and civilians hold memorials at CPV cemeteries throughout the northeastern region, including the Resist-America and Aid-Korea Martyrs Cemetery in Shenyang. In October 1980 (the thirtieth anniversary of the CPV's entry into the Korean War) Wang Ping (political commissar of the PLA's General Logistics Department who had served as CPV political commissar in Korea) took part in a Pyongyang mass rally celebrating China's participation in the war. In Beijing, CCP vice chairman Li Xiannian, PLA chief of the general staff Yang Dezhi, and Foreign Minister Huang Hua attended a commemorative banquet at the North Korean embassy. In his speech Yang reaffirmed China's North Korean security commitment.[29]

In July 1983, the thirtieth anniversary of the "Victory of Korea's Fatherland Liberation War" (Armistice Day), the North Korean embassy in Beijing entertained China's political and military leaders: Xi Zhongxun (member of the CCP Political Bureau), Vice Premier Li Peng, and PLA deputy chief of the general staff Xu Xin. Similarly, Hong Xuezhi (director of the PLA General Logistics Department who had been CPV deputy commander in Korea) led a friendship delegation to Pyongyang. Vice Minister of National Defense Paek Hak Rim thanked the CPV for "heroism" and "proletarian internationalism"; Hong praised North Korea's successful struggles against "U.S. aggressors" and urged the United States to withdraw its troops from South Korea. Kim Il Sung decorated Hong, members of his delegation, and members of the CPV liaison office to the Armistice Commission at Panmunjom. Moreover, in November 1982, Kim Il Sung and Kim Jong Il gave instructions to expand the Korea-China Friendship Tower on Pyongyang's Moranbong Hill, which had been originally erected on the ninth anniversary of the CPV's entry into the Korean War. No other country maintained such close associations with either China or North Korea.[30]

Often overlooked in discussions of the Chinese–North Korean military relationship is the large number of senior PLA officers who served in the Korean War, a situation absent in Soviet–North Korea relations. The CPV included millions of China's most experienced officers and soldiers; about 300,000 of them received special medals and awards from the North Korean government. The powerful nine-member Central Military Commission, set up in June 1983, included Yang Dezhi and Hong Xuezhi—the only two members in active military service. A Long March veteran, Yang served as commander of the Nineteenth Army Group, CPV chief of staff, and deputy commander during the Korean War and then replaced Deng Hua as CPV commander in October 1954; later he commanded PLA operations against Vietnam and became chief of the PLA's General Staff. Peng Dehuai once said that Hong Xuezhi (CPV deputy commander), another Long March participant who was in charge of logistic matters, should receive half the credit for the CPV's successful campaigns in Korea. After Korea he served as the director of the PLA's General Logistics Department. In subsequent years the CMC, chaired by Jiang Zemin, included other former CPV leaders including Chi Haotian, Zhao Nanqi, and Zhang Zhen.[31]

The Korean War veterans have been influential in the CCP's highest decision-making organs—the Political Bureau and the Central Committee (see table 1). Seven individuals—Peng Dehuai (minister of national defense), Xu Shiyu (commander of the Nanjing and Guangzhou Military Regions), Huang Yongsheng (chief of the General Staff), Li Desheng (commander of the Shenyang and Beijing Military Regions), Zhang Tingfa (air force commander), Yang Dezhi (chief of the General Staff), and Qin Jiwei (minister of national defense)—served on the Political Bureau between the mid-1950s and the late 1980s. A large number of those who had fought in Korea were elected or reelected to the Central Committee. They constituted 7.2 percent of all regular members of the Central Committee in the late 1950s, 16.4 percent in 1969, 17.4 percent in 1973, 17.4 percent in 1977, 15.2 percent in 1982, and 3.4 percent in 1987.[32] When the PLA promoted seventeen leaders to the rank of full general (*dajiang*) in September 1988, thirteen of them were Korean War veterans (see table 2). The Korean War group produced at least thirteen cabinet ministers (including three ministers of national defense), two chiefs of the General

TABLE 1
NUMBER OF KOREAN WAR VETERANS IN THE CHINESE COMMUNIST PARTY
(1956–1987)

	8th CC[a] (1956–58)	9th CC (1969)	10th CC (1973)	11th CC (1977)	12th CC (1982)	13th CC (1987)
CC Regular members						
—Total members	97	170	195	201	210	175
—KW[b] veterans	7	28	34	35	32	6
	(7.2%)	(16.4%)	(17.4%)	(17.4%)	(15.2%)	(3.4%)
CC Alternate members						
—Total members	96	109	124	132	138	111
—KW veterans	9	22	20	23	8	0
	(9.3%)	(20.2%)	(16.1%)	(17.4%)	(5.8%)	(0%)
PB[c] Regular members						
—Total members	20	21	21	23	25	17
—KW veterans	1	2	2	3	3	1
PB Alternate members						
—Total members	6	4	4	3	3	1
—KW veterans	0	1	0	0	1	0

[a] CC - Central Committee
[b] KW - Korean War
[c] PB - Political Bureau

SOURCE: Tan Zheng, *Zhongguo renmin zhiyuanjun renwulu* (Biographical Directory of the Chinese People's Volunteers) (Beijing: Zhonggong dangshi chubanshe, 1992).

Staff, and about thirty commanders of the military regions. The Shenyang Military Region adjacent to the Sino–North Korean border included a particularly large number of Korean War veterans. Others led the PLA General Staff Headquarters and the Departments of General Political Affairs and General Logistics and held high positions in the air force, navy, armored forces, artillery corps, and other fields.

Although it is difficult to assess the way the Korean experience has shaped the perceptions and attitudes of these military leaders toward Korea, the declaration that China and North Korea share a "militant friendship" cemented with blood is more than a figure of speech. For many Chinese participants, the Korean War was their only extensive foreign military assignment. Even if their sympathy and solidarity with the North Korean cause is not appreciably greater than that of their civilian counterparts or military colleagues without a Korean War connection, they often have a vested interest in Korea and some intimate knowledge of and expertise in Korean military affairs. Their reminiscences about their Korean War experiences are usually positive.[33]

The Chinese Korean War veterans have been active in visiting North Korea, hosting North Korean military delegations, sending special greetings to "Korean comrades in arms," articulating China's security promises for North Korea, and meeting with Kim Il Sung. Conversely, Kim maintained close personal ties with the CPV leaders. For example, on the death of Yang Yong (a former CPV commander) in January 1983, Kim Il Sung sent the following message of condolence to Hu Yaobang and Deng Xiaoping: "The Korean people deeply grieve the loss of Comrade Yang Yong, a communist fighter and comrade in arms . . . the exploits performed by him for the Chinese revolution and Korea-China friendship will be cherished long in the hearts of the Chinese and Korean peoples." (North Korean leaders expressed similar sentiments about the death of another former CPV commander—Yang Dezhi—in November 1994.) Although the Korean War veterans' representation in the Thirteenth and Fourteenth CCP Central Committees drastically declined, China's active military leaders (as of 1994) who served in the Korean War—such as Chi Haotian (minister of national defense), Zhang Zhen (vice chairman of the Central Military Commission), Zhao Nanqi (president of the Academy of Military Sciences), Li Jiulong (commander of the Chengdu Military Region), Gu Hui (commander of the Nanjing Military Region), Zhu Dunfa (commander of the Guangzhou Military Region), and Fu Quanyou (commander of the Lanzhou Military Region)—will surely continue to form an influ-

TABLE 2
PEOPLE'S LIBERATION ARMY LEADERS PROMOTED TO THE RANK OF FULL GENERAL
(SEPTEMBER 1988)

Names	Current Positions	Participant in the Korean War
Hong Xuezhi	CMC[a] member	Yes
Liu Huaqing	CMC member	No
Qin Jiwei	CMC member, minister of national defense	Yes
Chi Haotian	Chief of the General Staff	Yes
Yang Baibing	Director, General Political Development	No
Zhao Nanqi	Director, General Logistics Department	Yes
Xu Xin	Deputy chief of the General Staff	Yes
Guo Linxiang	Deputy director, General Political Development	No
You Taizhong	Deputy secretary of the MDIC[b]	Yes
Wang Chenghan	Political commissar, Academy of Military Sciences	Yes
Zhang Zhen	President, National Defense University	Yes
Li Desheng	Political commissar, National Defense University	Yes
Liu Zhenhua	Political commissar, Beijing Military Region	Yes
Xiang Shouzhi	Commander, Nanjing Military Region	Yes
Wan Haifeng	Political commissar, Chengdu Military Region	No
Li Yaowen	Navy political commissar	Yes
Wang Hai	Air force commander	Yes

[a] Central Military Commission
[b] Military Discipline Inspection Commission

ential group in the PLA leadership structure, at least for the next few
years. Michael D. Swaine, a Chinese military affairs analyst, suggests that
"enduring personal relationships among senior officers and party leaders
are forged through common involvement in armed conflicts and various
crucibles of fire such as the major campaigns of the Chinese Civil War and
the Korean War."[34]

POLICY CLEAVAGES

Yet China's developing friendly and cooperative relations with North
Korea during the 1980s did not vitiate the gap between them over a number of crucial Korean issues. A persistent source of cleavage concerned the
relative priorities of peace and unification in Korea. Whereas the Chinese,
preoccupied with their own policy preferences, attached a higher priority
to Korea's stable peace and military balance than to its unification, Kim Il
Sung sought Korea's territorial reintegration as his primary policy goal
and was thus bent on inciting internal disorder and revolutionary change
in South Korea. The Chinese, however, asked the United States' help in
bringing about South Korea's political stabilization.[35]

This Chinese position on Korea conflicted with the policy toward
Taiwan: China-Taiwan relations did not equate with those between North
and South Korea. After all, Taiwan was one of China's twenty-two provinces, and China did not fear any imminent threat or viable military competition from Taiwan. The imbalance in power potentials and diplomatic
functions between Beijing and Taipei was not comparable to the Seoul-
Pyongyang rivalry. Even if the Chinese refused to renounce the use of
force in their unification policy, they appeared to be supremely confident
that it was only a matter of time until they would absorb Taiwan by peaceful means. The North Koreans had exactly the opposite perspective—
namely, the longer they waited, the more difficult it would be for them to
take over South Korea. Hence there was a strong incentive for North Korea
to disrupt or even destroy South Korea's political system.

The Chinese did not wish to see another Korean war because, condi-
tioned by their explicit treaty obligations, they might find it difficult not
to offer at least indirect assistance. Such an involvement could undermine
their economic modernization programs and strain their cooperative ties
with the United States and Japan. If, however, they decided not to support

North Korea, the Soviet Union might reap a distinct advantage in North Korea at China's expense. If the Chinese had learned any lessons from the intransigence of a unified Vietnam, they might wonder whether a unified Korea under the fiercely independent-minded Kim's auspices would necessarily be conducive to their long-range national interests.

During the 1980s, therefore, the immediate objective of China's policy in Korea was to lessen tensions and bring about dialogue rather than confrontation among all parties. For this reason, the Chinese informed the United States and Japan at every opportunity that Kim Il Sung had neither the intention nor the capability of invading South Korea and that they were genuinely interested in easing tension in Korea. Deng Xiaoping told Utsunomiya Tokuma (a member of the House of Councillors and president of the Japan-China Friendship Association) that it would be a "foolish policy" to let tensions rise in Korea and thus drive Kim Il Sung to the Soviet Union. Deng added that, in terms of its military and economic capabilities, North Korea could not invade South Korea. Hu Yaobang agreed with Sasaki Ryosaku (chairman of the Democratic Socialist Party), who argued that peace was more important than unification in Korea. Premier Zhao Ziyang told both President Ronald Reagan and Prime Minister Nakasone Yasuhiro that China was opposed to "all acts by any quarter that would aggravate the tension" in Korea. At times the Chinese qualified their security guarantee to North Korea by implying that they would come to North Korea's defense only if it were attacked by others. In June 1987, Deng Xiaoping told Yano Junya (chairman of the Clean Government Party) that, even if U.S. forces withdrew from South Korea, South Korea would still be more powerful militarily than North Korea and bluntly stated, "If North Korea invades South Korea, China will not support it." He went on to say that "China wants a stable and peaceful environment in the Korean Peninsula." Yet the Chinese leaders maintained that their ability to influence North Korea's behavior should not be overestimated, suggesting that China's search for Korea's peace and stability was considerably constrained by Kim's *chuche* ideology as well as by the Soviet Union's countervailing influence.[36]

Another serious source of Beijing-Pyongyang policy differences was the way in which each dealt with the United States and Japan. In international politics cooperation between two military and diplomatic coalitions tends to increase suspicion and tensions in intracoalition relations. The Chinese–North Korean coalition was no exception; the two allies approached the United States and Japan from diametrically opposite directions during the early 1980s. Gone was the solemn common pledge that Zhou Enlai and Kim Il Sung had made in their 1970 joint communiqué to fight against U.S. "imperialists" and Japanese "militarists." The primary threat to China's national security was no longer the traditional American policy of military containment but came rather from the Soviet Union, which deployed some fifty divisions, nuclear-equipped missiles, modern tanks, and fighter aircraft along their 4,500-mile-long common border. Soviet military might in Asia was augmented by its growing Pacific Fleet and by another trans-Siberian railway. The Chinese recognized that their normalized relations with the United States and Japan and their favoring a strong American military presence in the Asian and Pacific region served as a deterrent to Soviet power. They welcomed the U.S.-Japan Mutual Security Treaty and Japan's modest defense buildup plans. The Sino-Japanese Treaty of Peace and Friendship concluded in 1978 committed both sides to mutual cooperation and an antihegemonist stand. Furthermore, the Chinese were prepared to purchase military weapons and nuclear power plants from the United States and to rely on American and Japanese capital and technology for their four modernizations programs.

This rapid Chinese rapprochement with the United States and Japan made the North Koreans uncomfortable because they continued to regard U.S. "imperialists" and Japanese "militarists" as mortal enemies who presented the main obstacle to their unification scheme. The North Koreans opposed the U.S.-Japan security treaty as an aggressive military alliance directed against the Korean Peninsula and were particularly perturbed by the warm welcome that both Prime Minister Nakasone and President Reagan received during their visits to China in the spring of 1984. Reagan and his Chinese hosts wanted to avert another Korean War and to assist inter-Korean reconciliation; Secretary of State George Shultz went from Beijing to Seoul to explain the results of Reagan's China visit to Foreign Minister Lee Won Kyung. North Korea considered the Nakasone government the most reactionary ruling party in the entire postwar era and castigated the Japanese promise of $4 billion in loans to South Korea as thinly disguised "military funds." (The Tokyo-Pyongyang relationship had deteriorated markedly after North Korean agents killed a number of high-level South Korean leaders at Rangoon in October 1983.) More important, the North Koreans hurled a barrage of harsh invectives at Reagan, characterizing him as "the most bellicose nuclear war fanatic" and "the sworn enemy of our nation." Although pressured by North Korea's escalating anti-Washington and anti-Tokyo vituperations, the Chinese were unwilling to sacrifice their global and regional interests to satisfy North Korea. The Chinese thus assumed a correct public posture by supporting North Korea's proposals in their meetings with American and Japanese representatives and assuring their apprehensive ally that China had not sold out North Korea's vital security interests. They probably also attempted to persuade Kim Il Sung that he could expect some tangible benefits—such as a diplomatic breakthrough and improved relations with the United States or Japan—from Chinese negotiations on his behalf with these two countries.[37]

The acceleration of China's cooperative relations with the United States and Japan contributed to Kim Il Sung's decision to visit the Soviet Union and other Eastern European countries in late May and early June 1984. A senior American diplomat in Beijing observed in 1984 that, when Kim Il Sung announced his trips to the Soviet Union and the Eastern European countries, the Chinese were "scared to death" but were reassured after CCP general secretary Hu Yaobang's summit meetings with Kim Il Sung in May 1984.[38]

In the aftermath of Kim's Moscow visit, the Soviet Union reportedly delivered a number of MiG-23 fighter aircraft to North Korea, sent Soviet naval vessels to call on North Korean ports, and dispatched high-level Soviet delegates—both military and civilian—to Pyongyang, including those who helped celebrate the fortieth anniversary of Korea's liberation from Japan in August 1985. Most likely in return for the Soviet Union's promising to assist North Korean nuclear programs, Kim agreed to sign the nuclear nonproliferation treaty in 1985. When Kim Il Sung paid another visit to Moscow in October 1986, China's Xinhua News Agency reported that Kim and Mikhail Gorbachev would discuss military matters. It was unusual for China to reveal a major agenda item for the Kim-Gorbachev meeting in advance—an indication of China's uneasiness about Gorbachev's new initiatives in the Asian-Pacific region. In fact, a spokesman for the Chinese Ministry of Foreign Affairs openly expressed concern about the visit of a Soviet aircraft carrier (*Minsk*) to Nampo, saying that all nations should promote peace in Korea.[39]

The continuing U.S. military presence in South Korea was an irritant in China's evolving relations with North Korea and the Soviet Union. A Soviet scholar argued that a principled Soviet Union opposed U.S. troops stationed in South Korea but that China deviated from that position. Notwithstanding its official statements, however, China probably favored the presence of some U.S. military strength in South Korea to preserve military balance and political stability on the Korean Peninsula and to counterbalance Soviet strategic ambitions in Asia. Asked about this assumption, North Korean ambassador to China Chon Myong Su angrily responded that both in public meetings and in private conversations, the Chinese supported North Korea's opposition to the U.S. military presence in South Korea.[40] He asserted that North Korea maintained equally good "class-based fraternal relations" with China and the Soviet Union.

Nevertheless, a careful study of China's public statements and documents reveals that China was somewhat reluctant to support North Korea's demand for "immediate and complete withdrawal" of all U.S. military personnel and equipment from South Korea. Henry Kissinger reports that Mao Zedong and other Chinese leaders "never really pressed us to remove our forces from Korea" because they "correctly judged that the visible presence of American power was crucial for maintaining a balance of power in Asia and Europe."[41] The Chinese frequently called for "complete withdrawal" (*quanbu chezou*) of U.S. troops from South Korea, but only on rare occasions did they refer to "immediate withdrawal" (*liji chezou*).[42] As an analyst at *Beijing Review* stated:

> It is clear that to secure a peaceful settlement of the problem of Korea, the United States should create favorable conditions for the reunification of Korea, put its armed forces out of South Korea *as early as possible* and leave the problem of reunification to the Korean people.[43]

This position was consistent with China's policy interests in Korea. In a meeting with President Reagan in April 1984, Hu Yaobang publicly expressed China's opposition to the stationing of U.S. troops in South Korea. "This," he told the president, "does no good to your reputation," a relatively mild statement whose primary audience was probably Kim Il Sung rather than Reagan. Shortly thereafter, Hu reported to a Pyongyang mass rally that he had urged President Reagan to pull U.S. troops out of South Korea. Asserting that he and Kim reached a "complete consensus" regarding Korean affairs, Hu failed to mention either complete or immediate withdrawal of U.S. troops but stated that "this problem must be settled in the process of realizing the independent and peaceful reunification of Korea."[44]

In the early 1980s the Chinese did not attack the U.S.–South Korea Mutual Security Treaty and were reticent about U.S. nuclear weapons deployed in South Korea, perhaps because they recognized the value of nuclear deterrence or because they did not want to heighten North Korean anxiety. The Chinese supported Kim Il Sung's proposal for a nuclear-free zone over Korea, and, in response to the "Team Spirit" exercises jointly conducted by the United States and South Korea, the Chinese Ministry of Foreign Affairs charged that such large-scale military maneuvers threatened peace and stability in Korea. China joined North Korea in rejecting a U.S. invitation to send observers to the Team Spirit exercises, but the Chinese were probably less concerned with the scale of these exercises than with their provocative effects on North Korea, which declared a state of semiwar during the exercise. Similarly, the Chinese protested the United States' supplying "sophisticated weapons" (e.g., F-16 jet fighters, the Stinger air defense system, M-55-1 light tanks, and M-88 tank retrievers) to South Korea precisely because they felt that new weapons might upset the precarious military balance in Korea or prompt North Korean requests for more Chinese and Soviet military aid. Again, China's ability to reduce military tensions or introduce arms control measures in Korea was less than effective. The Chinese, skeptical about the feasibility of America's complete military disengagement from South Korea, hoped that the United States would lower its military profile in South Korea or reduce its troop levels.[45]

As far as Kim Jong Il's hereditary succession was concerned, the Chinese had initial reservations but by the early 1980s had decided to respect Kim Il Sung's wishes, partly out of concern about North Korean political stability in the post-Kim era. They were also pragmatic about interfering in the internal affairs of fraternal parties. Deng Xiaoping declared:

A party may often make comments on the activities of a foreign fraternal party according to some existing formulas or some rigid patterns. Facts have shown that this approach can get one nowhere. Conditions vary from country to country, the level of political awareness varies from people to people, and the class relations and relative strength of class forces in one country are different from those in another. . . . In short, we must respect the way the parties and peoples of different countries deal with their own affairs. They should be left alone in blazing their own paths and exploring ways to solve their own problems. No party can act as a patriarchal party and issue orders to others.[46]

In addition to the above, the Chinese probably embraced Kim Jong Il to blunt a pro-Moscow tendency among North Korea's young technocrats, who viewed China's economic and technological conditions with contempt and looked to the Soviet Union as an effective supplier of what they needed most. When the Chinese delegation, led by Peng Zhen (chairman of the Standing Committee of the National People's Congress) and Hu Qili (member of the CCP Secretariat), visited Pyongyang in September 1983, *Renmin Ribao* (September 8, 1983) prominently reported their public meeting with Kim Jong Il, thus recognizing his elevated leadership status. It remained unclear, however, whether the Chinese could transfer their close personal rapport with Kim Il Sung (and his partisan colleagues) to Kim Jong Il (and his generational cohorts).

Sino-Soviet Reconciliation

In retrospect, by the end of the 1980s the Chinese had decided to improve their relations with the Soviet Union and to press on their North Korean colleagues the overriding importance of peace and development in an emerging new international order. In a speech at a Pyongyang banquet on April 24, 1989, General Secretary Zhao Ziyang emphatically told Kim Il Sung that it was possible to create a sustained environment for international peace, thereby rejecting the traditional Leninist proposition that conflicts were inevitable in world politics. Zhao stated that the strongest trends in the world were to turn confrontation (*duikang*) into dialogue (*duihua*) and tension (*jinzhang*) into moderation (*huanhe*). He added that China paid close attention to the moderation (*huanhe*) and stability (*wending*) of the Korean situation. Zhao thus urged Kim to heed and follow the dominant international trend. In their meeting on April 26, Kim assured Zhao that "dialogue is better than confrontation" and "moderation is better than tension" and that North Korea, too, needed a peaceful and stable international environment for its socialist construction.[47]

The historic summit meeting between Mikhail Gorbachev and Deng Xiaoping, which took place on May 16, 1989, in Beijing, normalized all aspects of relations between China and the Soviet Union. In a joint communiqué, the two sides promised to develop their relations on the basis of five "universal principles"—mutual respect for sovereignty and territorial integrity, mutual nonaggression, noninterference in each other's internal affairs, equality and mutual benefit, and peaceful coexistence.[48] They expressed readiness to resolve all disputes through peaceful negotiations and to refrain from using or threatening to use arms against each other. More specifically, China and the Soviet Union agreed to reduce the military forces along their common border areas to a minimum, to negotiate a fair and reasonable settlement of their boundary disputes, and to promote economic, commercial, scientific, technological, and cultural relations in a planned way. The two countries also agreed that "peace and development are the two most important questions in the world of today" and indicated their desire to relax military confrontation and settle regional conflicts. Even though the communiqué did not make a specific reference to the Korean question, it was clear that both China and the Soviet Union wished to see the easing of tension as well as the continuation of dialogue between North and South Korea.

There were many reasons for China and the Soviet Union wanting to normalize relations toward the end of the 1980s. First, both Deng and Gorbachev had downgraded ideological exhortations and revolutionary fervor as determinants of their domestic and foreign policies and had adopted a realistic approach to carrying out their respective reform programs. Whereas Gorbachev attached higher priority to political reform than to economic modernization, Deng emphasized economic reform over political restructuring. They agreed to stop the sterile debates over ideological issues such as "revisionism" and "dogmatism" and to seek mutual cooperation in practical matters. Second, both leaders recognized the expensive and counterproductive consequences of an endless arms race and direct military confrontation. The Soviet Union was particularly interested in pursuing a series of arms control and disarmament measures on intermediate range nuclear forces (INF), strategic arms reduction talks (START), Conventional Forces in Europe (CFE), and the Conference on Security and Cooperation in Europe (CSCE) and in extending these measures to the Asian-Pacific region. The Chinese did not fully accept all the global and regional disarmament efforts but certainly welcomed the idea of mutual military disengagement from the Sino-Soviet border areas.

Third, as recorded in the joint communiqué, both China and the Soviet Union accepted the priorities of "peace" and "development" in world affairs and reoriented their bilateral relationship in accordance with the prevailing trends of peaceful coexistence and developmental interdependence. Fourth, China and the Soviet Union attempted to reduce their differences over such countries as Cambodia, Afghanistan, and Korea. As far as the Korean Peninsula was concerned, China and the Soviet Union concluded that it was not in their best national interests to woo North Korea or to criticize each other's position, but the Soviets responded more eagerly and directly than did the Chinese to South Korea's northern diplo-

macy. In essence, the Chinese and the Soviets had already practiced a de
facto "two-Korea" policy in the late 1980s. The North Koreans, who
could no longer take advantage of the Sino-Soviet conflict, were the principal casualties of the new Sino-Soviet reconciliation.

To keep a lid on the potentially explosive situation on the Korean
Peninsula, China and the Soviet Union maintained frequent high-level
consultations and developed an understanding of, if not consensus about,
their respective policies toward Pyongyang and Seoul. Thus, in a meeting
between Foreign Ministers Eduard Shevardnadze and Qian Qichen, on
September 1, 1990, in Harbin, in addition to the gulf crisis, and questions
about German unification, Afghanistan, and Cambodia, they had an "in-
depth dialogue" regarding the situation in the Korean Peninsula. They
agreed that "without a solution to the Korean Peninsula question, it is
impossible to achieve genuine security and stability in Northeast Asia"
and that "the dialogue between North and South parts of Korea is important in the easing of the tensions."[49] Shevardnadze no doubt told his Chinese host that the Soviet Union had decided to establish diplomatic relations with South Korea and that he was to explain this decision to the
North Koreans during his forthcoming visit to Pyongyang. When the Soviet Union and South Korea signed an agreement to exchange diplomatic
relations on September 30, 1990, the Chinese did not issue an official
response; neither did they support North Korea's angry protest.

Although China and the Soviet Union placed a premium on peace and
stability in the Korean Peninsula, the North Koreans continued to be preoccupied with security because they believed that the U.S. "imperialists"
both intended and were capable of attacking North Korea with nuclear
weapons. In commemoration of the fortieth anniversary of the Korean
War, an editorial in *Nodong Sinmun* (June 25, 1990) declared:

> The [current] situation shows that reductions, detente, or peace, about
> which the U.S. imperialists and the puppets are babbling, is a worthless
> lie and they are running wild to ignite a fuse for war on the Korean
> Peninsula at all costs. Because of the vicious commotions by the U.S.
> imperialists and the South Korean puppets for anti-Republic confronta-
> tion and their reckless maneuvers to provoke a new war, a very danger-
> ous situation is prevailing in our country in which a nuclear war may
> break out at any time.

As "proof" of the U.S. military threat, the North Koreans cited the annual Team Spirit exercises between the United States and South Korea. In

response to those exercises, in 1991, North Korea's Ministry of Foreign Affairs stated that they were "a test nuclear war targeted against the northern half of Korea." The North Koreans contended that, because the United States was the only superpower remaining in the world that possessed an enormous and superior arsenal, there was no need to test its military preparedness in South Korea unless it planned to invade North Korea.[50]

Because North Korea felt increasingly isolated, betrayed, and insecure in a rapidly changing world, the Chinese made statements and gestures to demonstrate their military solidarity with their North Korean allies. In August 1990, for example, Defense Minister Qin Jiwei, who had fought in the Korean War, led a military goodwill delegation to Pyongyang and assured Kim Il Sung that the Chinese armed forces would continue to honor their security commitment to North Korea. On the fortieth anniversary of China's entrance to the Korean War, the General Political Department of the People's Liberation Army and the Ministry of Civil Affairs jointly sponsored a large-scale celebration in Beijing; Yang Dezhi (former commander of the Chinese People's Volunteers in Korea) spoke of the "great victory" of China's "Resist-America and Aid-Korea" campaign and the lasting friendship between China and North Korea. Participants in the celebration included Qin Jiwei (defense minister), Yang Baibing (director of the PLA's General Political Department and secretary-general of the Central Military Commission), Chi Haotian (PLA chief of the General Staff), Zhao Nanqi (director of the PLA's General Logistics Department), and other Korean War veterans (such as Yang Chengwu and Song Shilun).[51]

At the banquet hosted by North Korean ambassador Chu Chang Jun on October 24, 1990, Vice Premier Wu Xueqian stated that the victory of the Chinese and Korean people in their joint resistance against "U.S. aggression" greatly contributed to peace in Asia and the world as a whole. China also sent a number of goodwill missions to Pyongyang to mark the anniversary, including a party and government delegation led by Li Tieying (state councilor), the CPV delegation headed by General Zhang Zhen (president of the National Defense University), and a delegation of CPV heroes led by General Yao Xian (Beijing Military District's Air Force commander). Most important, an editorial in *Renmin Ribao* (October 25, 1990) claimed that the United States had invaded Korea forty years ago and pledged that China would forever uphold friendly and cooperative relations with North Korea as "comrades in arms" and "brothers." (This statement was a departure from China's current tendency of *not* blaming the United States for the origin of the Korean War.) When Premier Li Peng visited Pyongyang in May 1991, he was accompanied by PLA chief of General Staff Chi Haotian, another Korean War veteran.[52]

After the U.S. victory in the Persian Gulf war, China and the Soviet Union deemed it necessary to strengthen their cooperative ties as a counterweight to the rapidly growing influence of the United States in global and regional military affairs. The Soviet Union exhibited a patent inability to assist its client state, Iraq, in resisting the overwhelming technological superiority of the American forces, and China was profoundly disillusioned with the U.S. policy of economic sanctions following the Tiananmen Square incident. In this context the summit meetings between Mikhail Gorbachev and Jiang Zemin (general secretary of the Chinese Communist Party), which were held during May 15–19, 1991, in Moscow, were to reaffirm the importance of their bilateral relations and to spell out their positions on a wide range of salient issues. The joint communiqué issued on May 19, 1991 stated:

> They note with satisfaction that thanks to their joint efforts, the friendly and co-operative relations between the two countries are developing steadily in the political, economic, trade, scientific and technological, cultural, military and other fields. Treasuring the achievements already made, both sides express readiness to further develop the relations of friendliness, good-neighborliness, mutual benefit and co-operation. This not only accords with the interests and aspirations of the peoples of the two countries, but also contributes to the maintenance of peace and stability in the whole world.[53]

Unlike the May 1989 joint communiqué, this communiqué prominently mentioned the steady development of military cooperation and made it clear that "normal and friendly contacts will be maintained between the military forces of the two countries." Moreover, Gorbachev and Jiang gave special attention to the question of security and stability in the Asian-Pacific region, observing that "hot spots and unsettled conflicts" remained. They declared that both countries were ready "to make joint efforts for turning the Asian-Pacific region into a zone of openness, cooperation and prosperity." They also stated:

> China and the Soviet Union hold that relaxation of the situation on the Korean Peninsula is of great importance for the security and stability in Northeast Asia. Both sides welcome the positive changes that have re-

cently taken place on the Peninsula, reaffirm their support for the realization of a peaceful reunification of Korea through dialogue and consultations between the North and South. They express the hope that the North and South will continue their dialogue for further improvement of mutual relations, and call for both sides to refrain from taking any acts that might impede detente on the Peninsula and a peaceful reunification of Korea.

(Perhaps, in the aftermath of Premier Li Peng's meeting with President Kim Il Sung in Pyongyang, Gorbachev and Jiang wanted to ensure that North Korea would accept the separate admissions of North and South Korea to the United Nations.) Eight days after Jiang's Moscow visit, North Korea announced that it would join the United Nations as a separate member.

THE END OF THE COLD WAR

After the disintegration of the Soviet Union and the birth of the Russian Federation led by Boris Yeltsin, who viewed North Korea negatively, Kim Il Sung had no other country but China on which he could rely in military and foreign affairs. For all practical purposes, China became an indispensable patron for North Korea's survival. In the post–cold war era, North Korea and China shared several common interests. First, in view of the successive demise of many socialist regimes, the leaders of North Korea and China strongly defended their socialist systems, particularly the preeminent status of the Korean Workers' Party and the Chinese Communist Party, both of which opposed the concept of multiparty rule and the "peaceful evolution" of a socialist system. After having devoted their entire adult lives to revolutionary activities, neither Kim Il Sung nor Deng Xiaoping was prepared to give up supreme power or preside over the dissolution of his regime(as East German leaders did). Unlike Gorbachev in either revolutionary commitment or temperament, they were anxious to form an international united front with the few remaining socialist states—Vietnam, Cuba, and Laos.

Second, as the victims of external economic sanctions and diplomatic isolation, both North Korea and China were inclined to sympathize with each other and to favor mutual aid in diplomatic and economic matters.

Thus, Chinese foreign minister Qian Qichen warned Japanese foreign minister Watanabe Michio in November 1991 that "it is not good for many nations to pressure one country [North Korea] into a corner" (made in regard to an international campaign to stop North Korea's nuclear weapons program). The two allies cooperated for some time in a variety of joint economic activities.

Third, the leaders of North Korea and China were fiercely nationalistic and uncompromisingly protective of their respective heritage and sovereignty and thus rejected any form of external interference in their domestic affairs. For example, North Korea and China supported each other in resisting the U.S.-led campaign for human rights. Fourth, both countries shared the perspective that a military balance should be maintained between North Korea and South Korea.

In October 1991, soon after the abortive coup in Moscow, Kim Il Sung arrived at Beijing by special train on his thirty-ninth visit to China; his welcoming party included China's top leaders—General Secretary Jiang Zemin, President Yang Shangkun, and Premier Li Peng. He also had an unannounced meeting with Deng Xiaoping for two hours on October 5. Deng reportedly assured Kim that China would continue to honor its security commitment to North Korea.[54] Jiang congratulated Kim on North Korea's admission to the United Nations and on the significant progress made in inter-Korean negotiations and stressed that détente and stability in the Korean Peninsula had a direct bearing on the overall situation in Northeast Asia. He told Kim:

> No matter how the international situation might change in the future, China would, as always, do its utmost to further strengthen the friendship between the two countries.[55]

After a series of meetings with Chinese leaders in Beijing, Kim traveled to Jinan and Nanjing, where he inspected some modern industrial plants, including a joint venture company, and visited the tomb of Confucius, where he praised the Confucian teachings on morality. According to a Chinese Foreign Ministry spokesman, Kim and his Chinese hosts discussed North Korea's nuclear program; the Chinese supported Kim's proposal for a nuclear-free zone in Korea and hoped that the nuclear issue would be peacefully resolved. In response to Kim's request for economic assistance, Li Peng reportedly described the shortage of food, clothing, and housing in China and urged North Korea to adopt the Chinese model for economic reform. Deng and Li agreed to increase China's oil supply to North Korea and to postpone carrying out financial transactions in hard currencies. As part of the aftermath of Kim's China visit, the North Koreans accelerated a plan to open "a zone of free economy and trade" patterned after the Special Economic Zone in Shenzhen, pushed for the Tumen River Project, and showed an interest in inter-Korean negotiations. This conciliatory attitude presumably paved the way for the North-South agreements in December 1991.[56]

The Chinese were enthusiastic about the inter-Korean reconciliation. The Chinese Foreign Ministry praised the "Joint Declaration on the Denuclearization of the Korean Peninsula" as an outcome of the efforts made by the two Korean sides and hoped that the goal of Korean denuclearization would be realized as soon as possible.[57] A Chinese commentator stated:

> The agreements put an end to 47 years of mutual distrust and hostilities and opened up new vistas for national reconciliation. . . . As long as the two sides take the national interests as their prime concern, they can surely surmount their ideological and social differences.[58]

As North Korea and South Korea separately joined the United Nations and, in effect, recognized each other's legitimacy by means of the bilateral accords, the Chinese began to take a set of careful but purposeful steps toward a de jure two-Korea policy. While South Korean foreign minister Lee Sang Ock was still in Beijing in April 1992, President Yang Shangkun, accompanied by Vice Premier Wu Xueqian and Deputy Chief of the PLA General Staff Xu Xin, arrived at Pyongyang to participate in the gala celebration for Kim Il Sung's eightieth birthday. For the Chinese, who do not publicly celebrate Deng Xiaoping's birthday, it was a gesture designed to boost Kim's beleaguered position in the international community. (Yang was one of the few heads of state to come to North Korea at that time, and no Russian government representative came.) In a special message to Kim Il Sung, the Central Committee of the Chinese Communist Party wished him a "Happy Birthday" and applauded his glorious achievements.[59]

Yang told Kim that the recent reconciliation between Pyongyang and Seoul not only conformed to the basic interests of all Korean people but also promoted peace and stability in Asia and the world. Kim responded that the inter-Korean accords would create a favorable environment for Korea's independent and peaceful reunification. An editorial in *Renmin Ribao* (April 18, 1992) noted a "positive change" in inter-Korean relations and predicted that the Sino–North Korean friendship "will forever flourish from generation to generation." Unlike *Renmin Ribao, China Daily*, an English-language publication in Beijing, never mentioned Kim's birthday in reporting on Yang's visit to North Korea. This conspicuous silence perhaps indicated the cynicism with which Chinese intellectuals looked at Kim's personality cult. One of them emphatically stated that "no Chinese likes either Kim Il Sung or Kim Jong Il," but, he remarked, whenever Deng Xiaoping, Yang Shangkun, or other senior Chinese leaders visited Pyongyang, they were overwhelmed by the extravagant treatment they received.[60]

It is also likely that the Chinese placated Kim's need to be viewed heroically, thus persuasively influencing his policy. Despite their own uncomfortable diplomatic status following the Tiananmen Square tragedy, the Chinese remained North Korea's most effective advisers, encouraging and facilitating its contacts with Japan and the United States. The North Koreans considered Beijing a convenient and hospitable venue for governmental talks with Japan and the United States.

It has been reported that, to bolster North Korea's defense capability, the Chinese agreed to make up, at least partially, for the loss of Moscow's support by offering a package of economic and military assistance to North Korea following Kim Il Sung's meeting with Deng in October 1991.[61] This suggests the seriousness of the Chinese desire to preserve a military balance between North and South Korea and to prevent North Korea from feeling insecure and isolated, which could lead to dangerous consequences in the Korean Peninsula.

The Chinese thus frequently assured their North Korean counterparts that China would uphold the Treaty of Friendship, Cooperation and Mutual Assistance with North Korea and would maintain the spirit of friendship cemented by blood between the two allies. On the thirtieth anniversary of the security treaty, in July 1991, for example, Jiang Zemin, Yang Shangkun, and Li Peng sent a message to Kim Il Sung in which they stressed the "strong vitality" (*qiangdade shengmingli*) of the treaty and the "common destiny" (*gongtongde mingyun*) between the two countries.[62] In Beijing, North Korean ambassador Chu Chang Jun sponsored a banquet to celebrate the occasion; Chinese vice president Wang Zhen attended, and Defense Minister Qin Jiwei delivered a congratulatory speech. On the same day the North Koreans held a banquet in Pyongyang hosted by Prime Minister Yon Hyong Muk, organized a military rally, and began the Pyongyang-Beijing "friendship week." Undoubtedly the North Koreans were more enthusiastic about the treaty with China than with the Soviet

Union, and, indeed, the future of the Moscow-Pyongyang military alliance looked uncertain.

On the forty-first anniversary of China's entrance to the Korean War in October 1991, Ambassador Chu held a reception in Beijing for Defense Minister Qin and other Chinese dignitaries, and Choe Kwang (chief of the General Staff of the Korean People's Army) hosted a similar reception in Pyongyang. About the same time China's navy commander Zhang Lianzhong, together with Qu Zhenmou (commander of the Beihai Fleet), visited North Korea; they were decorated by Kim Il Sung. With the collapse of the Soviet Union under way in December 1991, Defense Minister O Chin U hurried to Beijing for consultations with Yang Shangkun, Qin Jiwei, and Liu Huaqing (vice chairman of the Central Military Commission). The two sides evidently discussed the crisis in the Soviet Union, U.S.–North Korean talks, and the progress of inter-Korean military negotiations. In his capacity as chairman of the Central Military Commission, Jiang Zemin sent a warm congratulatory message to Kim Jong Il for his appointment as KPA supreme commander. The Chinese dispatched Zhang Wannian (commander of the Jinan Military Region) and Zhao Shufeng (deputy chief of staff of the Shenyang Military Region) to Pyongyang in April 1992 to celebrate the sixtieth anniversary of the KPA's founding. Another military delegation led by Yang Baibing (secretary-general of the Central Military Commission and director of the PLA General Political Department) went to Pyongyang in June 1992; Yang had a series of meetings with Kim Il Sung, Kim Jong Il, O Chin U, and Choe Kwang. Even after China normalized diplomatic relations with South Korea, there was no sign of significant change in China's security commitment to North Korea.[63]

The Chinese took a contradictory stand on the issue of North Korea's nuclear program during 1991 and 1992. On the one hand, they publicly rebuffed U.S. secretary of state James Baker's proposal in November 1991 that the United States, China, the Soviet Union, and Japan team up in a multilateral action to stop North Korea's nuclear weapons program. Foreign Minister Qian stated that "we do not wish to see any international pressure" on North Korea and that the world should leave it up to North and South Korea to work out their problems. The Chinese also rejected a Franco-British initiative in the U.N. Security Council to pass a resolution against North Korea's nuclear development. On the other hand, however, the Chinese opposed the proliferation of nuclear weapons, especially in the Korean Peninsula, and privately indicated that they would persuade

North Korea to accept the International Atomic Energy Agency's (IAEA's) inspection of its nuclear facilities.[64]

In March 1992, China finally acceded to the Nuclear Nonproliferation Treaty (NPT), which it had earlier denounced as a hoax perpetuated by the two superpowers. Foreign Minister Qian expressed China's adherence to the treaty's objective to prevent nuclear proliferation but proposed that

all nuclear-weapons states undertake not to be the first to use nuclear weapons at any time and under any circumstances . . . [and that they] undertake to support the proposition of establishing nuclear weapon–free zones.[65]

(This position was similar to the North Korean demand to the United States.)

It was difficult, however, for China to apply its nonnuclear policy to the Korean Peninsula primarily because North Korea adamantly refused to accept the IAEA's inspections of its suspected nuclear dump sites in Yongbyon. When North Korea announced that it intended to withdraw from the NPT regime in March 1993, the Chinese were faced with a dilemma. China favored a denuclearized Korea and a negotiated resolution of the North Korean nuclear issue but opposed any U.N.-sponsored economic sanctions against North Korea or an air strike against North Korean nuclear facilities because it felt that either action might lead to a serious military confrontation in the Korean Peninsula. Foreign Minister Qian stated that "we support patient consultations to reach an appropriate solution."[66]

In response to a draft resolution that the United States and other Western powers introduced at the U.N. Security Council urging North Korea to reaffirm its adherence to the NPT and to comply with its safeguards agreement with the IAEA, Chinese ambassador Li Zhaoxing stated on May 11, 1993:

China, as a State party to the Treaty on the Non-Proliferation of Nuclear Weapons, has all along opposed nuclear proliferation and supported denuclearization of the Korean Peninsula. China does not wish to see nuclear weapons on the peninsula, whether in the North or in the South, or to have them introduced there by a third party. In our view, the nuclear issue concerning the Democratic People's Republic of Korea is mainly a matter between the Democratic People's Republic of Korea and the International Atomic Energy Agency (IAEA), between the Democratic People's Republic of Korea and the United States, and between the Democratic People's Republic of Korea and the Republic of Korea. It should therefore be settled properly through direct dialogue and consultation between the Democratic People's Republic of Korea and the three other parties concerned, respectively. In this connection, China opposes the practice of imposing pressure.

The resolution passed, however, by a vote of thirteen to zero with China and Pakistan abstaining.[67]

While the Chinese continued to protect North Korean interests at the United Nations and the IAEA, they urged North Korea to cooperate with the IAEA and encouraged high-level negotiations between the United States and North Korea in New York and Geneva. The Chinese also maintained close consultations with the United States, Japan, and South Korea. For this purpose Foreign Ministers Qian and Han Sung Ju visited each other's capitals in May and October 1993, respectively. And the nuclear issue was high on the agenda for the summit meeting between Presidents Jiang Zemin and Kim Young Sam in March 1994.[68]

At the U.N. Security Council, China played a decisive role in blocking another U.S.-sponsored resolution on the North Korean nuclear question and in drafting a statement issued by the president of the council on March 31, 1994. The statement once again called on North Korea to allow IAEA inspections of its nuclear facilities and to renew its discussions with South Korea for implementing the Joint Declaration on the Denuclearization of the Korean Peninsula. Despite China's painstaking diplomatic activities, however, North Korea angrily rejected the statement as "unjustifiable demands."[69]

The nuclear crisis escalated in May and June 1994 when the United States prepared a draft U.N. resolution to impose economic and diplomatic sanctions against North Korea and the Chinese were compelled to undertake an even more active diplomatic role about Korea. This activism was also prompted by President Bill Clinton's decision to extend most favored nation status to China without linking it to human rights; in explaining his decision, Clinton noted that the United States and China shared an "important interest" in a nuclear-free Korean Peninsula. Annoyed by North Korea's recalcitrance and saber-rattling, the Chinese attempted to moderate their North Korean ally's policy during Choe Kwang's visit to Beijing. In the aftermath of South Korean foreign minister Han's visit to China, the Chinese also subtly changed their posture at the United Nations from the old formula of "opposing economic sanctions" to "not favoring economic sanctions" against North Korea. This implied that they might abstain from, not veto, the U.N. sanctions resolution. The Chinese counseled all parties to exercise self-restraint and urged Kim Il Sung to negotiate with the United States in good faith. In this sense China contributed to Kim Il Sung's agreeing to resume U.S.–North Korean negotiations and to hold a summit meeting with his South Korean counterpart during Jimmy Carter's meetings with Kim in June at Pyongyang.[70]

After Kim Il Sung's death, the United States and North Korea reached a comprehensive agreement on a nuclear issue at Geneva on October 21, 1994. A spokesman for the Chinese Ministry of Foreign Affairs enthusiastically welcomed it and stated:

> This outcome shows that dialogue and consultation are the only effective ways to solve the Korean nuclear issue. The implementation of the agreement will help an early realization of denuclearization on the Korean Peninsula, the maintenance of peace and stability there and the improvement of relations among the countries concerned. We hope that the parties concerned will continue their constructive efforts to ensure a smooth implementation of the agreement.[71]

At the Asia-Pacific Economic Cooperation (APEC) summit meeting in Indonesia in November 1994, President Clinton was "pleasantly surprised" by the vigor of President Jiang's support for the Geneva agreement,[72] and the two leaders promised to cooperate on its implementation. In view of their continuing security interest in Korea, the Chinese were not only relieved but satisfied with the outcome of their mediatory efforts, which had defused the escalating military crisis in the Korean Peninsula and assisted in North Korea's rapprochement with the United States.

Meanwhile, China took a reluctant step of accommodating the maneuver to transform the Korean armistice agreement into a more permanent structure for peace. In response to a request from North Korea, Vice Minister of Foreign Affairs Tang Jiaxuan announced on August 30, 1994, that China would withdraw from the Military Armistice Commission at Panmunjom (the commission had previously consisted of China, North Korea, and the United Nations Command). It was probably difficult for Tang to reject the North Korean request because China regarded itself as a guest in Korea. Ever since 1991, when a South Korean general replaced a U.S. general to represent the United Nations Command at the commission, North Korea had boycotted its meetings and attempted to abolish it. In fact, North Korea wanted to nullify the Korean armistice agreement altogether and negotiate a peace treaty with the United States but without South Korea's participation. The Chinese hoped, however, that "all relevant parties" would continue to abide by the Korean armistice agreement until a new peace system was set up. On the last day of a five-day visit to South Korea in November 1994, Premier Li Peng made it clear that China favored the change from the Korean armistice agreement to a peace treaty and wanted "all relevant parties," including North and South Korea, to take part in the negotiations for that change. Li's view differs from that of the two Korean governments. Whereas North Korea intends to exclude South Korea from the negotiations, South Korea prefers that both North and South Korea reach an agreement through direct negotiations and then seek its guarantee by the United States and China. It remains to be seen how China can help reconcile the inter-Korean differences and can assist a permanent peace in the Korean Peninsula.[73]

Although the Chinese continue to uphold their defense treaty with North Korea and to support its overall security interests, they are carefully exploring a preliminary consultation with South Korea in regard to military affairs. At their meeting on May 10, 1995, in Beijing, Premier Li Peng and South Korean prime minister Lee Hong Koo agreed to begin bilateral military exchanges and to promote multilateral confidence-building measures in the Asian-Pacific region.[74] Moreover, the two leaders emphasized the importance of inter-Korean dialogue as the most effective way to resolve the military issues—such as nuclear nonproliferation and the status of the Korean armistice agreement. It is clear that China intends to distance itself from North Korea's recalcitrant strategic positions in a subtle but unmistakable fashion and to play a constructive role in reducing military tensions in the Korean Peninsula.

Chapter Four

DIPLOMATIC ISSUES

• •

RELATIONS WITH PYONGYANG

On October 6, 1949, the People's Republic of China (PRC) and North Korea established diplomatic relations at the ambassadorial level, embarking on a period of friendship and cooperation as new members of the growing international socialist camp. This relationship, severely tested and significantly strengthened during the Korean War, developed into an intimate collaboration and made it possible for both to enjoy the wide-ranging benefits of close diplomatic consultations at the armistice negotiations and the Geneva conference.[1] It was unthinkable for China to deviate from its pro-Pyongyang diplomatic posture or to even entertain any form of a two-Korea solution for many years to come, particularly because of China's vehement opposition to a two-China policy.

The Treaty of Friendship, Cooperation and Mutual Assistance signed on July 11, 1961, provided a solid legal foundation for Sino–North Korean military and diplomatic solidarity and was followed by an amicable and constructive settlement of territorial issues. According to a reliable source, China and North Korea concluded secret negotiations over boundary issues in 1963.[2] The Chinese negotiators were instructed by Premier Zhou Enlai to be sympathetic and accommodating toward the North Koreans because of the overriding importance of the burgeoning Sino-

Soviet disputes. Tianchi (Chonji) Lake was easily divided: three-fifths went to North Korea and two-fifths to China. As for the Tumen and Yalu Rivers, both sides rejected the widely practiced method of using a hypothetical middle line to demarcate international rivers but instead adopted the "three-joint" (*santong*) principle: joint ownership, joint management, and joint use of the two rivers. (This principle was first used in the Soviet–North Korean agreement over the Tumen River.) The Chinese agreed to recognize North Korea's jurisdiction over about 80 percent of the islands on the two rivers, including the largest island on each river. In the case of Pidan Island (*chouduandao* in Chinese) at the mouth of the Yalu River, the North Koreans had originally indicated their willingness to cede it to China in appreciation for the assistance of the Chinese People's Volunteers (CPV) during the Korean War, but the Chinese had not responded because they regarded it as theirs in the first place. In 1963, however, the North Koreans insisted that they controlled Pidan Island; the Chinese finally accepted this new claim and relocated (and subsidized) about fifty Chinese households from the island to China.

The Chinese also reluctantly acceded to North Korea's wish to control 90 percent of the entry to the Yalu River, on the condition that China would have the right of free navigation in the area. A discussion over a certain section of the land on the Chinese side of the Yalu River ended when the Chinese corps of military engineers used dynamite to make an artificial waterway around the section and gave it to North Korea. Indeed, the Chinese offered so many concessions to North Korea that local leaders in Jilin and Liaoning Provinces protested. A Chinese scholar opined that, no matter what other mistakes Kim Il Sung might have made, he should receive credit for securing favorable territorial settlements from China. The Chinese negotiators, however, in addition to the primary consideration of Sino-Soviet competition, had other factors in mind when they offered their generous package to North Korea: They cherished the special blood-cemented relationship with their "younger brothers" and were eager to peacefully and harmoniously resolve border disputes with their neighboring countries, except India.[3]

Euphoria for the Sino–North Korean friendship and the cooperation displayed in the cordial visits by Choe Yong Kun and Liu Shaoqi in 1963 was short-lived, however. In 1966, China succumbed to the chaotic Cultural Revolution. Inflamed by Mao Zedong's extreme ideological exhortations, rampaging Red Guards commandeered the Ministry of Foreign Affairs, persecuted Liu Shaoqi, Deng Xiaoping, and other moderate leaders, and struck out on a radical, erratic, and xenophobic foreign policy. During that tumultuous era, then, China had difficulties with socialist and nonsocialist countries alike. The relationship between Beijing and Pyongyang was no exception; both sides recalled their ambassadors and hurled accusations against each other's leaders.[4] Armed with their own *chuche* ideology, the North Koreans refused to accept the self-proclaimed universal validity of the Cultural Revolution and Mao's political teachings and attempted to prevent adverse spillover effects on their population.

Unhappy with North Korea's recalcitrance, the Red Guards wrote several wall posters in 1967 and 1968 claiming that a group of North Korean generals had arrested Kim Il Sung. The Red Guards charged that the North Korean leader followed a revisionist line, served as a disciple of Khrushchev, ignored the Cultural Revolution, and sabotaged the Vietnamese people's just struggle. Most devastating was an article circulated by the Guangzhou Red Guards in February 1968:

> Kim Il-song is an out-and-out counterrevolutionary revisionist of the Korean revisionist clique, as well as a millionaire, an aristocrat, and a leading bourgeois element in Korea. His house commands a full view of the Moranbong, the Taedong River, and the Pot'ong River. . . . The estate covers an area of several ten thousand square meters and is surrounded on all sides by high walls. All sides of the estate are dotted with sentry posts. One has to pass through five or six doors before one comes to the courtyard. This really makes one think of the great palaces of emperors in the past.[5]

In a speech delivered the same month, Kang Sheng (a member of the Standing Committee of the CCP's Political Bureau) asked Chinese leaders in Jilin Province to stop the activities of Soviet and Korean revisionist special agents. A number of Chinese scholars and officials who had studied in Korea or visited Pyongyang were branded as North Korean spies. Many high-ranking Korean leaders in China, notably Zhu Dehai(Chu Dok Hae in Korean), were persecuted or purged. Driven by the Red Guards' violent suppression, many Koreans in China crossed the Tumen or Yalu Rivers to take refuge in North Korea. Border guards on both sides of the rivers occasionally exchanged gunfire. In 1968, there were "shooting incidents" over border disputes.[6]

In response, the Korean Central News Agency (Pyongyang) issued a statement on January 26, 1967:

The Red Guard papers, wall papers, and handbills in Peking and other parts of China have recently been making false propaganda that something like a "coup" broke out and political unrest has been created in our country. . . . This cannot but be an intolerable slander against the party, government, people, and people's army of our country. . . . The heroic people's army, under the leadership of our party, is defending rock-firm the socialist gains in the northern half of the country and is fully prepared to repulse any aggression of the enemy.[7]

The North Koreans asserted that there was no difference between the Red Guards and the Chinese government and warned that, if the Red Guards continued to slander and defame North Korea, the Chinese government would be held responsible for the consequences. An article published in *Kulloja* in March 1967 rejected flunkyism, big-nation chauvinism, and any domination of one nation by another.[8]

The North Koreans, however, were restrained in public statements about China during 1968 and 1969, in sharp contrast to their vituperative attacks against the Soviet Union in the early 1960s. They eagerly accepted China's last-minute invitation to Choe Yong Kun to attend the October 1, 1969, national celebration for the PRC's founding. At the conclusion of the celebration, Mao Zedong, in a gesture of reconciliation, responded to Choe Yong Kun's question, "Do you still think we are revisionists?" with "no."[9] A meeting between Zhou Enlai and Kim Il Sung in April 1970 paved the way for diplomatic normalization; ambassadors were exchanged that spring. The two sides agreed to praise each other's policy achievements and the correct leadership of Mao Zedong and Kim Il Sung publicly, to refrain from compelling each other to attack the Soviet Union, to uphold the principle of noninterference in domestic matters, and to cooperate in the conduct of foreign affairs.

THE UNITED NATIONS AND KOREA

In the early 1970s, the close Sino–North Korean diplomatic cooperation became manifest in new approaches to the United Nations. Both countries had heretofore a record of essentially hostile relations with the world organization. Once the PRC gained entrance to the United Nations (replacing the Republic of China in October 1971), however, the Chinese modified their contention that the United Nations was a "marketplace" for U.S. imperialists and Soviet revisionists to strike political bargains, that the United Nations was nothing but an instrument of U.S. aggression in Korea, and that any U.N. discussion of the Korean question was illegal.[10]

The Chinese then became the chief diplomatic champions for North Korea at the United Nations at the expense of Moscow's competing claim. In his first policy statement at the U.N. General Assembly in November 1971, Chinese vice minister of foreign affairs Qiao Guanhua, who had participated in the Korean armistice negotiations, reiterated his support for North Korea's April 1971 eight-point program for peaceful national reunification.[11] On behalf of North Korea he demanded the withdrawal of U.S. troops from South Korea, the dissolution of the United Nations Commission for the Unification and Rehabilitation of Korea (UNCURK), and the nullification of all "illegal" U.N. resolutions on the Korean question. In U.N. discussions of the agenda items on Korea, China articulated and spearheaded the North Korean position.

When inter-Korean negotiations were under way in 1971 and 1972, the United States, Japan, and other pro-Seoul member states successfully maneuvered to postpone consideration of the Korean question at the United Nations on the grounds that such a discussion would interfere with the negotiations between the Koreas. In his second speech at the United Nations in October 1972, Qiao Guanhua contended that "a postponement [of the U.N. discussion] is neither in the interests of the Korean people nor conducive to relaxation of tension on the Korean Peninsula." He asserted that the continuing operations of UNCURK and the United Nations Command (UNC) were anachronistic and posed a threat to North Korea. He dropped his previous demand that the United Nations nullify all "illegal" resolutions on the Korean question, however, and assumed a more moderate and conciliatory posture than before. The U.N. General Assembly adopted another one-year moratorium on the Korean question by a vote of seventy to thirty-four with twenty-one abstentions.[12]

In 1973 the Chinese helped remove the twelve-year-old "Stevenson" formula (which discouraged North Korean participation in U.N. debates on the Korean question) and invite both North Korea and South Korea to participate in U.N. debates without being able to vote. Huang Hua, Chinese ambassador to the United Nations, hailed the participation of a North Korean delegation in the international organization as a victory and accused South Korea of sabotaging the independent and peaceful reunification of Korea, stepping up arms expansion, and intensifying its fascist rule.[13] He also called UNCURK and the UNC tools of foreign intervention in Korea and demanded the complete pullout of U.S. forces from South Korea.

In the larger context of Beijing's new détente policy toward the United States and Japan, however, Huang fully cooperated with U.S. ambassador John Scali to extract a compromise from the two rival draft resolutions and to adopt a consensus statement on the Korean question at the U.N. General Assembly on November 18, 1973. (He also got the North Koreans to accept the consensus statement.) The statement noted that "a joint communiqué was issued by the North and the South of Korea on 4 July 1972" and hoped that "the South and the North of Korea will be urged to continue their dialogue and widen their many-sided exchanges and cooperation in the above spirit so as to expedite the independent peaceful reunification of the country." It also dissolved UNCURK immediately. The Chinese took great pride in passing the consensus statement but regretted that the UNC remained in South Korea.[14]

The 1973 mood of compromise was shattered the following year by a showdown in the U.N. General Assembly between pro-Seoul and pro-Pyongyang member states. The confrontation reflected the failure of inter-Korean talks and the absence of diplomatic compromise among major powers. Radical leaders led by Jiang Qing played an increasingly influential role in China's power struggles during 1974 and 1975, and Huang Hua was unable to be flexible in the U.N. debates on the Korean question. On December 17, 1974, the U.N. General Assembly passed a pro-Seoul resolution by a vote of sixty-one to forty-three with thirty-one abstentions. The resolution reaffirmed the consensus statement adopted during the previous session and expressed the hope that the Security Council would consider "those aspects of the Korean question which fall within its responsibilities, including the dissolution of the United Nations Command, in conjunction with appropriate arrangements to maintain the Armistice Agreement."[15] Against Chinese and North Korean wishes, however, the First Committee of the United Nations rejected, by a tie vote (forty-eight to forty-eight with thirty-eight abstentions), a pro-Pyongyang resolution mandating that the UNC dissolve itself and U.S. troops withdraw from South Korea.

In view of their precarious position in the United Nations, the United States and South Korea proposed in June 1975 to terminate the UNC by January 1, 1976, provided China and North Korea agreed to continue the armistice agreement. This proposal was rejected by China and North Korea because it did not require the withdrawal of U.S. forces from South Korea and because the armistice agreement was supposed to be a temporary cease-fire arrangement. In his speech at the U.N. General Assembly in September 1975, Qiao Guanhua declared:

> Korea cannot remain forever in a state of armistice. . . . The key to a peaceful settlement of the Korean question lies in the conclusion of a peace agreement to replace the Armistice Agreement and in the with-drawal of all U.S. troops.[16]

After heated debates and intense lobbying, the U.N. General Assembly in November 1975 adopted the two mutually contradictory resolutions—the pro-Seoul resolution by a vote of fifty-nine to fifty-one with twenty-nine abstentions and the pro-Pyongyang resolution by a vote of fifty-four to forty-three with forty-two abstentions.[17] Whereas the pro-Seoul resolution urged "all the parties directly concerned" (meaning the United States, China, South Korea, and North Korea) to embark on talks as soon as possible so that "the United Nations Command may be dissolved concurrently with arrangements for maintaining the Armistice Agreement," the pro-Pyongyang resolution called for the unconditional dissolution of the UNC and the withdrawal of all foreign troops stationed in South Korea under the flag of the United Nations and asked "the real parties to the Armistice Agreement" (meaning the United States and North Korea) to replace it with a peace agreement. The United Nations' adopting two contradictory resolutions ensured that neither resolution would be implemented and that no more U.N. resolutions on the Korean question would be adopted for many years to come.

RELATIONS WITH SEOUL

Depite China's persistent anti-Seoul posture at the United Nations and the insults it hurled against President Park Chung Hee's "fascist rule," Park overcame his deep-seated opposition to China's "aggressive policy" and made peaceful gestures toward China throughout the 1970s. In January 1971 he expressed a willingness to seek rapprochement with those socialist countries he characterized as "nonhostile." This was followed by Foreign Minister Kim Yong Sik's statement that "it is the policy of the government to approach the question of diplomatic normalization with the Soviet Union and Communist China with flexibility and seriousness. It can be realized if they recognize our sovereignty and refrain from hostile actions."[18]

In a major speech, "New Foreign Policy for Peace and Unification," on January 23, 1973, President Park stated:

> The Republic of Korea will open its door to all the nations of the world on the basis of the principles of reciprocity and equality. At the same time, we urge those countries whose ideologies and social institutions are different from ours to open their doors likewise to us.[19]

In addition to their repeated public statements, the South Koreans relied on friendly intermediaries such as the United States, Japan, and Canada to convey their peaceful intentions to China. Even though the Chinese carried on a modest indirect trade with South Korea for China's four modernizations programs in the late 1970s, they held to a rigid one-Korea policy and rebuffed Seoul's overtures. China forbade even casual social contact between Chinese and South Korean officials in third countries and prohibited all forms of cultural exchange. The Chinese were fully aware of North Korea's sensitivity to even the appearance of Beijing-Seoul contacts and saw no useful payoff from reciprocating South Korea's initiatives at that time. Moreover, the Chinese Ministry of Foreign Affairs issued a series of warnings against South Korea's "violations" of its seabed oil resources and fishing rights. In March 1980, Deng Xiaoping told a *Yomiuri Shimbun* delegation that it would not be in China's best interests to develop relations with South Korea and that it was unrealistic for China to recognize South Korea and for the United States to recognize North Korea.[20]

An unexpected significant breakthrough in Beijing-Seoul relations took place in May 1983 when six armed Chinese civilians hijacked a Trident airplane containing 105 crew members and passengers during a routine flight from Shenyang to Shanghai, opened fire against crew members, and forced it to land at a U.S. military base near Chunchon in South Korea. The Chinese, stunned by this first successful act of civilian air piracy in China, promptly dispatched a thirty-three-member negotiating team led by Shen Tu (director-general of the Civil Aviation Administration of China [CAAC] and a regular member of the CCP Central Committee) to Seoul. The United States and Japan, having good diplomatic relations with China, discreetly helped facilitate Beijing-Seoul communications. To avert a major political embarrassment, Chinese government delegates entered into unprecedented direct negotiations with their South Korean counterparts, headed by Gong Ro Myong (assistant minister of foreign affairs). A sudden pro-China fever gripped many South Koreans, especially those in government agencies and the mass media, who warmly welcomed and lavishly entertained the Chinese guests. A South Korean critic, however, lamented that China's aggression during the Korean War had been forgotten.[21]

As a result of their friendly but intense discussions, Shen and Gong signed a nine-article memorandum on May 10, 1983. Because this document listed Gong as representing "the Ministry of Foreign Affairs, the Republic of Korea," it implied China's tacit de facto acknowledgment, if not recognition, of South Korea's governmental authority. They settled all issues to their mutual satisfaction, except the legal status of the six hijackers. The Chinese asked for extradition to China on the grounds that theirs was the state where the hijacked plane was registered, the offense was committed within Chinese air space, and the hijackers and most of the victims were Chinese. The South Koreans, however, rejected this request and decided to try them at Seoul in accordance with their own law (the Air Flight Security Act of 1974), the 1970 Hague Convention for the Suppression of Unlawful Seizure of Aircraft, and the 1971 Montreal Convention for the Suppression of Unlawful Acts Against the Safety of Civil Aviation. Gong permitted the safe return of the Chinese passengers and crew and the aircraft to China, and Shen expressed his appreciation to the South Koreans "for the speedy and appropriate measures taken for the safety of the aircraft and the well-being of the crew and passengers, as well as for the medical care of the wounded." The memorandum stated that "both sides have expressed their hope to maintain the spirit of cooperation which was amply manifested in handling the incident, in future case[s] of emergency which may involve the two sides." The returned Chinese crew were treated as heroes and given awards. At a welcoming ceremony in Shanghai, Wu Qingdan, deputy secretary-general of the State Council, thanked the South Korean authorities for their cooperative attitude. This "hijack diplomacy" gave China a convenient excuse to shed its nonpolicy toward South Korea. Foreign Minister Wu Xueqian flew to Pyongyang on May 20 to explain the incident to Kim Il Sung and to reiterate that China would not practice a two-Korea policy and would continue to honor the traditional friendship and alliance between China and North Korea.[22]

In August 1983 a three-judge panel of the Seoul District Criminal Court sentenced the six hijackers to prison terms ranging from four to six years. The South Korean Ministry of Foreign Affairs transmitted its official communications about the hijacking trial to China via the CAAC's Tokyo Office. The PRC complained that the sentences were too lenient and inconsistent with the Hague and Montreal Conventions; the Republic of China (ROC) sent eighteen lawyers to Seoul and demanded that the hijackers be released to Taipei as "freedom fighters." About the same time another Chinese plane—a MiG-21 jet fighter flown by a Chinese test pilot—arrived in South Korea. The plane was an advanced model of the Chinese-built MiG-19 jet fighter that a North Korean pilot had brought to Seoul in February. The South Korean government let this Chinese defector go to Taipei and expressed a willingness to negotiate with the PRC government for the return of the MiG-21 to China. No intergovernmental negotiations were consummated, however.

Despite Wu's assurances to North Korea, the Shen-Gong memorandum may have helped moderate China's long-standing policy that refused to allow South Korean officials to attend international meetings in China. In August 1983 the Chinese issued a visa to a South Korean official so that he might attend a month-long seminar on aquaculture in Wuxi under the joint auspices of the United Nations Development Program and the Food and Agriculture Organization. Anticipating protests by North Korea, the Chinese made it clear that South Koreans would be admitted to China only to participate in conferences sponsored by the United Nations or its specialized agencies. This principle was applied to a few additional South Korean visitors to China in October and November.

The Chinese continued to demonstrate fair and realistic attitudes on a few other issues related to Korea. When the Soviet Union shot down a Korean Air Line plane in September 1983, China joined the United States and Japan in denouncing Soviet behavior at the United Nations and requesting reparations for its victims. North Korea endorsed the Soviet action as justified and accused the United States and South Korea of arousing "anticommunist war hysteria" following the incident. A month later the Chinese also dealt even-handedly with the Rangoon bombing incident. *Renmin Ribao* (October 10, 1983) first reported the bombing, together with a report on student demonstrations in Seoul. On November 6, 1983, *Renmin Ribao* carried reports of the Burmese government's announcement, which blamed North Korea for the bombing, and North Korea's response. The Chinese were afraid that the incident might increase political instability in South Korea or intensify inter-Korean hostility. On a number of occasions the Chinese indicated that they were opposed to any form of terrorism and to all acts that would increase tensions in the Korean Peninsula.[23]

This approach was also reflected in China's sports diplomacy toward Korea. In March 1984 a Sino–South Korean sporting event—the Davis Tennis Cup's preliminary games—took place for the first time in China at Kunming. The eight-member South Korean team was permitted to display its national flag at the airport and during the games. North Korea protested that Sino–South Korean exchanges would undermine the Sino–North Korean friendship, but China responded that sports exchanges did not necessarily lead to political relations. A month later the first Chinese athletes went to Seoul to compete in the Asian Junior Basketball Championships, as well as in the Second Asian Swimming Championships. The government in Taiwan boycotted these games because of China's participation and protested to the South Korean government that Chinese athletes were allowed to use their national flags and national anthem in Seoul. To expand its sports diplomacy with China, however, South Korea was clearly willing to forgo Taiwanese objections. In September a twelve-member Chinese delegation—which included Zhang Baifa (mayor of Beijing), Chen Xian (vice minister of the State Sports Commission), and He Zhenlian (member of the International Olympic Committee)—attended the Olympic Council of Asia meeting in Seoul, as well as a banquet hosted by President Chun Doo Hwan. He Zhenlian announced that China would take part in the Asian Games and the Olympic Games wherever they were held. Because China's ambition was to host the Asian Games and the Olympic Games, he wanted to demonstrate China's adherence to the standards of international sports programs. The Chinese ignored the Soviet decision to boycott the 1984 Summer Olympics in Los Angeles, but North Korea joined the Soviet boycott, hoping that it would adversly affect the next Olympics in Seoul.[24]

In March 1985 China and South Korea had another important opportunity for intergovernmental negotiations when a mutiny on a Chinese navy torpedo boat set it adrift on the high seas; it was found by a South Korean fishing boat and towed to Kunsan in South Korea. Three Chinese navy vessels had invaded South Korean territorial waters in pursuit but retreated when South Korean naval forces arrived. The South Korean government lodged a protest with China and demanded an official apology as a condition for the return of the torpedo boat and its crew. As a result of negotiations between the Xinhua News Agency and the South Korean consulate general in Hong Kong, the Chinese Ministry of Foreign Affairs delivered a memorandum to South Korea on March 26, 1985, in which it apologized for its three naval vessels violating South Korean territorial waters and promised to prevent the recurrence of such an incident. (The memorandum specifically referred to "the Republic of Korea" and "the People's Republic of China.") In response, the South Korean government turned over the torpedo boat, its thirteen surviving crew members (including two mutineers), and the bodies of the six dead to the Chinese navy in international waters. Satisfied with the swift settlement of a difficult incident, the Chinese expressed appreciation to South Korea for its cooperation. The South Korean government was criticized for handing over the two mutineers, but it contended that they had not asked for political asylum. This "torpedo diplomacy," coupled with the "hijack diplomacy" two years earlier, signaled to China that it could expect South Korea to act in an even-handed manner in regard to Chinese interests and added to South Korea's image as a nation with firm resolve and sophisticated diplomatic skills.[25]

The year 1985 saw an increase in the number of contacts and visits between China and South Korea. Two South Korean diplomats (Lee Si Young and Kum Chung Ho) attended a U.N. seminar on the Palestinian question in April. In October, Prime Minister Lho Shin Young exchanged greetings with Premier Zhao Ziyang at two U.N.-related functions.[26] At the first, a reception hosted by President Ronald Reagan, Lho introduced himself to Zhao and said that he hoped to improve relations between China and South Korea; Zhao smiled and responded that he was "pleased to meet with you." This was the first time that the prime ministers of these two countries met. At the second, a social function sponsored by U.N. secretary-general Javier Pérez de Cuéllar, the two greeted each other again. It is important that Zhao did not deliberately avoid or rebuff Lho.

While sustaining relations with South Korea in sports, trade, informal contacts, and crisis management, the Chinese attempted to become mediators between North Korea and the United States. After his secret meeting with Kim Il Sung at Dalian in August 1983, Deng Xiaoping (chairman of the CCP's Central Advisory Commission) conveyed Kim's conciliatory message to Secretary of Defense Caspar Weinberger during their meeting on September 28. Deng told Weinberger that North Korea had neither the intention nor the capability of invading South Korea and that China supported Kim's proposal for a Confederal Republic of Koryo. Subsequently, on October 8, 1983 (one day before the Rangoon incident), China notified the U.S. embassy in Beijing that North Korea had reversed its earlier opposition to the tripartite talks. The Chinese welcomed this reversal as a "constructive" and "positive" change in North Korean policy. They assumed that South Korea would take a reasonable position on the tripartite talks, as had been the case in the earlier "hijack diplomacy" incidents. The Rangoon crisis, however, dampened China's role as mediator between Pyongyang and Washington for a few months.[27]

On January 10, 1984, North Korea publicly proposed holding tripartite talks; the following day the Chinese Ministry of Foreign Affairs issued a statement that welcomed that proposal as easing tension on the Korean Peninsula and achieving peaceful Korean reunification. At the same time, during a meeting in Washington, Premier Zhao Ziyang urged President Reagan to accept the North Korean initiative. In response to Reagan's counterproposal—that the tripartite talks be expanded to include China—Zhao demurred in deference to North Korea's declared policy preference but indicated that, if the three-way talks were held, China might join them later. Reagan also supported the South Korean position (that talks first be held between top leaders of both Koreas) but said that it was not possible for the United States to recognize North Korea in exchange for China's recognition of South Korea. The South Koreans demanded that North Korea apologize for the Rangoon bombing, but they were not adverse to Reagan's idea of four-party talks, which might improve Seoul-Beijing relations. In April 1984, when Reagan paid his first state visit to China, Zhao told him that "it is still China's hope that tripartite talks will be held at an early date."[28]

Yet the Chinese were concerned about Kim Il Sung's visit to the Soviet Union and Eastern European countries and his criticism of the Reagan administration. In a widely publicized interview with a TASS delegation, Kim praised the Soviet Union for opposing a triangular military alliance among U.S. "imperialists," Japanese "militarists," and South Korean "puppets" and declared that "the socialist countries must naturally deal a blow at Reagan's bellicose policy."[29] In that thinly veiled criticism of China's cooperating with the United States to counterbalance the Soviet Union, he added, "Korea and the Soviet Union are comrades-in-arms that maintain the relationship of alliance. . . . There is no difference [of views] between our two countries." Kim's balancing act between Moscow and Beijing continued.

The Chinese, alert to the Asian Games and the Summer Olympic Games to be held in Seoul in 1986 and 1988, respectively, expressed the hope that both Koreas would reach a negotiated solution to the Seoul Olympiad under the auspices of the International Olympic Committee. In a letter to Juan Antonio Samaranch, president of the International Olympic Committee in September 1985, Zhong Shitong, president of the Chinese Olympic Committee, said that a North-South compromise on the Seoul Olympic Games would promote the relaxation of tensions, the achievement of peaceful Korean unification, and the Olympic spirit. In a December 1985 letter to Kim Yu Sun (chairman of the North Korean Sports Guidance Committee), Li Menghua (minister of the State Sports Commission) stated that the North Korean proposals for the Seoul Olympic Games deserved careful consideration.[30] Li fell short, however, of endorsing North Korea's proposal for cohosting the Olympic Games in Seoul and Pyongyang. The Chinese were pleased with the initial signs of inter-Korean compromise made at Lausanne, Switzerland, in July 1986 but dissociated themselves from North Korea's extreme alternatives—namely, either cohosting the 1988 Olympiad or boycotting it. To North Korea's chagrin, the Chinese sent a huge contingent of athletes to the Seoul Asian Games in 1986, despite an editorial in *Nodong Sinmun* (September 1, 1986) that condemned the Asian Games as a political plot to further South Korea's "dictatorial rule" and to perpetuate Korea's division. The games played an important role in fostering China's positive perception of South Korea.

SEOUL'S NORTHERN DIPLOMACY

Although China engaged in sports diplomacy and economic transactions with South Korea, in the late 1980s and early 1990s it lagged behind the Soviet Union and Eastern European countries in responding to Seoul's diplomatic and political overtures. Campaigning for president in 1987, Roh Tae Woo promised to give high priority to achieving diplomatic normalization with China and to developing the western coastal region facing China. For this purpose he sent Park Tong Jin (former foreign minister) to Tokyo to solicit Prime Minister Takeshita Noboru's assistance and to meet with Chinese officials stationed in Japan. Park also made several trips to China to look at the Shenzhen Special Economic Zone and to talk to a number of Chinese leaders, including Zhu Liang (director of the CCP's International Liaison Department). In his first speech at the U.N. General Assembly in October 1988, President Roh stated:

> I welcome as an encouraging development the fact that socialist countries such as China and the Soviet Union are showing a forward-looking

attitude in recent months concerning mutual exchanges and cooperation with the Republic of Korea in a number of fields. I find it significant that China, a nation which has traditionally been a good neighbor of Korea, is moving to overcome the wall of separation that has lasted for nearly half a century and is expanding its mutual exchanges and cooperation with the Republic of Korea.

He repeated the same message in an address to the Council on Foreign Relations and the Asia Society in New York.[31]

The initial Chinese reaction to Roh's signals, however, was less than encouraging. In a meeting with Japanese newspaper publishers at Beijing in July 1988, Premier Li Peng said that China did not plan to enter into diplomatic relations with South Korea but that Sino-Korean trade was being conducted through nongovernmental channels. The Chinese invoked the principle of separation between economic and diplomatic spheres—a principle that China had vociferously rejected in its relations with Japan before 1972. During a visit to Pyongyang in September 1988, President Yang Shangkun assured Kim Il Sung that China's participation in the Seoul Olympic Games did not signal the onset of Chinese diplomatic relations with South Korea. About the same time a spokesman for the Chinese Ministry of Foreign Affairs told foreign correspondents in Beijing that China and North Korea had a most intimate and friendly relationship and that China was making no preparations for diplomatic contacts with South Korea.[32]

In a report delivered at the Second Session of the Seventh National People's Congress on March 20, 1989, Premier Li Peng stated:

Maintaining good-neighbor, amicable relations and cooperation with neighboring and nearby countries in Asia is the consistent policy of our government. The traditional friendship between China and the Democratic People's Republic of Korea has been growing. We are concerned over peace and stability in the Korean Peninsula, support the reasonable proposal made by the Democratic People's Republic of Korea for the independent and peaceful reunification of Korea, and hope that positive results will come out of the dialogue and contact between North and South Korea. China does not have official ties with South Korea, but people-to-people contacts do exist in economic relations and trade.

No doubt General Secretary Zhao Ziyang conveyed the same message to Kim Il Sung during their meetings on April 25 and 26, 1989.[33]

Meanwhile, the Chinese watched with interest South Korea's rapidly developing relations with the Soviet Union and Eastern Europe. In an analysis of this development, Ruo Yu observed that when President Roh Tae Woo expanded his relations with the Soviet Union and East European countries (beginning with sport exchanges, progressing to economic co-operation, and culminating in the establishment of diplomatic contacts), those countries responded because they wanted to push ahead with their domestic and political reforms, to fine-tune their foreign policies, and to open avenues to the outside world. He stated:

> As for South Korea, its interests in this affair are mainly political. On the one hand, it is attempting to pump up its international prestige by si-phoning strength from the Soviet Union and East European countries. On the other, it is trying to discard the image of being "little brother" to the United States, because the image is not compatible with its economic strength. Also, the huge markets of the Soviet Union and East European countries have a strong allure for South Korea.[34]

Ruo Yu also argued that South Korea's northern policy provided a "new flexibility in regard to North Korea's relations with the United States and Japan" and concluded that, during and after the Seoul Olympic Games, South Korea's relations with the Soviet Union and Eastern Europe be-came "more direct, more open and even more political in nature." He estimated that in 1987 South Korean trade with the Soviet Union and Eastern Europe soared to $500 million. Ruo Yu contended that the Soviet Union sorely needed South Korean technology to exploit its Far East re-gions and Siberia and that the USSR was promoting its relations with South Korea to expand its influence in the Asian-Pacific region, a poten-tial source of Sino-Soviet conflict. The Chinese, however, noted that the Soviet Union could be intending to develop its vast but economically back-ward Far East "through a tripartite cooperation between it, China and Japan, with hopeful inclusion of South Korea." According to Ruo Yu, in an attempt to demonstrate its incipient diplomatic contacts, the Soviet Union sent a consular corps to Seoul during the Olympic Games, and President Roh Tae Woo agreed to receive the consul.

In December 1988 the Chinese reported that the Soviet Chamber of Commerce and Industry and the (South) Korean Trade Promotion Corpo-ration (KOTRA) signed a series of agreements to exchange trade offices between Moscow and Seoul. The Chinese also reported Hungary's agree-ments with South Korea, first to exchange resident liaison officers between Budapest and Seoul in October 1988 and then to establish diplomatic relations in February 1989. *Renmin Ribao* reported that North Korea had denounced Hungary's decisions and recalled its ambassador from Hungary. Against this background a top Chinese government official expressed fear that the accelerated pace of South Korea's northern policy might drive North Korea to retaliate against South Korea and called on Seoul to exercise caution and patience. The Chinese may thus have asked the Soviet Union and East European countries to slow down their diplomatic advances toward South Korea. A senior North Korean diplomat stationed in Beijing was confident that China, unlike Hungary, would never "betray" North Korea and that the leaders of both countries would continue to trust, understand, and support each other because they shared a "special relationship" cemented by blood.[35]

As suggested by Ruo Yu, the Chinese recognized that Seoul's northern policy could positively affect Pyongyang's opening to the United States and Japan. To keep Pyongyang from becoming diplomatically isolated, the Chinese acted as mediators between North Korea and the United States and Japan.[36] They continued to promote the tripartite talks and welcomed the U.S. decision to allow its diplomats to make contact with their North Korean counterparts. They also facilitated an opportunity for U.S.–North Korean diplomatic talks in Beijing.

In Pyongyang, General Secretary Zhao Ziyang expressed the hope that the United States would upgrade its level of diplomatic representation with North Korea. In February 1989, the Chinese had presented North Korea's policy preferences to President George Bush. In his meetings with Chinese leaders, Kim Il Sung denounced all forms of the "two-Korea" conspiracy, but Zhao Ziyang refrained from offering any public comments on the matter. The Chinese also applauded the Japanese government's decision to lift a ban on contacts between Japanese and North Korean diplomats and Prime Minister Takeshita Noboru's statement that "it is time for Japan to improve relations with North Korea." The issue of Japanese–North Korean relations was discussed at meetings between Takeshita Noboru and Li Peng in August 1988 and April 1989. During those meetings, at President Roh's request, Takeshita explained South Korea's desire to improve relations with China. The Chinese reasoned that, if North Korea improved its relations with the United States and Japan, it would not only help North Korea but also further China's relations with South Korea. The Chinese favored the expanding cross contacts and cross relations among all parties concerned. In May 1989, for example, South Korean finance minister Lee

Kyu Sung attended the twenty-second annual convention of the Asian Development Bank in Beijing; he was the first South Korean cabinet member to visit China. The Chinese did not, however, support cross recognition because it was strongly opposed by North Korea.[37]

The Chinese were also opposed to the idea of South and North Korea's simultaneous admission to the United Nations General Assembly. If South Korea alone applied for United Nations membership, China would most likely veto the application in the Security Council. China opposed maintaining the United Nations Command and the United Nations Cemetery in South Korea and made every effort to honor and protect North Korea's diplomatic interests in the world organization. In September 1988, for example, a spokesman for the Chinese Ministry of Foreign Affairs rejected a proposal that the agenda for the forthcoming United Nations General Assembly include an item to celebrate the fortieth anniversary of the founding of South Korea.[38] The spokesman explained that the controversy this item would generate would not ease tensions in the Korean Peninsula or the present international situation. The Chinese thus preferred to avoid what promised to be an unproductive round of debates and resolutions about the Korean question in the United Nations and were probably apprehensive that, as South Korea's international status steadily improved, they would not be able to muster enough supporters for North Korea in the General Assembly. Yet the Chinese had no qualms about dealing with the two Germanys in the United Nations or about accommodating both Koreas in various United Nations functional organizations such as the World Health Organization, the United Nations Educational, Scientific and Cultural Organization, the United Nations Industrial Development Organization, and the Food and Agriculture Organization.

After Mikhail Gorbachev's Beijing visit in May 1989, both China and the Soviet Union desisted from accusing each other of befriending South Korea or betraying North Korea in diplomatic and economic fields. A Sino-Soviet joint communiqué declared:

> The normalization of Sino-Soviet relations is not directed at any third country, nor does it harm its interests. . . . The two sides took the view that peace and development are the two most important questions in the world of today.[39]

The two socialist countries disavowed any intention of seeking hegemony of any form in the Asian-Pacific region and agreed to adhere to the

Five Principles of Peaceful Coexistence as "the universal principles guiding state-to-state relations." If applied to their respective relations with South Korea, these "universal" principles were bound to help Seoul's northern policy in the long run.

In retrospect, it seems clear that, about the time when Kim Young Sam, a leader of the ruling Democratic Liberal Party of South Korea, visited Moscow in March 1990, Gorbachev had already decided to establish diplomatic relations with South Korea. The Soviet leader did, however, require some time to iron out the bureaucratic and procedural problems in the Soviet Union before carrying out his decision. In a joint communiqué issued by the Democratic Liberal Party and the Institute for World Economy and International Relations, the two sides stated that the normalization of relations between the Soviet Union and South Korea was essential to the peaceful reunification of Korea and peace in East Asia. In response, the North Koreans denounced Kim Young Sam as a "political prostitute" and warned that "if the Soviet Union establishes diplomatic relations with South Korea, this will legally acknowledge that two states exist in Korea and will further fix division on the Korean Peninsula."[40]

This warning did not prevent the Soviet Union and South Korea from conducting intensive negotiations, including Anatoly F. Dobrynin's secret visit to Seoul, which paved the way for the Gorbachev-Roh meeting in San Francisco on June 4, 1990. Gorbachev indicated in the meeting that he was determined to reject North Korean pressure and to implement his decision for diplomatic normalization with South Korea. During September 2–3, 1990, Foreign Minister Shevardnadze made a "working visit" to Pyongyang and told North Korean foreign minister Kim Yong Nam that the Soviet Union would establish diplomatic relations with South Korea on January 1, 1991, and convert barter trade with North Korea into a cash payment in hard (convertible) currency. A furious Kim Il Sung refused to see Shevardnadze. If the Soviet Union did not rescind its decision, Kim Yong Nam told Shevardnadze, North Korea would develop nuclear weapons, support Japan's position on the northern territorial issue, and recognize the independence of some Soviet republics (presumably, the Baltics).[41]

In an extraordinary move, North Korea published a six-point memorandum discussing why diplomatic ties between the Soviet Union and South Korea would be an obstacle to Korean reunification. The memo argued that, among other things, diplomatic relations would mean a tripartite alliance, with the Soviet Union joining the United States and South Korea in a conspiracy to topple the socialist system in North Korea. It declared:

> If the Soviet Union establishes diplomatic relations with South Korea, the [North] Korean-Soviet alliance treaty will automatically be reduced to a mere name. This will leave us no other choice but to take measures to provide us for ourselves some weapons for which we have so far relied upon the alliance. This will lead the arms race to an acute phase on the Korean Peninsula and carry the situation there to the extreme pitch of strain. Worse still, this will aggravate the situation of the Asia-Pacific region in general.

The Shevardnadze mission was mistreated and humiliated in North Korea; thus on September 30, 1990, the Soviets normalized diplomatic relations with South Korea. Roh visited Moscow in December 1990, and Gorbachev visited Cheju Island in April 1991.[42]

The North Koreans condemned the Soviet "betrayal and hypocrisy" and accused Moscow of "openly joining the United States in its basic strategy aimed at freezing the division of Korea into two Koreas, isolating us internationally and guiding us to 'opening' and thus overthrowing the socialist system in our country."[43] They argued that the Soviet Union had established diplomatic relations with South Korea in a desperate attempt to rescue its economy from the brink of bankruptcy:

> The Soviet Union sold off the dignity and honor of a socialist power and the interests and faith of an ally for 2.3 billion dollars. The Soviet beginners who are making painstaking efforts to acquire the basic knowledge of the method of capitalist economic management, while turning the socialist economic system into a market economic system, may feel satisfied, having learned that selling of an immaterial commodity, that is, the establishment of diplomatic relations, at a "high price" is a profitable capitalist dealing.

Faced with the Soviet Union's rapprochement with South Korea, North Korea campaigned against diplomatic cross recognition. At a news conference in February 1991, Foreign Minister Kim Yong Nam stated:

> Diplomatic relations are not trade or commercial relations like selling and buying goods. Cross-recognition is, therefore, a senseless view regarding diplomatic relations as a cargo, and it is very wrong. Cross-recognition has never been and can never be found in the history of world diplomacy.

... It is a product of the ruse of great powers to encroach on the interests of small countries, regarding them as an object of bargaining. The word, cross-recognition, itself rolled off the tongue of the United States.[44]

The North Koreans were apprehensive that, if cross recognition were not firmly rejected, the door would be open for China's diplomatic normalization with South Korea. The Chinese did not object to cross recognition but wanted it handled carefully so that North Korea's integrity and prestige were not irreparably damaged.

Unlike the Soviet Union and the Eastern European countries, China was reluctant to accommodate South Korea's northern diplomacy at this time for a number of reasons. First, in view of the collapse of socialist regimes in Eastern Europe and the crisis in the Soviet Union, China and North Korea wanted to protect their socialist systems and fend off the winds of "bourgeois liberalization," "peaceful evolution," and "multiparty pluralism" that were blowing eastward. In their summit meeting in Beijing in November 1989, Deng Xiaoping and Kim Il Sung agreed to preserve the supremacy of their respective communist parties and stressed their firm commitment to the socialist road. (Evidently Jiang Zeming and Kim Il Sung concluded in March 1990 that Gorbachev's perestroika policy was ultimately responsible for the declining fortunes of socialist countries in the world.) Deng and Kim also pledged to consolidate the comradeship and friendship between China and North Korea and to support each other's domestic and foreign policies.[45]

Second, Deng Xiaoping appreciated that when the United States, Japan, and other industrialized countries condemned his suppression of prodemocracy demonstrations at Tiananmen Square in June 1989, North Korea was one of the few countries that expressed public support. Deng regarded Kim as a true friend who came to help him at a time of critical adversity and therefore felt that China should not betray or abandon North Korea, as had the Soviet Union.[46]

Third, as was mentioned in chapter 2, unlike the USSR, China fought in the Korean War to save North Korea from territorial extinction and suffered in human as well as economic terms. This legacy solidified the "militant friendship" between the two allies and sustained China's vested interests in North Korea. The Chinese feared that, if North Korea were to be completely isolated in the international community, another Korean War might erupt.

Fourth, China's economic and ethnic conditions were not desperate, unlike Gorbachev's dire predicament. The Chinese were confident of their ability to manage political instability, economic stagnation, and minority nationalities. For all practical purposes, China overcame the economic sanctions imposed by the United States, Japan, and other Western countries after the Tiananmen Square tragedy. More important, China enjoyed a growing economic linkage with South Korea without diplomatic normalization.

In 1990 and 1991 the Chinese seized several opportunities to assure their uneasy North Korean comrades that their "traditional friendship" and "revolutionary loyalty" would endure from generation to generation. They invited President Kim Il Sung to Shenyang, Premier Yon Hyong Muk to Shenzen, and Vice President Li Jong Ok and Minister of Foreign Affairs Kim Yong Nam to Beijing and dispatched several members of the Political Bureau of the Chinese Communist Party—General Secretary Jiang Zemin, Song Ping, Minister of National Defense Qin Jiwei, and State Councilor Li Tieying—to Pyongyang. The Chinese celebrated all major anniversaries important to North Korea and praised North Korea's "brilliant achievements" and correct unification policy. On the forty-second anniversary of the Democratic People's Republic of Korea's (DPRK's) founding, for example, an editorial in *Renmin Ribao* declared that China and North Korea were socialist states with "strong vitality" (*qiangdade shengmingli*) and that their "militant friendship" (*zhandou youyi*) cemented in blood would be strengthened despite all challenges. The editorial supported President Kim's proposal for the Confederal Republic of Koryo and his independent and self-reliant foreign policy.[47]

Premier Li Peng conveyed the same reassurances to the North Korean leadership during his four-day official goodwill visit to Pyongyang in May 1991. At a banquet hosted by Premier Yon Hyong Muk, Li Peng stated:

> The world today is by no means tranquil despite a relaxation of tension in U.S.-Soviet relations and a reduction of military confrontation. Hegemonism and power politics still exist but new regional conflicts may still happen, the North-South contradictions are becoming ever more outstanding and the vast number of developing countries are faced with even more rigorous challenges.[48]

Li told Kim Il Sung and Kim Jong Il that, no matter what happened in world affairs, China would always stand by North Korea and continue to support Kim's proposed Confederal Republic of Koryo based on the formula of "one nation, one state, two systems, and two governments."[49]

Compared with Jiang Zemin's speeches during his Pyongyang visit in March 1990, Li Peng's statements were more moderate and constrained. He did not specifically ask the United States to withdraw its troops from South Korea or to accept the proposal for tripartite talks. He also noted that "positive changes have taken place on the Korean Peninsula in recent years, particularly the trend of relaxation of the tension."

In an attempt to ease tension in the Korean Peninsula and to avert further North Korean diplomatic isolation, I believe that Li Peng persuaded Kim Il Sung to accept the simultaneous admission of North and South Korea to the United Nations using the following arguments:

1. As became apparent during the Persian Gulf conflict, the United Nations will play an increasingly important role in dealing with the problems of international peace and security, including the future of Korea.

2. An overwhelming majority of U.N. member states are inclined to accept the concept of universality and to favor South Korea's forthcoming membership application.

3. As a nation opposed to any manifestation of "big-power chauvinism," China will find it difficult to veto South Korea's application in the U.N. Security Council and to thereby upset many member states in the General Assembly.

4. If only South Korea is admitted to the United Nations, North Korea will face an insurmountable diplomatic setback and will lose the direct opportunity to influence U.N. discussions and decisions regarding the Korean question.

5. If North Korea, together with South Korea, can join the United Nations, North Korea will obtain worldwide recognition of its governmental legitimacy and will improve its relations with Japan and the United States.

6. Once admitted, North Korea will be eligible to receive a variety of financial, scientific, and technological assistance programs sponsored by the United Nations and its specialized agencies.

7. The cases of Germany and Yemen show that dual memberships in the United Nations are not an inherent obstacle to Korean reunification.

On Li Peng's return to Beijing, a spokesman for the Chinese Ministry of Foreign Affairs said that Li and his North Korean hosts discussed "the question of joining the United Nations by both North and South sides of Korea" and that Li wished that the two sides of Korea would find a way acceptable to both sides through dialogue and consultation.[50] This statement suggested that North Korea was prepared to accommodate Li's wish. A few days after Li's visit to Pyongyang, the North Korean government announced its decision to apply for admission to the United Nations.

CHINA'S TWO-KOREA POLICY

As soon as the Asian Games ended in Beijing (China captured the largest number of medals, followed by South Korea), Zheng Hongye, chairman of the China Chamber of International Commerce(CCOIC), and Lee Sun Ki, president of the Korea Trade Promotion Corporation (KOTRA), signed an agreement to exchange resident trade offices between Beijing and Seoul.[51] The offices were entrusted with consular responsibilities and accorded semidiplomatic privileges. The Chinese emphasized that the exchange was nongovernmental and without diplomatic significance, but the South Koreans regarded it as a historic first step toward diplomatic normalization. The South Korean side selected a senior diplomat, Roh Jae Won (who had served as vice minister of foreign affairs and as ambassador to Canada) to head KOTRA's Beijing office; CCOIC sent its vice chairman, Xu Dayu, to lead its Seoul office. In view of North Korea's uneasiness, for a while Roh was not permitted to enter or contact the Chinese Ministry of Foreign Affairs or to hold formal diplomatic receptions. Yet on behalf of their governments, the two trade organizations negotiated and signed a number of economic accords, including a trade agreement, which granted each other most favored nation status (December 1991) and an agreement on the encouragement and reciprocal protection of investments (May 1992).

Meanwhile, in September 1991, Chinese and South Korean foreign ministers—Qian Qichen and Lee Sang Ock—met for the first time at the United Nations and briefly discussed their bilateral relations. In response to Lee's inquiry, Qian expressed interest in improving functional relations with South Korea in an unobtrusive manner. A month later Qian, along with Li Lanqing (minister of foreign economic relations and trade), came to Seoul to attend the Asia-Pacific Economic Cooperation (APEC) conference; Qian said he appreciated South Korea's role in ironing out delicate matters concerning the representation of China, "Chinese Taipei," and Hong Kong in APEC. Qian had a long meeting with Lee Sang Ock and paid a courtesy call on President Roh, who explained that South Korea had no intention of absorbing North Korea and asked Qian to transmit this view to North Korea. Lee explored the possibility of early diplomatic normalization, but Qian said that conditions were not yet ripe and that it would be pursued as U.S.–North Korean relations improved and inter-Korean talks were held. When Lee visited Beijing in April 1992 as outgoing president of the Economic and Social Council for Asia and the Pacific (ESCAP), he arrived in a plane flying the flag of the Republic of Korea and was invited to meet with Jiang Zemin and Li Peng. Qian and Lee agreed to make a joint effort to normalize bilateral relations and to meet again in September at the APEC meeting in Bangkok and the United Nations. Hence Kwon Byong Hyon (former South Korean ambassador to Myanmar) and Zhang Ruijie (former Chinese ambassador to Sri Lanka), leaders of their respective negotiating teams, conducted three rounds of negotiation sessions (May 14–16 and June 2–4 in Beijing and June 20–21 in Seoul).[52]

The Chinese finally responded to South Korea's argument that, in normalizing its diplomatic relations with South Korea, China would assert a bona fide role of leadership in Asia and recognize Beijing-Seoul relations for their intrinsic merits, rather than as an extension of inter-Korean relations and North Korea's relations with the United States and Japan.[53] A variety of government leaders and private individuals, including Deng Xiaoping's son (Deng Zhifang) and Roh Tae Woo's relatives, were enlisted to smooth the road for diplomatic negotiations. To undertake their new two-Korea diplomacy, the Chinese adapted to changing political and economic exigencies on the Korean Peninsula and elsewhere by transcending their earlier commitment for a one-Korea formula. In addition to the success of South Korea's northern diplomacy toward the Soviet Union (Russia) and Eastern Europe, the simultaneous admission of the two Koreas to the United Nations conclusively established the legitimacy of the South Korean government. Moreover, the fact that the two Korean prime ministers in December 1991 signed the "Agreement on Reconciliation, Nonaggression and Exchanges and Cooperation" and the "Joint Declaration on the Denuclearization of the Korean Peninsula" laid the foundation for peaceful coexistence between the two Korean governments.

No longer could the Chinese justify the fiction that the Republic of Korea did not deserve their de jure recognition.

In the post–cold war era, especially after German unification and the collapse of the Soviet Union, the Chinese felt that they should assume a role in managing global and regional affairs, including the Korean question. After the Tiananmen Square incident led to a deterioration of relations with the United States and Western Europe, the Chinese emphasized an Asia-centered diplomacy that would lower the importance of their relations with the United States and Western Europe and solidify their traditional base in the Asian-Pacific region. In their competition with Taiwan, which had recently reestablished diplomatic relations with Niger (with a promise of $50 million in loans) and opened consular relations with the Baltic states, the Chinese hoped that South Korea, the only Asian country that still maintained diplomatic relations with Taiwan, would terminate those relations. Although the resident offices of CCOIC and KOTRA had expanded bilateral commercial relations, which amounted to $5.8 billion (twice as much as South Korea's trade with Taiwan) in 1991, the Chinese concluded that there was no substitute for embassies to legalize and strengthen the growing economic and cultural ties between China and South Korea.

Conservative senior CCP leaders, some Korean War veterans, and a small number of cadres in the CCP's International Liaison Department and in the Ministry of Foreign Affairs resisted the timing of the Beijing-Seoul diplomatic rapprochement. According to Parris H. Chang, a specialist in Chinese affairs, they argued that China's adopting a two-Korea policy might, in turn, justify a two-China policy by other countries, deepen North Korea's sense of isolation and vulnerability, and contribute to the collapse of the North Korean system. They also said that, because of the existence of the trade offices, there was no urgency to establish full diplomatic relations between the two countries. A Chinese analyst was quoted as saying that "we already have an affair going on, a relationship could be a burden." Deng Xiaoping decided, however, to move ahead with diplomatic normalization with South Korea, in part because he wanted to rekindle momentum for China's modernization campaign and open-door policy before the Fourteenth National Congress of the Chinese Communist Party, which was scheduled for October 1992. To serve China's long-term interests, he was prepared to forgo the assurances he had given Kim Il Sung over the years. Deng also may have wanted to formalize a framework of mutually beneficial relations with South Korea before President

Roh Tae Woo's retirement. He may also have been concerned that Bill Clinton's anti-Beijing rhetoric with respect to human rights could endanger Sino-American relations and complicate China's Korea policy as well.[54]

The Chinese carefully and gradually prepared the way so that Kim Il Sung would be convinced of the inevitability of the Beijing-Seoul diplomatic normalization and would not voice too much public opposition. (The vitriolic North Korean reaction to the Soviet Union's establishment of diplomatic relations with South Korea was widely remembered.) During his visit to China in October 1991, Kim Il Sung was likely given broad hints about China's forthcoming diplomatic relations with South Korea. According to a reliable source, when Kim asked Deng and Jiang not to recognize South Korea until North Korea's diplomatic talks with Japan were successfully concluded, "they just smiled." In April 1992, when Lee Sang Ock met with Li Peng at Beijing, President Yang Shangkun left for North Korea to celebrate Kim's eightieth birthday and met with Kim at Pyongyang. Yang probably notified Kim of the outcome of the Lee-Qian discussions. In addition to journeys to Pyongyang made by China's Ding Guangen (alternate member of the CCP Political Bureau and member of the Central Secretariat) in May and Yang Baibing (member of the Central Secretariat, secretary-general of the Central Military Commission, and director of the PLA's General Political Department) in June, Qian Qichen made a secret trip to Pyongyang in June to give a detailed advance report to Kim Il Sung. One of Qian's main arguments was that China's diplomatic normalization with South Korea would help North Korea's diplomatic relations with Japan and the United States, stabilize the Korean Peninsula, and contribute to North Korea's system maintenance. Kim grudgingly expressed his understanding, if not acceptance, of China's decision on South Korea.[55]

Once the North Korean factor was taken care of, bilateral negotiations progressed rapidly and smoothly.[56] Compared with the complicated diplomatic issues that China had negotiated with Japan (such as Japan's aggression in China, the state of war, war reparations, and the Japan-Taiwan peace treaty) or the United States (such as the U.S.-Taiwan security treaty and the U.S. military presence on Taiwan and in the Taiwan Straits), China's negotiations with South Korea presented no difficult problems. The South Korean negotiators, latecomers on the Chinese diplomatic scene, enjoyed the distinct advantage of understanding the Chinese position. They were well prepared, armed with internal studies, consultants' reports, and the cumulative record of China's earlier diplomatic negotiations. The United States and Japan received advance notice from the South Korean government, but neither country was directly involved in the Beijing-Seoul talks. Gone was the ubiquitous presence of the Sino-Soviet rivalry in Korean affairs.

On August 24, 1992, at the Diaoyutai State Guesthouse in Beijing, Qian and Lee signed a joint communiqué in which China and South Korea agreed to recognize each other and to immediately establish diplomatic relations. The communiqué stated:

> The governments of the Republic of Korea and the People's Republic of China agree to develop the enduring relations of good neighborhood, friendship and cooperation on the basis of the principles set forth in the Charter of the United Nations and the principles of mutual respect for sovereignty and territorial integrity, mutual nonaggression, noninterference in each other's internal affairs, equality and mutual benefit, and peaceful coexistence.

The communiqué declared that the government of the Republic of Korea "recognizes" the government of the People's Republic of China as the sole legal government of China and "respects the Chinese position that there is but one China and Taiwan is part of China."[57]

On signing the joint communiqué, Lee announced at a press conference that South Korea would sever diplomatic relations with Taiwan. Chinese president Yang Shangkun hailed the communiqué as a major event in the history of the two nations' relations, and Korean president Roh Tae Woo said that the new relationship would bear great significance in world history and contribute to the peaceful reunification of Korea. The communiqué settled on a mild term—*respect*—in regard to the Taiwan question and incorporated both China's adherence to the Five Principles of Peaceful Coexistence and South Korea's emphasis on the principles of the United Nations Charter. When the South Koreans raised the issue of China's participation in the Korean War, the Chinese refused to apologize, argued that they were compelled to enter the war because their security was threatened, and insisted that they had greatly suffered as a result. (Domestic political factors also played a role in China's refusal to apologize to South Korea.) In any event, the two sides agreed not to repeat the unfortunate past. Unlike the Soviet Union, which had extracted a promise of $3 billion in loans from South Korea in return for diplomatic normalization, China did not make such a request of South Korea.[58]

The Taiwanese leaders, distressed by the Beijing-Seoul diplomatic establishment, felt mistreated and betrayed by South Korea. They had valued their long history of close cooperation with the Koreans during their common struggles against Japanese aggression and international communism and had fully supported South Korea at the U.N. Security Council during the Korean War. In anticipation of the diplomatic negotiations between China and South Korea, Taiwan president Lee Teng-hui sent his secretary-general, Chiang Yen-shih, to Seoul in May 1992. He asked President Roh to curb further political relations between Beijing and Seoul. The Taiwanese proposed that South Korea have diplomatic relations with both China and Taiwan, but the South Koreans rejected this measure because of China's adamant opposition. On August 18, Foreign Minister Lee privately informed the Taiwanese ambassador to Seoul that "substantive progress" had been made in Chinese–South Korean negotiations. This information was leaked to the press in Taiwan the following day, and, just as they had done against Japan in 1972, the angry Taiwanese staged a violent demonstration in front of the South Korean embassy in Taipei. The South Koreans understood from China that, even after diplomatic relations were suspended with Taiwan, South Korea would continue to have relations with Taiwan in economic, cultural, and other nongovernmental areas. To avoid legal and diplomatic complications, the South Koreans decided to turn over the ROC embassy's property (worth $1.7 billion) in Seoul to the PRC.[59]

Thus the Chinese managed to eliminate a major vestige of the cold war era in East Asia and establish a balanced position in the Korean Peninsula. Compared with the United States and Japan, both of which lacked a diplomatic presence in North Korea, and Russia, which had unfriendly relations with North Korea, China enjoyed the best of two worlds—retaining the traditional framework of diplomatic and military ties with North Korea and entering into a new economic and diplomatic partnership with South Korea. The Chinese capacity to influence Korean affairs was dramatically enhanced. Fully represented in both Korean capitals, they had a direct avenue through which they could ward off another Korean War and support inter-Korean reconciliation and cooperation. But the Chinese solidified their position of pragmatic diplomatic leadership in the Asian-Pacific region at the cost of Taiwanese aspirations. A Chinese scholar of Asian affairs mentioned, however, that China was mistaken not to link its diplomatic normalization with that between Japan and North Korea. Another analyst added that North Korea should not be driven into diplomatic isolation.[60]

The South Koreans were immensely pleased with the outcome of their northern diplomacy. President Roh visited Beijing toward the end of September 1992, thus fulfilling a campaign promise made five years earlier.[61] On the eve of the forty-third anniversary of the PRC's founding, Roh and Yang Shangkun issued a joint press communiqué that stated that "relaxation of tension on the Korean Peninsula will not only serve the interests of the whole Korean people but also be favorable for the settlement of peace and stability of the Northeast Asian region as well as the whole of Asia." Yang expressed "hope for early realization of the goals set forth in the Joint Declaration on the Denuclearization of the Korean Peninsula." The South Koreans secured a friendly and cooperative international environment in Asia, except North Korea, and established diplomatic relations with all permanent members of the U.N. Security Council. They banished the forty-two-year-old specter of the Korean War and opened a new era of mutually beneficial relations with China, thus weakening the political foundation of the Chinese–North Korean military alliance. Bolstered by their high-level diplomatic status and their recent economic and political gains, the South Koreans prepared to deal with North Korea and to exercise independent and assertive roles in their own affairs. More practically, they hoped to penetrate the growing China market.

The Beijing-Seoul diplomatic ties were a major setback to the North Koreans, to whom China was their most dependable ally and supporter. North Korea, bitter about what it considered betrayal and abandonment by China, in protest limited cultural exchange programs with China and drew up a "black list" of Chinese officials and scholars regarded as pro-Seoul.[62] Border crossings were restricted for several months, and North Korean celebrations for the forty-second anniversary of China's entry into the Korean War were subdued. Yet the North Koreans did not publicly express as much displeasure toward China as they had toward the Soviet Union, mainly because they could not afford to alienate or antagonize China, who was now their irreplaceable patron and guardian following the demise of the Soviet Union. China's top leaders, especially Yang Shangkun and Qian Qichen, did come to Pyongyang to explain their diplomatic intentions to Kim Il Sung in advance and to reiterate their respect and support for his policies. Their tactful handling of Kim softened the impact of China's new diplomacy on North Korea. Kim undoubtedly missed the days when he could play off China against the Soviet Union, but North Korea had to shed its sense of isolation and adapt to the rapidly shifting international situation.

The relationship between China and North Korea improved appreciably during 1993, in part because North Korea required Chinese support for its nuclear policy at the United Nations and the International Atomic Energy Agency. In an attempt to soothe Kim Il Sung, the Chinese designated a rising political star, Hu Jintao (member of the Standing Committee of the CCP Political Bureau and member of the Secretariat) to lead the well-publicized activities for the fortieth anniversary of the Korean armistice agreement. On July 25, 1993, Hu presided over a ceremony to open the impressive Memorial Hall for the Resist-America and Aid-Korea War at Dandong, a border city on the Yalu River. The calligraphy by Deng Xiaoping was unveiled in the presence of Chi Haotian (minister of national defense), Hong Xuezhi (vice chairman of the Chinese People's Political Consultative Conference), Chen Muhua (vice chairman of the Standing Committee of the National People's Congress), and other high-level Chinese leaders. In his speech, Hu praised the "great and just war against the aggressors."[63] In the next few days, Hu, accompanied by Chi Haotian, met with Kim Il Sung and Kim Jong Il in Pyongyang, stressed the continuity of their traditional friendship, and attended the Korean armistice agreement celebration. A delegation of former CPV members headed by Liu Anyuan (political commissar of the Nanjing Military Region) also came to the festivities. Kim Il Sung was reassured by China's avowal of regard for the Sino–North Korean bonds forged during the Korean War and by the close rapport between Hu Jintao and Kim Jong Il, who were the same age. Hu replaced another young Chinese political leader, Hu Qili, whose personal ties with Kim Jong Il were close until Tiananmen Square. Kim Il Sung was also pleased by the appointment of Qiao Zonghuai as the Chinese ambassador to Pyongyang; Qiao was a son of the late Qiao Guanhua, who had participated in the Panmunjom negotiations and defended North Korean diplomatic interests at the United Nations in the early 1970s.

When Kim Il Sung died in July 1994, Deng Xiaoping issued condolences to the Central Committee of the Korean Workers' Party and expressed his "deep grief" at the loss of a "close comrade in arms" (*qinmide zhanyou*). He sent a wreath to the North Korean embassy in Beijing and ordered the flags flown at half-mast in Kim's memory. President Jiang Zemin, Premier Li Peng, and Qiao Shi (chairman of the Standing Committee of the National People's Congress) jointly stated:

Comrade Kim Il Sung always strove to preserve and promote the traditional friendship of the peoples of China and Korea with great zeal. He maintained deep friendship with the older generation of Chinese revolutionaries and incessantly pushed forward the friendly and co-operative relations between the two countries. Though Comrade Kim Il Sung is dead, his lofty image will always remain in the hearts of the Korean people. The Chinese people will always remember him. It is our strong belief that the Korean people will surely carry out his behest, unite closely around the Workers' Party of Korea led by Comrade Kim Jong Il, and continue their efforts in building their country well and achieving a lasting peace for the Korean Peninsula.[64]

The Chinese promptly recognized Kim Jong Il as the new supreme leader in North Korea to assist in the smooth transition of power in Pyongyang. They concluded that Kim Jong Il had accumulated a sufficient degree of internal support in North Korea, but they were concerned about his illnesses. China agreed to donate 100,000 tons of grain to North Korea.[65]

The death of Kim Il Sung moved Chinese policy toward North Korea beyond intimate personal ties to bring about a more normal relationship between the two countries. Once Kim Il Sung's forty-four-year rule was over, the Chinese hoped that his successors would pursue a pragmatic open-door foreign policy and improve inter-Korean relations. Jiang Zemin and Li Peng may have conveyed such hopes to Vice President Li Jong Ok, who came to Beijing to celebrate the forty-fifth anniversary of the PRC's founding on September 27, 1994. Jiang Zemin and Kim Jong Il exchanged greetings for the anniversary; the North Koreans hosted a banquet at the People's Palace of Culture in Pyongyang.[66]

While Kim Jong Il and his associates were preoccupied with solidifying their regime and charting a new direction for domestic and foreign affairs in the post–Kim Il Sung era, Premier Li Peng began a five-day official visit to Seoul on October 31, 1994. After Presidents Roh's and Kim's state visits to China, President Jiang was expected to reciprocate by visiting Seoul, but Li came instead, mainly because of North Korean sensitivities. Before his Seoul trip, Li had proposed a visit to Pyongyang; in addition to attempting to placate North Korea's concern, Li had wanted to ascertain the precise conditions of Kim Jong Il's deteriorating health. The North Koreans, however, had not welcomed Li's visit at that time because Kim Jong Il was in mourning and also because they were unhappy with China's growing economic and diplomatic cooperation with South Korea.[67]

In his meetings with President Kim and Prime Minister Lee Yong Duk in Seoul, Li stated that China wished to develop good relations with both South Korea and North Korea and that such relations would be conducive to regional and global peace. He also suggested that the two Korean governments resume high-level dialogue and settle all questions, including nuclear issues, by peaceful means. In turn, President Kim explained that political stability and economic recovery in North Korea were important to the peace in the Korean Peninsula and to the development of Sino–South Korean cooperation. He asked for China's assistance in ensuring that North Korea fully implement the Geneva agreement on nuclear issues.[68]

On his return from Seoul, Li Peng evidently submitted a glowing report on South Korea to the Political Bureau of the Chinese Communist Party, recommending that China transcend its obsession with North Korea's negative reactions and aggressively expand its relations with South Korea in all areas, including military affairs. China was not yet prepared to allow a South Korean consulate-general in Shenyang because of North Korea's opposition; unlike Shanghai and Qingdao, where South Korea had already opened consulates-general, Shenyang, where North Korea had its consulate-general, was regarded as a sensitive city close to the Sino–North Korean border. The exchange of top-level leaders between China and South Korea continued in 1995—notably, Qiao Shi in April and South Korean prime minister Lee Hong Koo in May. Lee received an extraordinarily warm and enthusiastic welcome in China and met with Jiang Zemin, Li Peng, Qiao Shi, and other Chinese leaders. Jiang accepted Lee's invitation to visit South Korea by the end of 1995. Lee's and Jiang's trips served to illustrate China's long-range diplomatic goal—to maintain a pragmatic and advantageous two-Korea posture but to consolidate its new political and economic ties with South Korea.[69]

Chapter Five
ECONOMIC RELATIONS

• •

A s we saw in chapter 4, China's changing diplomacy toward the Korean Peninsula was closely associated with its economic relations with Pyongyang and Seoul. For a quarter century after the Korean War, China adopted a rigid one-Korea policy in diplomatic, military, and economic fields. During this time, the Chinese provided Kim Il Sung with generous grants and loans and conducted a moderate amount of bilateral trade with North Korea but had no such economic ties with South Korea. The Chinese characterized South Korea as an economic colony of the United States and Japan and as an "abyss of suffering" because of its industrial bankruptcies, foreign debts, labor exploitation, and popular discontent during the 1960s and 1970s.[1] This biased policy stemmed from four main factors: (1) Maoist China's autarkic policy model, which attached little importance to economic relations with nonsocialist countries, (2) China's militant friendship and cooperation with North Korea, (3) North Korea's importance in the context of Sino-Soviet competition, and (4) China's assessment of North and South Korea's economic performances.

The Chinese, however, initiated a gradual change in their economic relations with both Koreas toward the end of the 1970s because, transcending the Maoist economic model, they recognized South Korea's phenomenal economic achievements. Guided by the expedient notion of the separation of economic and political spheres, they entered into indirect trade with South Korea in 1979 and explored a number of cooperative

projects with South Korean businesspeople. Yet they were somewhat constrained by North Korean protests and the Soviet Union's criticism. Not
until after the Seoul Olympic Games (1988) and the Gorbachev-Deng summit meeting (1989) was China able to openly assume an aggressive economic stance toward South Korea, despite North Korea's persistent disapproval. Economic considerations thus played a central role in the evolution of China's de facto and de jure two-Korea policy.

CHINA AND NORTH KOREA

In retrospect, China's economic interest in North Korea has always been
secondary to its own overall strategic and political objectives, but China
has nonetheless served as a useful partner for North Korean economic
programs. When Kim Il Sung led an eight-member delegation to Beijing in
November 1953, the two governments signed an agreement on economic
and cultural cooperation stipulating that both sides "shall extend to each
other all possible economic and technical aid, carry out the necessary economic and technical cooperation and endeavor to promote cultural exchange between the two countries." China promised a grant of 800 million yuan to restore North Korea's war-torn economy. Dae-Sook Suh
maintains that "the Chinese were more generous than the Soviet Union
and canceled all North Korean debts to China, including materials supplied by the Chinese during the Korean War from 1950 to 1953." With
the escalation of the Sino-Soviet conflict after 1960, the Chinese used financial assistance and trade to woo Kim Il Sung away from the Soviet
camp but often found it difficult to compete with the Soviet Union's superior financial and technological capabilities. Kim, capitalizing on the Sino-
Soviet rivalry, extracted the maximum possible economic benefits from
both allies; by 1976 he had received an estimated $967 million in grants
and loans from China and $1,534 million from the Soviet Union.[2]
    China shared about 20 percent of North Korea's total foreign trade
throughout the 1970s and 1980s. This share represented a small portion
of China's growing foreign trade and decreased appreciably during that
time—from 2.5 percent in 1970 and 1.7 percent in 1980 to 0.8 percent in
1985 and 0.6 percent in 1989. Crude oil was a major Chinese export to
North Korea; the China-Korea Friendship Pipeline, completed by joint efforts in January 1976, transported oil from Daqing to North Korea. In the

aftermath of Premier Hua Guofeng's visit to Pyongyang in 1978, China evidently agreed to increase its annual oil export to one million metric tons (about 1 percent of China's total annual output) but to sustain the cut-rate "friendship price" ($4.50 a barrel). China also sent engineers and technicians to North Korea to construct oil refineries, petrochemical plants, and other related industries. To diversify its oil suppliers, however, North Korea turned to the Soviet Union, Iran, and other Middle Eastern countries. The Chinese commitment for regular oil exports was spelled out in the long-term trade agreement (1982–86) that Minister of Foreign Economic Relations and Trade Chen Muhua and Vice Premier Kong Chin Tae signed in October 1982. Another long-term trade agreement (1987–91) was signed in September 1986 that was especially important for North Korea's ambitious Third Seven-Year Economic Plan (1987-93).[3]

The two governments held frequent economic meetings, concluded agreements in a variety of fields (trade, hydroelectric power, navigation, railways, civil aviation, communications, publications, educational exchange, public health, and science and technology), and arranged payments. They expanded cooperative ties among industries, cities, institutes, and other economic units. A large number of North Korean students, scientists, technicians, bureaucrats, and other professional personnel visited China every year, studied at Chinese universities and research institutes, and held scientific and technical exchange programs with their Chinese counterparts.

Some suggested that North Korea was emulating China's Great Leap Forward Movement and its people's communes when it launched the Chollima Undong (Flying horse movement) and agricultural cooperatives in 1958. In fact, Kim Il Sung said that the Great Leap Forward Movement had demonstrated "the great creative power of the 650 million Chinese people," and he extolled the people's communes as an important step in China's transition to a communist society.[4] The Taekam Korea-China Friendship Cooperative Farm near Pyongyang had a sister relationship with the Hongxing (Red star) China-Korea Friendship People's Commune in Beijing, which Kim Il Sung often visited during his trips to China. If Tokyo served as a major gateway for South Korea's connections with the world, so did Beijing serve the same function for North Korea.

The Yalu and Tumen Rivers constitute a convenient channel for active border trade—especially between Dandong and Sinuiju and between Tumen City and Namyang and Onsong. Along the Yalu River both sides have long benefited from hydroelectric power stations at Shuifeng (Supung,

700,000 kW), Yunfeng (Unbong, 400,000 kW), Weiyuan (Wiwon, 390,000 kW), and Taipingwan (Taepyongman, 190,000 kW). The binational Yalu River Hydroelectric Corporation meets yearly to decide power distribution and financial matters and to agree on repairs, renovation, and expansion. Electricity generated by the joint stations is usually evenly split between the two sides. Railway connections across both rivers provide bilateral transportation. The border railways also are important because Chongjin and other North Korean ports serve as entrepôts for China's economic relations with third countries.[5]

In the late 1980s, however, the Chinese became increasingly concerned about North Korea's economic difficulties, especially in view of South Korea's robust performance (see table 3). Unlike their Chinese counterparts, the North Koreans had been unable to reform their autarkic economic system or to open their doors to the international economic community. Despite the inclusion of some worthy moral and political ideals in Kim Il Sung's *chuche* ideology, it nonetheless stifled North Korea's ability to promote technological innovation and managerial adaptation. Heavy defense expenditures and counterproductive political campaigns exhausted North Korea's financial resources. As a result, the Third Seven-Year Economic Plan failed to fulfill its projected outputs; the actual growth rate (about 3 percent) of its gross national product (GNP) per year fell far short of the 7.9 percent target during the 1987–89 period. In the same period the estimated total volume of North Korea's foreign trade remained at $4.8 billion (1989), and its outstanding foreign debts increased from $5.2 billion to $6.8 billion. For its external economic activities, North Korea routinely relied on the Soviet Union and, to a lesser extent, on China.

The Soviet Union under Mikhail Gorbachev's leadership, however, could not support North Korea economically, mainly because its own house was in utter disarray. Unlike their Chinese comrades, the Soviets became openly critical of North Korea's inefficient and irresponsible economic performance. Vasily V. Mikheev, a young scholar at the Institute for International Economic and Political Studies, contended:

> We must consider the profound stagnation in the economy of the DPRK and the chronic decline in the living standards of the majority of the population in recent years. . . . Shortages, disbalances in the national economy, lack of motivation for labor, the noncompetitiveness of DPRK goods on world markets—all this deprives us of any hopes for large-scale achievements through cooperation with the DPRK.[6]

TABLE 3

ECONOMIC PERFORMANCE OF NORTH AND SOUTH KOREA
(1985–1994)

	1985	1987	1989	1991	1994
GNP (in billions of dollars)					
South Korea	$89.7	128.9	211.2	280.8	328.7
North Korea	$15.1	19.4	21.1	22.9	20.5
GNP growth rate (%)					
South Korea	7.0%	13.0	6.8	8.4	5.6
North Korea	2.7%	3.3	2.4	-5.2	-4.3
Total foreign trade (in millions of dollars)					
South Korea	$61,420	88,300	123,840	153,390	166,040
North Korea	$3,090	4,150	4,800	2,720	2,640
Trade with China (in millions of dollars)					
South Korea	$1,161	1,679	3,143	5,812	11,560
North Korea	$488	513	562	610	623

SOURCE: National Unification Board (Seoul) and Bank of Korea (Seoul)

He claimed that in 1989 North Korea barely fulfilled 45 percent of its trade obligations toward the Soviet Union. North Korea owed about 22 billion rubles (about $4 billion) to the Soviet Union by the end of 1990. Mariana Trigubenko, another scholar in the same institute, estimated that North Korea's per capita GNP was no more than $400 in 1989; this figure was significantly lower than the Central Intelligence Agency's estimate of about $1,000.[7] According to her study, in 1989 North Korea's GNP decreased by 5 percent and its industrial and agricultural outputs declined by 10 percent and 1 percent, respectively. As Shevardnadze notified his North Korean hosts in September 1990, North Korea would now be required to use hard currency in its commercial transactions with the Soviet Union and to pay the world price for crude oil imports from the Soviet Union. For this purpose the two governments signed a new trade agreement on November 2, 1990. Crude oil amounted to about 40 percent of North Korea's annual imports from the Soviet Union. This stringent new trade arrangement further strained North Korea's economic and political relations with the Soviet Union.

Stunned by the Soviet Union's withdrawal of economic assistance, the North Koreans had no choice but to ask for China's help. On the conclusion of Shevardnadze's Pyongyang visit in September 1990, Kim Il Sung made an unannounced trip to Shenyang to meet with Deng Xiaoping and Jiang Zemin. Among other things, Kim appealed to his Chinese friends for urgent economic cooperation, particularly an increase in China's crude oil exports to North Korea at the "friendship price." Despite their limited resources, the Chinese presumably responded sympathetically to Kim's desperate request.

In November 1990, during Premier Yon Hyong Muk's Beijing visit, Vice Premiers Wu Xueqian and Kim Tal Hyon (concurrently chairman of the External Economic Affairs Commission) signed an agreement on China's economic assistance to North Korea. Yon met with Jiang Zemin at the Shenzhen Special Economic Zone and carefully inspected this model of China's economic modernization policy. Other North Korean leaders— such as Kang Song San (Yon's predecessor), Kim Yong Nam (vice premier and minister of foreign affairs), and Han Jang Kon (minister of commerce)—also visited Shenzhen. Jiang explained to Yon that Shenzhen's success proved that China could pursue an open-door economic policy and preserve the socialist road at the same time. He also said that economic reform and socialist thought supported each other and that socialism could not develop amid economic difficulties, suggesting that North

Korea should not be afraid to reform its economic system and open its doors to the outside world. The North Koreans gradually and carefully studied and followed the Chinese experiments, passing a series of laws on joint venture, foreign investment, and taxes for foreign investors and foreigners and establishing a few free economic and trade zones such as Najin and Sonbong. They also collaborated with China on the Tumen River Development Project. Yet they were reluctant to adopt the Chinese model as a whole because they suspected that it might undermine the *chuche* ideology and create political problems similar to those evidenced at Tiananmen Square. They were aware of the adverse social consequences of a capitalistic system in Shenzhen, and they did not have enough territory to insulate the free economic and trade zones from the rest of North Korea.[8]

Whereas China had a deficit in its trade with North Korea during the 1984–86 period, it had a surplus of $40 million in 1987 (see table 4). This surplus grew to $111 million in 1988, $192 million in 1989, $233 million in 1990, and $439 million in 1991. To make up for the drastic decline in their trade with the Soviet Union/CIS, the North Koreans increased their imports from China, but their ability to export goods to China dwindled appreciably—from $233 million in 1988 to $85 million in 1991.

There was a significant drop in Moscow's exports of crude oil and coal/coke to North Korea between 1990 and 1991, and China's relative importance to North Korea's economic survival and military preparedness, particularly with respect to its crude oil requirements, loomed larger than ever (see table 5).[9] China's share in North Korea's total foreign trade increased from 24 percent in 1991 to 28 percent in 1992 and 34 percent in 1993, and China's grain exports constituted more than 10 percent of North Korea's total domestic needs in 1992 and 1993. The volume of two-way trade increased from $696 million in 1992 to $890 million in 1993. In addition to crude oil, grains, and coal/coke, China exported electrical appliances, electronics, rubber products, soap, sugar, cotton, plastics, and chemicals to North Korea and imported steel, cement, minerals, and marine products from North Korea. Because North Korea continued to suffer from a negative GNP growth rate and a shortage of foreign currency reserve in 1994, the volume of its trade with China decreased by 30.6 percent. Yet China shared 37 percent of North Korea's total foreign trade and 60 percent of North Korea's total oil import and 80 percent of its grain import. Other major trading partners for North Korea were Japan and South Korea; Russia was relegated to the fourth position.

TABLE 4
CHINA'S TRADE WITH NORTH KOREA
(IN MILLIONS OF DOLLARS)

	Total Volume	China's Exports	China's Imports	Balance
1970	$115.1	$ 60.9	$ 54.2	$ 6.7
1975	481.9	284.1	197.8	86.3
1980	677.5	374.2	303.3	70.9
1981	531.0	300.0	231.0	69.0
1982	585.4	281.4	304.0	−22.6
1983	527.7	273.4	254.3	19.1
1984	498.2	226.2	272.0	−45.8
1985	488.3	231.4	256.9	−25.5
1986	509.8	233.3	276.5	−43.2
1987	513.3	277.1	236.2	40.9
1988	579.0	345.3	233.7	111.6
1989	562.7	377.4	185.3	192.1
1990	482.7	358.2	124.5	233.7
1991	610.4	524.7	85.7	439.0
1992	696.5	541.4	155.4	385.7
1993	890.0	600.0	290.0	310.0
1994	623.7	424.5	199.2	225.3

Because North Korea was unable to pay for its cumulative trade deficits, the Chinese were compelled to reschedule North Korea's delinquent obligations or forgive some of them altogether. Thus trade assumed the form of expensive aid programs for North Korea. As China outgrew its ideologically prescribed economic policy and pursued a "socialist market economy," it faced a growing cleavage with North Korea in terms of ideological solidarity and economic orientation. The Chinese abolished the "friendship price" in their oil exports to North Korea during 1991. The following year the Chinese stipulated that Sino–North Korean trade would be settled in hard currencies, but they were unable to fully implement this policy because they recognized that extreme economic hardship might

TABLE 5
NORTH KOREAN IMPORTS OF OIL, COAL/COKE, AND GRAIN

	1989	1990	1991	1992
Total imports (in millions of dollars)				
From USSR/CIS	$1,641	1,669	194	264
From China	$ 371	394	577	595
Imports of crude oil (in thousands of metric tons)				
From USSR/CIS	500	440	40	190
From China	1,140	1,100	1,100	1,100
From Iran	820	980	750	220
Imports of coal/coke (in thousands of metric tons)				
From USSR/CIS	939	827	184	NI
From China	1,597	1,792	1,913	1,493
Imports of grain (in thousands of metric tons)				
From China	303	270	223	649

SOURCES: Chong-Sik Lee, *The Political Economy of North Korea* (1994), and Yong-Sup Han, "China's Leverages over North Korea," *Korea and World Affairs*, Summer 1994.

lead to system collapse in North Korea. They did not anticipate an immediate end to their growing North Korean economic burden. The importance of intergovernmental economic relations between China and North Korea will most likely decrease, but border trade across the Tumen and Yalu Rivers will probably increase. In particular, Jilin Province is expected to form a cooperative economic link with Chongjin, Sonbong, and Najin.

CHINA AND SOUTH KOREA

Ironically, although China faced an increasingly burdensome economic relationship with North Korea, it developed a gradual but constructive economic partnership with South Korea. This reversal took place because, in the post-Mao era, the Chinese economic imperative—namely, the four modernizations program and open-door policy—eroded the traditional primacy of China's military alliance and diplomatic coalition with North Korea. To modernize China in agriculture, industry, science and technology, and national defense, Deng Xiaoping and his associates shed the Maoist ideological penchant for autarkic, populist, egalitarian, and self-reliant economic policies and introduced a number of new and drastic measures that can indeed be called China's "second revolution." First, the Chinese relaxed strict central control over domestic and foreign economic activities and allotted a degree of decision-making power to local governmental units and industrial and agricultural organizations. Second, they combined a system of planned economy with market mechanisms so that competitive factors would rectify the negative aspects of socialist systems and bureaucratic control. Third, they adopted a responsible and accountable system for economic management and permitted tangible material incentives to stimulate performance. Fourth, they promoted a large group of young, well-educated, and professionally oriented technocrats to leadership positions and encouraged and rewarded innovation and creativity in education, science, and technology. Most important, the Chinese opened their doors to the international economic community, especially the United States, Japan, Western Europe, and other nonsocialist countries. Unlike their Maoist predecessors, Deng Xiaoping and other reform-minded Chinese leaders eagerly solicited and welcomed capital investments, joint ventures, public and private loans, technological transfers, and collaborative resource development from abroad. For this purpose they established special economic zones on the coast and readjusted their legal practices. They also joined the World Bank, the International Monetary Fund, the Asian Development Bank, and other international financial institutions. From 1979 to 1988, China concluded 16,325 contracts utilizing a total foreign capital of $79.1 billion; there were 15,955 direct foreign investment contracts ($28.2 billion), which included 8,532 joint ventures ($9.8 billion) and 370 loan agreements ($46.9 billion).[10]

The Chinese GNP grew from 374.2 billion yuan in 1978 to 842.1 billion yuan in 1987, a 2.25-time rise in one decade. The ratio of foreign trade to China's GNP increased from 9.7 percent in 1978 to 27.9 percent in 1987, when the total amount of its foreign trade reached $82.7 billion. The Chinese proudly noted:

> From 1978–87, China's total foreign trade expanded dramatically, not only exceeding the world's average growth rate but comfortably outstripping South Korea—one of Asia's economic "dragons"—during its period of economic take-off. Although China's share of world trade remains small, it has rapidly moved up the league table of trading nations: from 28th position to 12th in terms of total trade, from 32nd to 14th in export volume and from 27th to 11th in imports.[11]

From their new pragmatic perspective, it was no longer possible for the Chinese to dismiss South Korea as a mere colony of the United States and Japan. Although China continued to state publicly that "the economy [in South Korea] is now chaotic and inflation and employment grow worse by the day," both CCP general secretary Hu Yaobang and Premier Zhao Ziyang privately acknowledged in 1980 that China's open-door policy was inspired in part by South Korea's developmental experiences. At the same time Qian Jiajun—a noted Chinese economist—explained that between 1961 and 1978 South Korea's GNP made a seventeenfold jump, unemployment declined from 8.2 percent to 3.6 percent, and exports recorded the world's fastest growth rate (42 percent per year). He recommended that China learn from South Korea's successful economic tactics—such as the government's efficient intervention in economic affairs, utilization of foreign capital and technology, enterprise merger and reorganization, encouragement for study abroad, and labor force exportation. In another article in Shanghai's *Shijie Jingji Daobao* (World economic journal), Zhang Wen discussed "Nine Measures Adopted by South Korea to Promote Exports." He said that the amount of South Korea's exports was only $55 million in 1962 but that it grew to $842 million in 1970 (a 1,400 percent increase in eight years) and to $12.7 billion in 1978 (another 1,400 percent increase in eight years). He added, "In recent years, the growth rate has slightly dropped, but the export amount still reached $20.9 billion in 1981, an increase of 20 percent over 1980."[12]

As to the nine measures, he listed (1) establishing ten industrial bases such as Masan and Ulsan for export, (2) attaching importance to investigation and research and strengthening marketing and sales, (3) making use of financial levers, (4) playing an active role in contracting to build foreign projects, (5) attaching importance to Korea's reputation in the economic community and practicing a grading system, (6) being strict and fair in meting out rewards and punishments, (7) ensuring direct intervention by the government in economic polices (and the president's personal involvement in trade promotion), (8) supporting large commercial firms, and (9) sending people to foreign countries for study and inspection.

The Chinese favorable evaluation of South Korea's economic advancement served as a basis for indirect trade between the two countries; the volume increased from $19 million in 1979 to $188 million in 1980 and $280 million in 1981. Even though the latter amount constituted a meager share (0.34 percent) of China's total foreign trade, it was more than half the estimated volume of Chinese–North Korean trade. In view of North Korean sensitivities, the Chinese adopted a policy of separating economic from diplomatic issues. Trade negotiations with South Korea were usually channeled through third-party intermediaries or the trading firms that South Korean companies incorporated in Hong Kong or elsewhere. Hong Kong became a principal entrepôt for indirect Chinese–South Korean trade. In an effort to conceal its commercial contracts, the Chinese frequently removed South Korean trademarks or disguised the origins and destinations of goods traded. It was reported that "third-country vessels, sometimes manned and owned by South Koreans but bearing flags of third countries, were required to camouflage their destinations through the use of two bills of lading, one of which was destroyed halfway through the journey." Ships from China were required to call on ports in Japan before proceeding to South Korean harbors. At times, however, the Chinese permitted the direct shipment of goods (such as coal) between China and South Korea. It was not difficult to come across a Daewoo automobile in Beijing, to buy a Goldstar television set in Shanghai, or to see a large advertisement for South Korea's Borneo furniture in Guangzhou.[13]

In an attempt to strain Beijing-Pyongyang relations, the Soviet newspaper *Izvestia* reported in March 1981 that China had betrayed North Korea's interests by promoting trade with South Korea "on an official basis." The Chinese Ministry of Foreign Trade issued a statement categorically denying the report and reaffirming China's disapproval of any "two Koreas" machinations and its nonrecognition of the South Korean authorities. The Chinese countercharged that the Soviet Union was flirting with the South Korean regime, abetting the plot to create "two Koreas" and inviting South Korean "government ministers," economic delegations, scholars, and sportsmen as "honored guests" to Moscow. The trade issue was presumably high on the agenda of Premier Zhao Ziyang's discussions with Kim Il Sung and Li Jong Ok in December 1981. In public statements made in Pyongyang, Zhao emphasized China's rejection of the "two-Korea" policy pursued by the United States and South Korea.[14]

After Zhao's visit to Pyongyang and Kim Il Sung's visit to Beijing in September 1982, indirect trade between China and South Korea declined appreciably—$139 million in 1982 and $120 million in 1983. This downward trend was not only a result of pressure from North Korea and the Soviet Union but was also an extension of China's economic retrenchment policy, which scaled down its excessively ambitious Ten-Year Economic Plan (1976–1985) and imposed restrictions on foreign imports.

In 1984, however, the amount of China's trade with South Korea climbed to $434 million, approaching that of its trade with North Korea ($498 million). In 1985 it grew to $1,161 million, in 1986, $1,289 million, in 1987, $1,679 million, and in 1988, $3,087 million (see table 6). This trend reflected China's decision to strengthen its open-door policy, enunciated at the Third Plenum of the Twelfth Central Committee in October 1984. Growth also occurred when the Chinese attended the Asian Games (1986) and the Summer Olympic Games (1988) in Seoul, which North Korea boycotted.

Determined to emulate the South Koreans, the Chinese set aside the Marxist or Maoist ideological framework and carefully and objectively analyzed the South Korean model of economic development. A number of Chinese publications, magazines, and newspapers openly praised South Korea's economic success. In *Jingji Cankao* (Economic reference), edited by the Xinhua News Agency in October 1986, the Chinese referred to South Korea, Taiwan, Hong Kong, and Singapore as Asia's "four dragons" and noted that South Korea had dramatically increased its foreign exports by exploiting the Japanese yen's appreciation. They suggested that China as a big dragon should study the South Korean record. A similar point of view was expressed in the CCP's theoretical journal, *Hongqi* (Red flag).[15]

Moreover, in the prestigious Chinese literary journal *Renmin Wenxue* (People's literature), Li You (a *Beijing Ribao* reporter and a member of the Chinese Writers' Association) wrote a lengthy report on his observations of the Seoul Asian Games.[16] He praised the neatness and modernity of Seoul, the bustling South Gate market, the majesty of the Kyungbok Palace, the modern facility of *Chungang Ilbo* (a major South Korean newspaper), and the beautiful students at Ewha Women's University. He ob-

TABLE 6
CHINA'S TRADE WITH SOUTH KOREA
(IN MILLIONS OF DOLLARS)

	Total Volume	China's Exports	China's Imports	Balance
1979	$ 19	$ 15	$ 4	$ 11
1980	188	73	115	-42
1981	280	75	205	-130
1982	139	91	48	43
1983	120	69	51	18
1984	434	205	229	-24
1985	1,161	478	683	-205
1986	1,289	621	699	-47
1987	1,679	866	813	53
1988	3,087	1,387	1,700	-313
1989	3,143	1,705	1,438	267
1990	3,821	2,268	1,553	715
1991	5,812	3,441	2,371	1,070
1992	8,218	3,725	4,493	-768
1993	9,078	3,927	5,151	-1,224
1994	11,660	5,460	6,200	-740

served that Korean girls always smiled and wore modern dress but observed traditional customs. He mentioned that South Korea's annual per capita GNP reached $2,000 and that 90 percent of the automobiles in Seoul were made in Korea. According to him, Seoul, unlike Beijing, did not have any Crowns, Toyotas, or Fiats. He also noted that whereas China preferred to import consumer goods from abroad, South Korea used foreign capital and technology to enhance its industrial competitiveness. He was impressed that many South Koreans volunteered to work for the Asian Games. He vividly described the opening and closing ceremonies that emphasized Korean traditions. He also reported on the tight security measures and the allegations that the judges at the games were unfair. In summation, he pointed out South Korea's high technology, efficient organization, modern transportation system (especially highways), and good service. His overall message contradicted the reports emanating from North Korea on economic conditions in South Korea.

Exchanges of economic delegations between China and South Korea were under way at this point. Several influential South Korean business-men—such as Kim Woo Jung (chairman of the Daewoo Corporation), Han Bong Su (president of the Korea Trade Promotion Corporation), and Nam Kung Yon (chairman of the Korean Shipbuilding Association)—had visited China by the mid-1980s; other prominent leaders, including Lee Sun Ki (president of the Korea Trade Promotion Corporation), Moon Hi Gap (senior economic assistant for President Roh Tae Woo), and Lee Kyu Sung (minister of finance), did so in the late 1980s. The International Private Economic Council of Korea (IPECK) was organized to facilitate private economic cooperation between South Korea and socialist coun-tries and to invite and host Chinese delegations to Seoul. In 1988 Shandong Province opened the first representative office of a Chinese local govern-ment in Seoul. The Chinese were now prepared to forgo the cumbersome, inefficient methods of clandestine negotiations and indirect trade and con-duct open, direct commercial transactions with South Korea. As Dan C. Sanford suggests, by 1988 "the economic exchange between the PRC and the ROK traveled the route from being a closed secret, then an open se-cret, and finally no secret whatsoever."[17]

Even though the volume of trade between the two countries fluctu-ated widely from 1979 to 1988, South Korea's imports from China via Hong Kong registered a steady increase, suggesting that South Korea had an underlying political purpose for continuing to purchase Chinese goods even when the Chinese were unable or unwilling to reciprocate. The Chi-nese exported agricultural products (corn, millet, oil), natural resources (coal), textiles, silk, jute fibers, cotton yarn, and other raw materials to South Korea and imported intermediate technology goods—steel prod-ucts, electronics, electrical appliances, textiles, machine tools, petrochemi-cals, and chemical fertilizers—from South Korea.[18]

In accordance with their Seventh Five-Year Plan (1986–90), the Chi-nese intended to implement the four modernizations policy with vigor and pragmatism. They projected an average annual growth rate of 7.5 percent in total industrial output value and 4 percent in total agricultural output value (see table 7). The plan outlined several goals:

> In the five-year period, the total volume of import and export will grow at an average rate of 7 percent, reaching US $83 billion by 1990. Export will grow at a rate of 8.1 percent and import at a rate of 6.1 percent. We shall continue to increase exports of petroleum, coal, non-ferrous

TABLE 7
THREE OF CHINA'S FIVE-YEAR ECONOMIC PLANS
(1981–1995)

	Sixth Plan (1981–1985)	Seventh Plan (1986–1990)	Eighth Plan (1991–1995)
Average annual growth rate in agricultural output	4–5%	4%	5%
Aveage annual growth rate in industrial output	4–5%	7.5%	6.8%
Targets at final years			
Coal (in millions of tons)	700	1,000	1,230
Steel (in millions of tons)	39	55–58	72
Crude oil (in millions of tons)	100	150	145
Electricity (in billion kW/h)	362	550	810
Grain (in millions of tons)	360	425–450	455

metals, grain, cotton, etc. In addition, we shall gradually increase the proportion of manufactured goods in the total volume of export. So far as imports are concerned, priority will be given to computer software, advanced technologies and key equipment, as well as to certain essential means of production that are in short supply on the domestic market.[19]

After the sudden dismissal of Hu Yaobang as CCP general secretary in January 1987, the seventh plan appeared to be in jeopardy. On Premier Zhao Ziyang's assumption of the CCP's acting general secretaryship, however, he assured a visiting foreign dignitary that "the personnel change will not affect our line and policies but will enable us to implement them more correctly" and that "we will expand, instead of reducing, our cooperation with foreign countries in trade, economic, technical, monetary and other fields. This cooperation will be expanded in width and depth." At the fifth session of the Sixth National People's Congress, held in March and April 1987, he stated:

We shall open wider to the outside world and explore new possibilities for the effective use of foreign funds, the import of advanced technology and the earning of foreign exchange through export. In this way our open policy will play a greater role in China's economic development and socialist modernization. Using foreign funds and attracting foreign businessmen to launch joint ventures, cooperative enterprises or wholly foreign-owned ones is a major component of our open policy.[20]

In this connection the Chinese looked on South Korea as an increasingly attractive economic partner for a variety of reasons. First, as part of its northern diplomacy, South Korea was eager to accommodate China's economic preferences to the extent of sacrificing its own short-term financial interests; China indeed enjoyed a lion's share (85.2 percent) of South Korea's total trade with socialist countries during 1989.[21] Second, the Chinese found the intermediate technology of South Korea more suitable to their practical needs than the expensive high-technology of the United States, Japan, and Western Europe. Third, they felt more comfortable with the sociable and outgoing South Koreans than with the Japanese, who were still under close scrutiny because of their past colonial ambitions and who frequently assumed an air of economic superiority, or with the Taiwanese, who faced political obstacles to direct trade with China. Fourth, the geographic proximity and cultural affinities between China and South Korea reduced transportation costs and barriers to communications. South Korea was particularly well situated to assist China's developmental plans, which focused on its coastal regions (such as Shandong Province) and northeastern provinces (such as Liaoning Province). To avoid direct political confrontation between Beijing and Pyongyang, a convenient face-saving device was adopted: decentralizing economic decision-making authority to the provincial governments, coupled with enterprise autonomy. The South Koreans devised the Yellow Sea Development Project, which called for utilizing their southwestern coastal areas as an outlet for economic cooperation with China. Fifth, China made use of the highly educated and professionally competent Koreans (about two million) residing in China who were ready to interact with their South Korean counterparts. The reconciliation between China and the Soviet Union as indicated by the Gorbachev-Deng summit meeting in May 1989 removed a thorny political impediment to Sino–South Korean economic cooperation.

Even the Tiananmen Square incident did not dampen China's burgeoning economic partnership with South Korea but rather enhanced its relative importance. When the United States, Japan, and the European Community imposed varying degrees of economic sanctions against them, the Chinese appreciated President Roh's refusal to join the international campaign against China and his efforts to expand bilateral economic relations. In particular, South Korea provided assistance to China's tourist industries, which had been adversely affected by the Tiananmen tragedy, and promised substantial financial and technological assistance for the Asian Games in Beijing in September and October 1990. A Western reporter observed that "a flood of South Korean advertising and contributions for the Asian Games is intended to promote Beijing-Seoul ties that could benefit the economies of both nations and contribute to peace on the Korean Peninsula."[22] Yet the Chinese government was not yet willing to accept South Korea's proposal for exchanging trade offices between Beijing and Seoul; rather it suggested that South Korea could do so with China's provincial governments. Nor did the Chinese allow South Korean companies to open offices in Beijing. The absence of diplomatic relations hampered the smooth development of trade and other economic relations between the two countries.

China did agree, however, to open regular shipping routes between Chinese and South Korean ports and to export Daqing crude oil to South Korea. In 1989 trade between China and South Korea remained at about the same level ($3.1 billion) as that of the previous year; in 1990 it reached $3.8 billion. The volume of Chinese imports from South Korea during both years failed to match that of 1988 because of Tiananmen and China's retrenchment policy, but Chinese exports to South Korea greatly expanded.

Once the Asian Games had been successfully completed, on October 20, 1990, the China Chamber of International Commerce (CCOIC) and the Korea Trade Promotion Corporation (KOTRA) signed a memorandum of understanding. Article One stated: "For the purpose of promoting bilateral exchanges and cooperation in the fields of trade, investment, science, technology, etc., the two Parties have decided to mutually establish representative offices in Beijing and Seoul as soon as possible." Each representative office (*daibiaochu* in Chinese and *taepyobu* in Korean) consisted of twenty persons and had consular responsibilities and diplomatic immunities. This important step institutionalized Chinese–South Korean economic relations and paved the road for diplomatic normalization. On behalf of their respective governments, the two trade offices negotiated a trade agreement that offered most-favored-nation (MFN) status to each other. Article Two stated that the MFN provision "shall not apply to the preferences and advantages either party's government grants or may grant to its neighboring countries to facilitate border trade." The Chinese required this clarification to protect their special border trade with North Korea, and the South Koreans expected that it would prove helpful in future inter-Korean economic relations.

The South Korean government played an important role in bringing China, along with Taiwan and Hong Kong, to the Asia-Pacific Economic Cooperation meeting in Seoul in November 1991. At this meeting, Foreign Minister Qian Qichen and Minister of Foreign Economic Relations and Trade Li Lanqing met with President Roh Tae Woo. The volume of bilateral trade jumped by 51.9 percent to $5.8 billion in 1991 and by 41.4 percent to $8.2 billion in 1992. This rapid expansion sharply contrasted with China's economic relations with North Korea, which remained a burden on China's financial resources, during the early 1990s. South Korea, however, stimulated China's growing economic activities both at home and abroad.

NEW MODES OF TRADE AND INVESTMENT

Diplomatic rapprochement between Beijing and Seoul heightened expectations for an increase in bilateral economic cooperation. The two governments formally replaced the representative offices of the CCOIC and the KOTRA in each other's capital and took over all agreements concluded between them. For this purpose Li Lanqing and Han Bong Su (minister of trade and industry) met at Beijing in September 1992. On diplomatic normalization a group of South Korean businessmen organized the Korea-China Economic Council to promote and coordinate South Korea's new mode of economic exchange with China.[23] Headed by Kim Sang Ha (president of the Korean Chamber of Commerce and Industry), the council embraced the leaders of all *chaebol* and the representatives of the four major business associations—the Federation of Korean Industries, the Korean Foreign Trade Association, the Korea Federation of Small Business, and the Korea Employers' Federation. In 1993, the year following their diplomatic normalization, China became South Korea's third-largest trading partner (after Japan and the United States) and South Korea was China's sixth-largest trading partner (after Japan, Hong Kong, the United States, Taiwan, and Germany).

Although the amount of Chinese exports to South Korea remained relatively stable from 1991 to 1993, China's imports of South Korean goods increased dramatically during the same period—by 52.6 percent in 1991, 89.4 percent in 1992, and 14.6 percent in 1993. Several factors accounted for this increase. First, the Chinese economy had a high rate of growth and thus a general increase in its overall imports (26.3 percent in 1992 and 28.9 percent in 1993). This trend helped boost South Korean exports to China, especially steel, machinery, chemicals, and rubber products. Second, the trade agreement, which went into effect in February 1992, applied most-favored-nation status to South Korea and lowered the tariffs imposed on South Korean goods by 5 percent to 30 percent. Diplomatic normalization brought with it a legal and institutional infrastructure favorable to Chinese–South Korean commercial transactions. Direct trade gradually eliminated the cumbersome, uncertain, and costly aspects of indirect trade, which declined from 78.1 percent of total trade in 1988 to 57.7 percent in 1991 and 42.3 percent in 1992. Third, an increase in South Korea's investments in China, especially in light manufacturing industries, was accompanied by the purchase of South Korean facilities and materials. The high value of the Japanese yen indirectly enhanced the comparative utility of South Korean products in the Chinese market.

China's ability to increase its exports to South Korea, however, was limited. The South Korean economy, unlike its Chinese counterpart, only grew at a moderate rate during 1991. In 1992 its total imports increased by 0.3 percent. Chinese exports became affected by the general slowdown in South Korean foreign trade. When South Korea's imports of corn and other agricultural goods from China had reached the saturation point, China was unable to substitute alternative products in demand in South Korea. Moreover, the South Korean government continued to impose restrictions on imports of Chinese agricultural products and light industrial goods that threatened their South Korean competitors. The growing gap in bilateral trade ($768 million in 1992 and $1,224 million in 1993) became a source of dispute between China and South Korea. China's trade deficit decreased considerably in 1994, however, because South Korea's import of Chinese goods increased by 39 percent.

In general, China continued to export primary raw materials (such as crude oil, minerals, and agricultural products) and labor-intensive industrial goods (such as textiles and chemicals) to South Korea and to import capital- and technology-intensive commodities (such as steel, machinery, electronics, electrical appliances, synthetic fiber, chemical products, and nonferrous metals) from South Korea. Even though China and South Korea enjoyed a mutually beneficial vertical complementarity in their trade relations, a horizontal complementarity existed in a few select categories such as textiles, chemicals, and minerals. Even in the latter categories, South Korea tended to sell high value-added goods to China and to buy low-priced items.

The Pohang Iron and Steel Corporation (POSCO), which ran up against a stiff protectionist wall in the United States during 1992 and 1993 and suffered a drastic decline in its exports to the United States and Japan (whose share of South Korea's total steel exports fell from 54.5 percent in 1991 to 40.8 percent in 1992), made impressive inroads into the China market owing to China's construction boom and rapid industrialization, especially in automobiles and electronics. The trade agreement also lifted China's discriminatory tariffs on South Korean steel products. A POSCO official said that China had become its savior, boosting its sagging foreign sales. POSCO was engaged in collaborative efforts with the Baoshan Iron and Steel Corporation, China's largest steel mill, and was instrumental in creating a steel cooperation council between the two countries. In return for Chinese imports of South Korean steel, South Korea imported semifinished steel products from China. In addition, POSCO decided to invest $8.4 million in a cold-rolled coil-processing center at Tianjin and $60 million in a joint venture for continuous galvanizing sheets in China.[24] South Korea's synthetic fiber and apparel industry became an increasingly attractive category in China. China's labor-intensive textile industries flourished, requiring additional raw materials from South Korea. Chinese consumers, prompted by more disposable income and a rising fashion consciousness, began to favor high-quality imported clothing. And the textile industries in which South Korea invested preferred to purchase raw materials from South Korea.

Encouraged by the ease with which diplomatic and economic normalization between Beijing and Seoul had been established, the South Korean Ministry of Trade, Industry, and Energy projected in 1994 that the volume of bilateral trade would reach $28 billion ($16 billion in exports and $12 billion in imports) in 1997 and $56 billion ($30 billion in exports and $26 billion in imports) in 2001, when China's GNP is expected to exceed $1 trillion.[25] Just as they had profited from the special procurement boom in Vietnam during the 1960s and from the Middle East boom during the 1970s, the South Koreans wished to use the China market as a new venue for economic rejuvenation.

At the time of his state visit to Beijing in March 1994, President Kim Young Sam met with Jiang Zemin and agreed to establish a joint panel to promote industrial cooperation and joint ventures in such industries as telecommunications, automobile production, civil aircraft production, and high-definition television; the panel was chaired by South Korean trade minister Kim Chul Su and his Chinese counterpart Wu Yi. They agreed to conclude a pact on standardization to facilitate trade between the two countries and to develop standardized contracts to preempt disputes over trade issues. Premier Li Peng emphasized the economic issue during his five-day trip to South Korea in October and November 1994. The two governments signed cooperative agreements on civil aviation, civil passenger planes, and the peaceful utilization of nuclear science. The top leaders of all South Korea *chaebol* competed to meet with Premier Li and invite him to their model industries. The United States and Japan regarded the growth of Chinese–South Korean industrial cooperation as a potential threat to their economic interests in East Asia.[26]

As China's aggressive open-door economic policy continues to bear fruit, China has become a rival of South Korea in the international market. In total foreign trade, South Korea outperformed China from 1988 to 1991, but China outpaced South Korea by $7.5 billion in 1992. The Chinese have already overtaken their South Korean counterparts in exports to the European Community in 1989, Japan in 1990, and the United States in 1991. In 1988 China and South Korea shared 5.8 percent and 6.3 percent of the Japan market, but the numbers were reversed to 6.0 percent and 5.2 percent in 1991. China and South Korea shared 1.9 percent and 4.6 percent of the U.S. market in 1988, but the corresponding figures were 4.9 percent and 3.2 percent in 1992. In the United States, China not only surpassed South Korea in exporting labor-intensive light industry products (such as textiles and footwear) but also challenged South Korea in other advanced industrial categories. In 1992, for example, Chinese exports of color television sets to the United States jumped by 49.8 percent, to $117 million, but South Korean exports fell by 26.8 percent, to $146 million.[27] Likewise, Chinese exports of refrigerators to the United States increased by 20.9 percent, to 110 million sets in 1992, but South Korean exports decreased by 17 percent, to 130 million sets. Hence it is expected that although China and South Korea will continue to expand their bilateral trade in the years ahead, they will also vigorously compete against each other in the United States, Japan, Europe, and Southeast Asia. By capitalizing on its cheap labor, China can threaten the survival of small and medium-sized light industries in South Korea.

The rapid expansion of trade between China and South Korea was accompanied by an increase in the latter's investment in China. In 1985, in the first known case of South Korean investment in China, Hans Toy Company of South Korea used its subsidiary in Hong Kong to set up a toy factory in Guangdong Province; it was followed by a few other cases of indirect South Korean investments in China. In 1988 the governments of Shandong and Liaoning Provinces received permission from Beijing to open their doors to South Korea's direct investments. Despite their strong interest in the China market, South Korean businesspeople, unfamiliar with and uncertain toward the Chinese investment environment, were initially cautious. South Korean investments totaled eleven in 1988–89 and thirty-five in 1990 (see table 8). The number greatly increased in subsequent years, however, in part because the two countries agreed to exchange trade offices in October 1990, signed the trade agreement in December 1991, and normalized diplomatic relations in August 1992. Moreover, Zheng Hongye (CCOIC chairman) and Roh Jae Won (head of the KOTRA representative office in Beijing) signed the Agreement on the Encouragement and Reciprocal Protection of Investments on May 2, 1992, on behalf of their respective governments.[28]

The agreement stipulated that "investors of either state shall within the territory of the other state be accorded treatment no less favorable than that accorded to investors of their state in respect of the admission of investment and the matters in connection therewith." It further specified that investors be given sympathetic consideration with respect to their applications for entry, sojourn, residence, licenses, and permits and that investments and returns of investments not be nationalized or expropriated but receive constant protection and security. The two sides agreed on the procedures for repatriating profits to home countries and for using an arbitration board to settle disputes. On diplomatic normalization between Beijing and Seoul, both governments took over this agreement as an intergovernmental accord. They concluded other agreements in 1992 and 1993 in a wide range of areas—science and technology, construction, commercial arbitration, telecommunications, water resources, maritime transport, environmental protection, and postal and telephone service.

Supported by both governments, there was a dramatic increase in South Korea's direct investments in China—from 107 cases in 1991 to

Table 8
South Korean Investment in China

	1988–89	1990	1991	1992	1993	Total
Number of cases approved	11	35	107	260	630	1,043
Amounts approved (in millions of dollars)	$13.8	50.0	121.9	220.9	570.3	$976.9
Actual investment (in millions of dollars)	$12.8	48.3	91.0	168.6	153.9	$474.6

SOURCE: *Chungguk Pyonram* (China almanac) (1994), p. 634.

260 in 1992 and 630 in 1993. Even though South Korea lagged far behind Hong Kong, Macao, Japan, and Taiwan, the annual growth rate of its investments in China was impressive. In 1993 South Korea invested more in China than in any other country. The total amount of South Korean investment approved for China reached $976.9 million (1,043 cases) by the end of 1993. For the first half of 1994 the South Korean government issued permits for 1,551 cases of investment in China (a 98.8 percent increase over the corresponding period of 1993), which amounted to $1.35 billion (a 71.8 percent increase). The number of permits for South Korean investment in China for the first half of 1994 was more than that in any other country, but China ranked next to the United States in terms of the amounts permitted. The total amount of South Korea's actual investments in China reached $1.1 billion by the end of 1994; South Korea emerged as the sixth-largest investing nation in China. Conversely, Chinese investments in South Korea remained at $1.2 million (42 cases) by the end of 1993; these investments were mainly intended to penetrate the Korea market in agricultural products and light industries.

A growing number of South Korea's small and medium-sized companies chose China as the most suitable site for investment—placing it far ahead of Vietnam, Mexico, and the United States. Asked why they decided to invest in China, a large number (40.8 percent) of South Korean investors mentioned the cheap labor force. Others responded that their investments were designed to open new markets (24.8 percent), to establish bridgeheads for gathering economic intelligence and moving into the China market (11.2 percent), to increase indirect exports to third countries (8.8 percent), and to obtain semifinished products in China for complete production in South Korea (8.8 percent). They often replied that the China market was attractive because they were able to take advantage of its convenient location, cultural similarities, readily available raw materials, and inexpensive real estate.[29]

No doubt the abundance of a cheap labor force in China was particularly important to South Korean businesspeople because they had encountered a serious array of problems in South Korea since the late 1980s—labor shortages, rising wages, radical union activities, acute labor disputes, and frequent work stoppages. The wage differential between China and South Korea was significant at all levels. The average monthly wage of Chinese managers employed by South Korean investors was 455.5 yuan (about $80) in 1992, which amounted to only 10.2 percent of the average salary for their South Korean counterparts.[30] Monthly wages for skilled and unskilled workers in China were 349.7 yuan and 246.6 yuan, respectively, only 9.8 percent and 9.5 percent of the wages for comparable South Korean workers. Even if other costs for benefits (about 60 percent of wages) were added, the average expense for employing Chinese managers and workers was no more than 16 percent of that for using their South Korean counterparts. The number of Chinese employed by South Korean investors was estimated at thirteen thousand in 1992 and twenty thousand in 1993. Many of them were bilingual and bicultural Korean-Chinese.

The productivity of Chinese labor, however, was measured at only 63.4 percent of that of South Koreans, and the discipline and caliber of Chinese workers were brought into question. South Korean investors in China identified the indifferent attitude of Chinese workers as their most serious problem (see table 9).[31] They also pointed out that wages for Chinese workers were rising and that it was difficult to recruit qualified workers. Competition for skilled Chinese workers drove up their wages sharply. Yet the South Korean investors had no serious problems with Chinese government agencies, the branches of the Chinese Communist Party, or labor unions.

As to the difficulties of investing in China, a large number of South Korean businesspeople responded that it was difficult to obtain appropriate economic information (36.4 percent), to understand and overcome China's complex administrative procedures (23.5 percent), and to deal with the frequent changes in China's positions during negotiations (15.7 percent). Others said that it was difficult to handle South Korea's complex administrative procedures (11.4 percent) or to choose Chinese partners for joint ventures (10.6 percent). Asked about managerial problems in China, they responded that China did not have a sufficient infrastructure (29.5 percent), had a low level of labor discipline and labor productivity (24.8 percent), and did not provide high-quality raw materials on time (18.6 percent). Other problems included an increase in production costs, a shortage of local operational funds, and various restrictions in the China market. A few Korea-invested facilities encountered labor disputes, as illustrated by a strike of more than twelve hundred Chinese workers at a shoe company in Tianjin in February 1993.[32]

In 1992 China became the largest recipient of foreign direct investment among developing countries; in comparison with the corresponding figures in the previous year the number of investment projects almost trebled, to 49,000, and the total value of $58 billion almost quadrupled. Enterprises with foreign investment produced about 6 percent of China's

TABLE 9
PROBLEMS FACING SOUTH KOREAN INVESTMENT IN CHINA
(%)

	No Problem at All	Major Problem	About Average	Some Problem	Serious Problem
Worker's undisciplined attitude	3.1	7.7	24.6	40.0	24.6
Wage increase	3.1	12.3	41.5	26.2	16.9
Difficulties in recruitment	20.0	29.2	27.7	15.4	7.7
Chinese government's interference in management	29.2	38.5	12.1	7.7	1.5
CCP's interference in management	46.2	35.4	13.8	3.1	1.5
Labor union's interference in management	43.1	41.5	13.8	1.5	0

SOURCE: An Chong Sok, *Hanguk kiupui daechung tuja siltae wa hyanghu kwajae* (The situation of South Korean industries' investment in China and its future tasks) (1993), p. 57.

total industrial output. The number of foreign investments reached 135,000, with a total contract value of $170 billion by June 1993. Now that foreign-invested firms share an increasing portion (27.5 percent in 1993) of China's total exports, the importance of foreign investments looms larger in China's economic performance. Because China's foreign direct investment regime is more liberal than that of South Korea, it may force South Korea to further liberalize its investment environment.[33]

Unlike the general tendency for foreign investments to be concentrated in the southern and central regions in China (up to 70 percent), a major characteristic of South Korean investments in China was their heavy emphasis on the northern and northeastern regions. The Bohai Sea area (Shandong Province, Tianjin, Beijing, and Hebei Province) and the northeastern region (Liaoning, Jilin, and Heilongjiang Provinces) attracted 86.0 percent of all South Korean investments (or 85.9 percent of total value) in China by the end of 1993 (see table 10). Except for Jiangsu and Guangdong Provinces and Shanghai, the regions south of the Yangzi River, especially the central interior, were largely untouched by South Korean investors. A number of factors account for this geographic pattern of investments. First, Shandong Province occupies a special position in economic relations with South Korea. In addition to its traditional links with Korea, Shandong obtained permission from the Beijing government to directly deal with South Korea and to issue entry visas to South Korean businesspeople and tourists even before diplomatic normalization. An overwhelming majority of the twenty-six thousand overseas Chinese in South Korea claimed Shandong as their ancestral province. In September 1990 Shandong's two ports—Weihai and Qingdao—opened direct shipping routes with Inchon.

The city of Qingdao has been called a "paradise" for South Korean firms. A Chinese reporter noted in 1993:

> The city now has 131 ROK funded enterprises, and most of them are exclusively ROK-funded. The total ROK investment in Qingdao comes to US $210 million, accounting for one-third of its total in China. Today, Qingdao not only has the largest number of ROK enterprises but also the largest number of ROK citizens in any place on China's mainland. There are estimated to be over 1,000 ROK nationals working in the city, and some of the young men have married local girls.[34]

The city attracted about eight hundred Korean-Chinese workers from the northeast, and many local Chinese youths learned Korean, which became

TABLE 10

GEOGRAPHIC DISTRIBUTION OF SOUTH KOREAN INVESTMENT IN CHINA
(BY THE END OF 1993)

	Number of Cases Approved	Percentage	Total amount (in thousands of dollars)	Percentage
Bohai Sea area				
Shandong	293	28.1	$374,331	38.3
Tianjin	109	10.5	131,053	13.4
Beijing	69	6.6	62,362	6.4
Hebei	27	2.6	23,553	2.4
Subtotal	498	47.7	591,299	60.5
Northeast region				
Liaoning	221	21.2	125,155	12.8
Jilin	99	9.5	46,186	4.7
Heilongjiang	79	7.6	76,900	7.9
Subtotal	399	38.3	248,241	25.4
Central China				
Jiangsu	44	4.2	45,897	4.7
Shanghai	19	1.8	18,612	1.9
Zhejiang	11	1.1	6,676	0.7
Subtotal	74	7.1	71,186	7.3
South China				
Guangdong	40	3.8	42,609	4.4
Fujian	10	1.0	16,195	1.7
Hainan	2	0.2	800	–
Subtotal	52	5.0	59,604	6.1
Other regions	20	1.9	6,594	0.7
TOTAL	1,043	100.0	976,923	100.0

SOURCE: *Chungguk Pyonram* (China almanac) (1994), p. 635.

the most popular foreign language in Qingdao. China accepted a South Korean consulate-general in the city in September 1994 and began direct air services between Seoul and Qingdao in December 1994.

Second, as a latecomer to the China market, South Korea found it difficult to expand its investments in the special economic zones and other coastal areas of the south because Hong Kong, Taiwan, and Japan had already established footholds there and because the costs for labor, real estate, and other facilities were higher in the south than elsewhere in China. In comparison, the more accessible Shandong and Liaoning Peninsulas offered many advantages to South Korean adventures.

Third, the three northeastern provinces, which had enjoyed a close and long historical relationship with the Korean Peninsula across the Yalu and Tumen Rivers, had an advanced industrial infrastructure inherited from the Japanese colonial era and embraced a vast majority of the Korean-Chinese population—63 percent in Jilin Province, 25 percent in Heilongjiang Province, and 11 percent in Liaoning Province.[35] Whereas North Korea constituted a geographic and political barrier, South Korean businesspeople felt familiar and comfortable in this region and could communicate with many inhabitants.

Fourth, because a majority of South Korea–invested plants and enterprises in China imported equipment and materials from South Korea, assembled or manufactured products in China, and exported them to South Korea or third countries, the Bohai Sea area had distinct advantages in terms of geography, transportation, and communications. Moreover, once a few South Korean businesspeople had made initial investments in the northern and northeastern regions, other businesspeople followed suit.

At the initial stage, South Korean investments in China focused on labor-intensive and short-term manufacturing enterprises of small or medium size. They processed or manufactured light industrial products such as textiles, apparel, toys, fur, footwear, leather, furniture, food, and electrical appliances. These commodities were primarily for export, but some were also consumed in China. A number of South Korea's declining or weak industries went to China to increase their competitiveness in the international market. South Korean investments in China in the manufacturing sector amounted to 91.9 percent of the total—twice as high as the average of South Korea's overall investments abroad. Investments in nonmanufacturing sectors were largely limited to such categories as restaurants, fishing, marine industries, and rock quarries. About 80 percent of all South Korean investments in China were less than $1 million each.

South Koreans almost equally divided their investments between wholly owned firms and joint ventures with Chinese counterparts. Whereas the enterprises wholly owned by South Koreans in China tended to emphasize exports, the joint ventures were mainly geared for consumption in China. A typical joint venture would involve the Chinese side offering land, buildings, and labor and the South Korean side providing capital, technology, and management.

Encouraged by the profitable experiments in China, South Korea's major industrial conglomerates (*chaebol*) began to show an increasing interest in large-scale, capital-intensive, and long-term investments in China—such as steel, cement, automobiles, containers, petrochemicals, electronics, chemical fiber, and telecommunications. For example, the Daewoo Group, the most active *chaebol* in China, decided to use $300 million for constructing a cement plant in Shandong Province and $2 billion for setting up an automotive parts plant at Changchun. It also acquired a 25 percent share in Youyi Shopping City, the largest department store in Beijing, and a 50 percent share in a joint venture (worth $300 million) for coal mines in Shandong Province. The Lucky-Goldstar Group is considering a $50 million investment in a joint venture for telephones in Shandong Province. Another major conglomerate—Samsung Group—won the bid for a $200-million ethylene project for the Jilin Chemical Industrial Corporation in September 1992 and signed another agreement to build a $40-million ethylene glycol plant for the China National Chemical Construction Corporation and the Jilin Chemical Industrial Corporation in May 1993. Moreover, the Samsung Group decided to invest more than $4 billion in constructing China's industrial complexes and distribution networks by 2000; thus Samsung chairman Lee Kun Hee was warmly received by Jiang Zemin and Li Peng in April 1995. Other major projects include investments by Sunkyong in an oil refinery at Shenzhen ($1.5 billion), by Ssangyong in another oil refinery at Qingdao ($1 billion), and by Jinro in a commercial and financial center at Beijing ($2 billion). In February 1995 the Korea Electric Power Corporation (KEPCO) and the China National Nuclear Corporation signed a memorandum of understanding on joint nuclear power plants; KEPCO hoped to develop a joint plant model with China based on the South Korean station and to participate in the construction of more than twenty nuclear power plants in China by 2010. The South Koreans also took part in the large-scale industrial parks in Tianjin and Shenyang and in the development of offshore oil fields in the Yellow Sea and the East China Sea.[36]

Even though the South Korean government did not promise a specific amount of loans to China at the time of diplomatic normalization in 1992 and could not compete with Japan's yen-denominated official development assistance programs, which would amount to $9 billion by 1995, China and South Korea quickly embarked on a course of financial cooperation. The Korea Exchange Bank became the first South Korean bank to open an office in China in 1992, and Cho Soon, governor of the Bank of Korea, visited China in October of the same year. There were twelve South Korean financial institutions represented in China by the end of 1993; in turn, the Bank of China and other Chinese banks established branch offices in Seoul. A commercial bank in South Korea offered $200 million in loans to the Jilin Chemical Industrial Corporation to support its ethylene project. The South Korean Export and Import Bank loaned $140 million to the Bank of China and $111 million to the Shandong Cement Works. In September 1993 the two governments signed a memorandum on bilateral financial cooperation that offered each other's banks the most-favored treatment in business location and operations and agreed to hold regular policy consultations. For the first time, in October 1994, the South Korean government announced plans to offer long-term and low-interest public loans (Economic Development Corporation Fund) to China—$10 million for expansion of an airport at Yanji in the Yanbian Korean Autonomous Prefecture of Jilin Province, $15 million for construction of a bridge in Tianjin, $8 million for expansion of a port in Shandong Province, and $10 million for modernization of a railway system in Heilongjiang Province. All four projects were in part intended to facilitate South Korea's economic operations in China.[37]

As far as economic relations with South Korea are concerned, the Chinese have almost completely transcended the erstwhile constraints of ideological and diplomatic considerations or the political sensitivities of North Korea and Russia. Relations are now primarily dictated by the naked and unabashed pursuit of economic interests. According to recent projections, in the next few years South Korean investments in China will probably shift from the northern and northeastern regions to the rest of China, from short-term, labor-intensive activities to long-term, capital-intensive enterprises, and from wholly owned projects to joint ventures.

Prospects for Sino–South Korean economic cooperation brightened in July 1994 when both governments achieved a breakthrough in their long and difficult negotiations over civil aviation. From the beginning of the negotiations in 1992 the Chinese had insisted that the air control boundary (or flight information region) between China and South Korea be set at longitude 125° east, along a line linking South Korea's Paekryong Island with North Korea's Sinuiju. This area would then be put under Chinese air control.[38] The South Korean negotiators had been adamant that the boundary at 124° that was endorsed by the International Civil Aviation Organization (ICAO) was the most appropriate solution. This boundary was used during the Asian Games (1986) and the Olympic Games (1988) when special charter planes flew between Beijing and Seoul. Because the air control boundary as quasi-sovereign airspace had far-reaching policy implications in regard to aerial territory and the continental shelf, South Korea had rejected China's compromise proposals to use 124° for the Beijing-Seoul route and 125° for the Shanghai-Seoul route or to fix the boundary at 124.5°. In a rare expression of common national interests, North Korea supported the South Korean position.

Another source of disagreement had been the number of carriers each side should be allowed to serve the route between Beijing and Seoul. Although Chinese negotiators had argued that only one carrier should use the route, their South Korean counterparts proposed to have no limit on the number of carriers because South Korea's two main air lines—Korean Air and Asiana Airlines—both wanted to participate in this potentially lucrative route.

In the end, however, the Chinese concluded that the civil aviation agreement was essential to the future of their economic relations with South Korea and agreed to accept the 124° boundary for all routes except for the Shanghai-Seoul connection and to let the two Korean airlines fly the direct route between Beijing and Seoul. The agreement allowed each side to operate nine flights a week between Beijing and Seoul; this route would be shared by Korean Air (five flights) and Asiana Airlines (four flights). It also specified the weekly schedule as follows: (1) each side has three flights between Seoul and Qingdao and Shenyang; (2) China operates three flights between Dalian and Seoul; (3) South Korea has three flights between Seoul and Tianjin; and (4) each side conducts six chartered flights between Shanghai and Seoul. The new arrangement reduced the flight time required between Beijing and Seoul from three hours and ten minutes to one hour and forty minutes, enabling South Koreans to fly to Beijing faster and less expensively than to Tokyo. The first regularly scheduled flights between China and South Korea began on December 22, 1994. This was a significant boost for tourist industries. Attracted by China's colorful traditions and cultural mystique, a growing number of South Koreans used both air

TABLE 11

EXCHANGE OF VISITORS BETWEEN CHINA AND SOUTH KOREA

(IN THOUSANDS)

	Chinese Visitors to South Korea	South Korean Visitors to China
1985	0.1	0.3
1986	0.7	0.5
1987	0.2	0.8
1988	3.0	5.8
1989	5.4	13.6
1990	25.2	31.9
1991	44.2	43.2
1992	45.0	43.0
1993	40.0	112.0
1994	63.0	235.0

SOURCE: *Chungguk Pyonram* (China almanac) (1994), p. 641, and Ministry of Foreign Affairs (Seoul).

lines and ferry boats to visit China (see table 11); in particular, they flocked to the Paektu Mountains and the Chonji Lake on the Sino–North Korean border—places that Koreans regard as sacred. There was a rapid increase in the number of Chinese visitors to South Korea in the 1990s, but many (about thirty-one thousand by December 1994) overstayed their time limit in South Korea. About 80 percent of them were ethnic Koreans who took advantage of their bilingual skills and of the labor shortage in South Korea to engage in illegal commercial activities and factory work.[39]

As demonstrated by the use of Nampo and Chongjin as an entrepôt for shipments between North Korea and South Korea, the robust growth of Sino–South Korean economic ties, especially in the Yanbian Korean Autonomous Prefecture of Jilin Province and in border cities such as Dandong (which faces Sinuiju across the Yalu River), cannot fail to have a positive effect on the future of inter-Korean relations. It may also lead to a triangular linkage among China, South Korea, and North Korea. If North Korea decides to open Nampo, Haeju, or Sinuiju on the Yellow Sea to free trade, the Yellow Sea basin area may become a useful venue for direct or indirect economic transactions among the three countries. On the other side of the Korean Peninsula a similar system of multilateral economic cooperation may take place in the Eastern Sea (or the Sea of Japan) with particular focus on the Tumen River Development Project. The Chinese, recognizing this area's potential as a "magnetic juncture" and "economic miracle" for China, North Korea, South Korea, Russia, Japan, and Mongolia, made Hunchun an open city to be linked with Najin in North Korea and Zarubino in Russia. A Chinese report explained:

> Businessmen and tourists the world over will soon be able to enter and leave here without a visa. Exports and imports will be duty-free. Likened to Hong Kong or Rotterdam, this will be a new economic and trade hub, a free Oriental harbour. Shipping voyages to North America and Europe will be shorter than from any other Chinese ports. Passengers and freight will cross Eurasia within three days, relying on an express railway linking the Pacific and Atlantic shores; a faster route to be sure.[40]

With this purpose in mind, both Jiang Zemin and Li Peng inspected the area, allocated substantial funds for Hunchun's development, and fully cooperated with the United Nations Development Project's preparatory efforts. The joint venture agreement—which China and North Korea signed in April 1994 to expand Najin's port facilities, to begin a wholly closed international passenger train service between Hunchun and Najin, and to open a new air route between Yanji and Sonbong—specified that "legal protection will be offered to South Korean joint ventures which registered in China but also have interests [in] financing infrastructure projects in Najin and Sonbong." A new highway linking Hunchun with Najin was opened in September 1995.

So long as China sustains its open-door orientation and high-growth policy, it is expected to induce South Korea's further engagement in the China market and to strengthen Sino–South Korean economic ties. As a result of transferring their capital, technology, and managerial expertise to China, the South Koreans may face a possible weakening of their domestic economic base and a boomerang effect from their investments in China. When China joins the World Trade Organization (WTO), expands its economic links with Taiwan, and takes over Hong Kong in 1997, it will present South Korea with formidable economic competition. South Koreans, however, are likely to receive more benefits than losses from their long-range economic relations with China by taking advantage of both vertical and horizontal complementarity. They can also learn from

China's advanced technology and experience in such areas as aerospace, lasers, linear accelerators, applied physics, communications, satellites, missile technology, and nuclear science. The two governments recently set up a China-Korea Joint Committee on Science and Technology and signed an agreement to conduct joint scientific research and exchange scientists and graduate students.[41]

The Chinese continue to regard South Korea as a constructive and cooperative partner for future economic programs. This expectation is well illustrated in the package of 434 items for Sino–South Korean economic cooperation that was presented to President Kim at Beijing in March 1994. Even if not all of these items are implemented, both governments are committed to developing an overall political and legal framework for economic and technological interdependence. In addition to normal diplomatic relations, a stable security environment is essential to sustaining this structure. Once the framework is firmly institutionalized in the years ahead, China and South Korea cannot afford to undo their important economic achievements. They are also likely to cooperate in multilateral economic activities and organizations—such as APEC and the WTO.

Chapter Six
CONCLUSION

• •

The preceding chapters suggest that the process of developing China's new two-Korea policy, which has gradually supplanted the relatively straightforward one-Korea policy pursued from the 1950s to the 1970s, has been complex and tortuous. The intense Sino–North Korean solidarity engendered by the Korean War has colored China's approach to the Korean question, but it has not prevented China from significantly restructuring its economic, diplomatic, and military relations with both Koreas during the 1980s and early 1990s. This dynamic transformation reflects (1) a change in Chinese domestic and foreign policy priorities, especially after the transfer of political leadership from Mao Zedong to Deng Xiaoping, (2) a decisive tilt of the inter-Korean power configurations in favor of Seoul, and (3) shifting quadrilateral relationships among China, the Soviet Union (Russia), the United States, and Japan.

The main thrust of the new Chinese Korean policy is economic. Gone are the days when China jealously guarded its exclusive economic relationship with North Korea and openly denounced South Korea as a bankrupt and abject colony of the United States and Japan, or when China and the Soviet Union accused each other of fraternizing with South Korea. Governed by the Deng Xiaoping–inspired four modernizations program, open-door policy, and socialist market economy, the Chinese have rapidly and unabashedly strengthened their new ties with South Korea in trade, investment, loans, technology, and management. Commercial and political considerations have prompted the South Koreans to jump on the China bandwagon. Although China and South Korea strenuously compete in the markets of the United States, Japan, and Southeast Asia, their interdependent economic links, based on vertical and horizontal complementarity, are bound to expand in the years ahead, presenting a formidable challenge to Japanese and U.S. economic interests in the Asian-Pacific region. It is conceivable that China will eventually join South Korea in sponsoring a Yellow Sea economic community or a variety of multilateral developmental programs such as the Tumen River Project. Yet China remains willing and able, despite its heavy burden, to assist in the economic survival of North Korea, now irreparably deprived of the Russian largesse.

The Chinese economic imperative, coupled with the passing of the cold war international system, has to a great extent determined China's decision to replace its doctrinaire one-Korea position with a pragmatic two-Korea diplomacy. Under Deng Xiaoping's tutelage the celebrated Maoist dictum of "politics in command" has been overshadowed by the ascendancy of economic consideration. The Chinese were instrumental in bringing about the simultaneous admissions of Seoul and Pyongyang to the United Nations and facilitating the inter-Korean Agreement on Reconciliation, Nonaggression and Exchanges and Cooperation in December 1991. In normalizing their diplomatic relations with South Korea, the Chinese received no explicit opposition from the United States, Japan, or Russia and managed to deal with Kim Il Sung's displeasure. In the process they also resolved a vexing semantic problem by referring to the Democratic People's Republic of Korea in official documents and mass media as *Chaoxian* and the Republic of Korea as *Hanguo*, instead of *Nanchaoxian* (southern Korea).[1] China's diplomatic posture in the Korean Peninsula signifies the diminishing relevance of its ideological and revolutionary exhortations and its militant solidarity in foreign relations. It is also indicative of conscious Chinese efforts to adopt an objective and realistic role in the management of Korean issues. The Chinese may indeed become useful mediators between North and South Korea and may serve to deescalate inter-Korean mistrust and tensions. If a multilateral diplomatic forum on Korea is held, China will probably play an active, central role. At the same time, China will undoubtedly continue to urge the United States and Japan to improve relations with North Korea so that a pattern of cross-recognition by all four major powers can be established on the peninsula. China will continue to support North Korea's diplomatic maneuvers in the United Nations and elsewhere, to the extent that the outcome does not compromise its vested interests in the Korean Peninsula.

Compared with the remarkable shift in economic and diplomatic relations with Korea, Chinese military policy has not substantially altered, despite the end of the cold war and the collpase of the Soviet Union. The lingering memory of the Korean War is still evident in China's strategic calculations. The Chinese view North Korea as a useful buffer zone that contributes to their national security and thus see their military alliance with North Korea as important. At the moment they are entering into a limited degree of military exchanges and consultations with South Korea, including the exchange of military attachés in their capitals, and they prefer to maintain the Korean armistice agreement until a more permanent peace structure can be set up in the peninsula. China's de jure two-Korea policy has, however, eroded its alliance system with North Korea, and there is a growing cleavage between the Chinese and North Korean military orientations. China's 1961 security treaty with North Korea, which amounted to a virtual extension of the Korean War, was a product of the cold war and Sino-Soviet rivalry. In view of today's vastly different circumstances, China must recognize that it has become a mechanism to provide North Korea with a sense of security and at the same time constrain North Korean military options.

With respect to the North Korean nuclear issue, the Chinese, as demonstrated in the United Nations and the International Atomic Energy Agency, have generally protected North Korean military and diplomatic positions but have failed to fully embrace the North Korean cause. China supports the Joint Declaration on the Denuclearization of the Korean Peninsula, signed in December 1991, and the uninterrupted implementation of the U.S.–North Korean Geneva agreement, concluded in October 1994. It is in their strategic interests that the Chinese continue to honor their security guarantee toward North Korea and favor a semblance of military balance on the Korean Peninsula. It is doubtful, however, that China will ever extend an unconditional military promise or nuclear umbrella to North Korea. China may gradually and cautiously reach an understanding on military issues with South Korea and support confidence-building measures and arms control proposals among all parties concerned. China will also be interested in exploring a regional collective security system focused on the Korean Peninsula.

For the sake of their overall policy objectives, especially economic growth and peaceful coexistence, the Chinese do not seem enthusiastic about a radical change in the status quo of the Korean Peninsula. China defines the current Korean situation as potentially explosive and mutually hostile across the demilitarized zone, but, in light of its two-Korea policy, does not believe that this divisive situation is adverse to its national interests. Now that the Soviet Union (Russia) has been, at least temporarily, eradicated as a strategic rival and possible spoiler in Korea, the Chinese are confident that a period of relative peace and stability is possible in the Korean Peninsula and that both the United States and Japan can be counted on to be cooperative in this regard.

No matter what they may say or imply in commemorating the Korean War, the Chinese prefer not to see armed clashes between North and South Korea resume or to witness a Vietnam-type unification of Korea. Another Korean War would spell disaster for China's domestic and foreign policies. If North Korea decides to launch another all-out attack against South Korea, it would be impossible for China to stop it immediately. In the event of prolonged warfare, North Korea would require China's assistance in such areas as military supplies, oil delivery, and logistic support. Given their legally binding treaty obligations and repeated security commitments, China might find it difficult to ignore North Korean requests for military assistance or to remain on the sidelines if North Korea's total defeat were imminent. Unlike their massive involvement in the Korean War, however, the Chinese would likely avoid direct military engagement and advocate a negotiated settlement. To prevent another war in Korea, the Chinese are expected to make every effort to discourage North Korean military aspirations, to restrain precipitous actions by the United States or South Korea, and to help ease the tensions in the peninsula.

Viewed from the perspective of China's present policy priorities, Korea's peace and stability are more important than unification.[2] The Chinese have no compelling reason to push for Korea's immediate political reintegration, even by peaceful means. On the contrary, they are concerned lest Korea become united following the German unification model—that South Korea absorb North Korea because of the growing disparity between their capabilities.

A German-type unification scenario in Korea would present the Chinese with a number of distinct disadvantages and problems. First, it would mean, in effect, that China's long-standing policy of buttressing North Korea's system had failed. After the successive demise of Eastern European socialist regimes and the Soviet Union, the downfall of yet another socialist government so close and dear to China would have demoralizing consequences and evoke the specter of "bourgeois liberalization" and "peaceful evolution" in China. This would also be a blow to China's unification formula of "one state and two systems." Moreover, the loss of North Korea as a buffer zone, accompanied by an influx of North Korean refugees or the presence of a North Korean government in exile, would probably pose a danger to China's border security.

Second, China may have a greater sense of uncertainty toward a unified Korea than toward a divided Korea. One cannot rule out the possibility that a unified Korean government could adopt a nationalistic outlook or an autarkic economic orientation, thus undermining China's substantive interests in Korea. The reversal of Sino-Vietnamese relations from revolutionary solidarity to armed hostility in 1979 is a painful reminder of this possibility, and the Chinese must take this contingency into consideration when formulating their Korea policy. They cannot be sure that a unified Korean government would not raise territorial issues over border areas and the continental shelf or attempt to influence the Korean minority in China. The enormous financial costs of Korean unification might imperil China's substantial economic stakes in Korea.

Third, the Chinese may be concerned that a rapid unification of Korea would destabilize the delicate balance of power in Northeast Asia and complicate China's regional strategic posture. A report prepared by the RAND Corporation asserts:

> Scenarios for Korea's future entail a diverse range of possibilities. In several such scenarios, the reunification process will prove far more tumultuous within the region than German reunification has proved in Europe. Moreover, the emergence of a unified, economically strong Korea could bring on a new era of competition to replace the tensions of the Cold War, centered on the possible advent of intense economic and diplomatic rivalry with Japan and the revival of historical suspicions of China and Russia. Instability would become all the more likely if a unified Korea saw the need to develop a nuclear weapons capability.[3]

This view appears to be overly alarmist, but China can hardly disregard the strategic consequences of Korean unification. Whereas the Federal Republic of Germany is anchored in and integrated with the European Union, NATO, and other institutions of Western internationalism and is content with the continuing U.S. military presence, a unified Korea could become a free-standing entity without regional economic or security arrangements. There is no assurance that a unified Korea would necessarily be friendly, cooperative, and peaceful toward China. If a unified Korea were to conclude a security treaty with the United States or allow a

U.S. military presence, China's desire to keep a preeminent foreign power out of the Korean Peninsula and to preserve the balance of strategic interests in the region would be thwarted.

If, however, the two Korean governments agree to unify themselves by peaceful and independent means, China, despite its reservations and concerns, would not be in a position to resist or cast a veto. The Chinese have long endorsed Kim Il Sung's proposal for the Confederal Republic of Koryo as a reasonable and practical step toward Korean unification but consider it unfeasible because of South Korea's opposition.

The Chinese are reluctant to champion immediate Korean unification following either the Vietnam or German model and thus opt for the Korean status quo and reducing tensions between Seoul and Pyongyang. China hopes that both Korean governments carry out the Agreement on Reconciliation, Nonaggression and Exchanges and Cooperation and the Joint Declaration on the Denuclearization of the Korean Peninsula and that the United States, Japan, and Russia join China in adopting and practicing a genuine two-Korea policy. To hasten the goal of inter-Korean reconciliation, the Chinese suggest that South Korea needs to recognize the difficulties faced by the post–Kim Il Sung leadership in North Korea and offer generous concessions and material benefits to North Korea.[4]

The long-range future of China's relations with the Korean Peninsula will depend on the leadership structure in the post-Deng era. If his successors inherit an irreversible commitment to China's four modernizations policy and maintain political stability amid resounding economic and social changes, they will prefer cooperation and accommodation over revolution and violence as the means of settling global and regional disputes and will uphold a moderate and realistic approach to Korea, at least through the turn of the century.

As they have so successfully done in the past decade, the Chinese will continue to adapt their policy to the changing balance between North and South Korea. If the two Korean governments can quell mutual tensions and honor the letter and spirit of their 1991 accords, China's two-Korea policy will stimulate inter-Korean cooperation. If, however, no significant breakthrough is achieved in the inter-Korean situation, it will be in China's best interest to counsel Seoul and Pyongyang to exercise self-restraint and moderation. China enjoys a normal diplomatic and political relationship with both Korean parties and provides vital support to North Korea. Thus, it is in a good position to exercise a constructive influence over the direction and substance of inter-Korean relations. Yet China cannot afford to patronize or reinstitute the hierarchical relations of the Middle Kingdom; both North and South Korea would resent any foreign power's overt condescension or dictation. The Chinese are well advised to manage their delicate policy toward Pyongyang with care because North Korean leaders in the post–Kim Il Sung era are increasingly suspicious of China's "socialist solidarity" and "militant friendship."[5] North Korea will attempt to utilize its new relations with the United States as a counterweight to China's growing linkage with South Korea. The South Koreans are not entirely assured of the long-term viability of China's current two-Korea policy.

At the present time, China shares a common interest with the United States, Japan, and Russia in making sure that the Korean Peninsula does not succumb to another wave of fratricidal struggles or big-power confrontations. If, however, this concert of major powers is disrupted in Korea, there will be a serious spillover effect upon China's two-Korea policy. Because the United States, the only surviving superpower, remains the most powerful presence in the Asian-Pacific region, China's changing relationship with it, rather than Japan or Russia, will determine the regional strategic setting for Korean affairs during the next few years. If the United States normalizes diplomatic and economic relations with North Korea, its relative status in the peninsula will loom larger than ever before. Hence it will be increasingly important to the peace and stability of the Korean Peninsula that China and the United States, combatants during the 1950–1953 period, closely coordinate their respective policies toward both Koreas and make a concerted effort to settle the Korean question in a rational and constructive fashion. If China has a hostile relationship with the United States, however, it is bound to have an adverse effect on the Korean situation.

Needless to say, it is ultimately incumbent on the leaders of both Koreas to learn from the tragic history of international victimization of Korea and to shape their own destinies toward each other and toward China and other major powers. The most desirable ways for both North and South Korea to bring about a bright future for the Korean people are to engage in bona fide dialogue and cooperation and to establish a viable system of checks and balances among the four major powers concerned with Korea. In view of the asymmetry of national interests and historical experiences of these powers in regard to Korea and the changing nature of policy priorities that they demonstrate toward their Korean partners, both North and South Korea should be able to use the competing external forces to build a mutually beneficial relationship that would eventually culminate in peaceful national reintegration. In this context China, along with the United States, seems to have both the intention and the capacity to provide a stable and supportive external environment for the Korean Peninsula.

NOTES

• •

CHAPTER ONE

1. For China's tributary system, see John K. Fairbank, ed., *The Chinese World Order* (Cambridge: Harvard University Press, 1968), pp.1–19.
2. See Chun Hae-jong, *Hanchung kwankye yongu* (A study of Korean-Chinese relations) (Seoul: Ilchokak, 1970), and Hae-jong Chun, "Sino-Korean Tributary Relations," in Fairbank, *Chinese World Order*, pp. 90–111.
3. See John K. Fairbank and Ssu-yu Teng, *Ch'ing Administration: Three Studies* (Cambridge: Harvard University Press, 1960), p. 113.
4. Carter J. Eckert, Ki-baik Lee, Young Ick Lew, Michael Robinson, and Edward W. Wagner, *Korea Old and New: A History* (Seoul: Ilchokak, 1990), p. 92.
5. O. N. Denny, *China and Korea* (Shanghai: Kelly and Walsh, 1888), p. 42.
6. For the text of the treaty, see *The Diplomacy of Japan 1894–1922*, vol. 1 (Tokyo: Kajima Institute of International Peace, 1976), pp. 262–69.
7. See Ki-baik Lee, *A New History of Korea*, trans. Edward W. Wagner and Edward W. Schultz (Seoul: Ilchokak, 1984), pp. 306–11.
8. For Syngman Rhee's relationship with the Korean Provisional Government, see Chong-Sik Lee, *The Politics of Korean Nationalism* (Berkeley: University of California Press, 1963), pp. 129–79; for Kim Il Sung's activities in the Northeast Anti-Japanese United Army, see Dae-Sook Suh, *Kim Il Sung: The North Korean Leader* (New York: Columbia University Press, 1988), pp. 11–29.
9. For a succinct overview of China's foreign policy, see Xie Yixian, "China's Foreign Policy," *Beijing Review*, February 13–26, 1989, pp. 12–17.

CHAPTER TWO

1. For an excellent study of Sino–Soviet relations, see Sergei N. Goncharov, John W. Lewis, and Xue Litai, *Uncertain Partners: Stalin, Mao, and the Korean War* (Stanford: Stanford University Press, 1993).

2. For a discussion of the domestic causes of Kim's action, see Dae-Sook Suh, *Kim Il Sung: The North Korean Leader* (New York: Columbia University Press, 1988), pp.111–23.

3. Allen Whiting, *China Crosses the Yalu: The Decision to Enter the Korea War* (Stanford: Stanford University Press, 1960), p.45. See Pu Shan's recollections in Warren I. Cohen, "Conversations with Chinese Friends: Zhou Enlai's Associates Reflect on Chinese-American Relations in the 1940s and the Korean War," *Diplomatic History*, summer 1987, p.288. Hao Yufan and Zhai Zhihai, "China's Decision to Enter the Korean War: History Revisited," *China Quarterly*, March 1990, p.99.

4. See Marshall Shulman, *Stalin's Foreign Policy Reappraised* (Cambridge: Harvard University Press, 1963), p.141. Adam Ulam, *The Communists: The Story of Power and Lost Illusions, 1948–1991* (New York: Charles Scribner's Sons, 1992), pp.81–82.

5. Kathryn Weathersby, *Soviet Aims in Korea and the Origins of the Korean War, 1945–1950: New Evidence from Russian Archives* (Washington, D.C.: Woodrow Wilson International Center for Scholars, 1993).

6. For a thesis that Chinese influence in North Korea was superior to that of the Soviet Union, see Bruce Cumings, *The Origins of the Korean War: The Roaring of the Cataract, 1947–1950*, vol. 2 (Princeton: Princeton University Press, 1990), pp. 350–76. For the Korean summaries of the declassified Russian diplomatic documents concerning the Korean War, see *Hangukchon munso yoyak* (The summary of documents concerning the Korean War) (Seoul: Ministry of Foreign Affairs, 1994) (hereafter cited as *Hangukchon*) and *Hangukchon pochung munhon* (The supplementary documents concerning the Korean War) (Seoul: Ministry of Foreign Affairs, 1994). The Mao–Kim Il meeting probably was designed to confirm other agreements that Kim Il Sung had concluded with the CCP in regard to their military cooperation. See Cumings, *The Origins of the Korean War: Roaring of the Cataract*, p.359, and Hiramatsu Shigeo, *Chugoku to Chosen senso* (China and the Korean War) (Tokyo: Keiso shobo, 1988), pp.34–44.

   The 166th Division, commanded by Pang Ho San (who had attended the Whampoa Military Academy), became the Sixth Division of the Korean People's Army; the 164th Division, commanded by Kim Chang Dok, became the Fifth Division. See Cumings, *Origins of the Korean War: Roaring of the Cataract*, p. 363, Hiramatsu, *Chugoku to Chosen senso*, pp.36–37, and Doo-Bok Park, *Zhonggong canjia hanzhan yuanyinzhi* yanjiu (A study on the causes of communist China's participation in the Korean War) (Taipei: Liming wenhuashiye gufen youxiangongsi, 1975), pp. 65–67.

7. For Shi Zhe's recollection, see Goncharov, Lewis, and Xue, *Uncertain Partners*, pp.325, 130. The quotation is not included in Shi's published memoir. For an interview with Shi, see Chen Jian, *China's Road to the Korean War* (New York: Columbia University Press, 1994), pp. 87–88. See Nikita Khrushchev, *Khrushchev Remembers*, trans. Strobe Talbott (Boston: Little, Brown, and Co., 1970), p. 368. For a critical review of *Khrushchev Remembers*, see John Merrill, *Korea: The Peninsular Origins of the War* (Newark: University of Delaware Press, 1989), pp. 21–29.

8. See *Hangukchon*, p. 19. Nie Rongzhen, *Nie Rongzhen huiyilu* (Memoirs of Nie Rongzhen) (Beijing: Jiefangjun chubanshe, 1984), p.744. The returnees from China (commanded by Chun Wu) constituted the KPA's Seventh Division. See Cumings, *Origins of the Korean War: Roaring of the Cataract*, p. 363, and Hiramatsu, *Chugoku to Chosen senso*, p. 37. Nie refers to 14,000 Korean soldiers, but Chen Jian mentions 23,000 soldiers in *China's Road to the Korean War*, p. 255.

9. The text of Stalin's telegram is translated in *Cold War International History Project Bulletin*, fall 1994, p. 61. For the meetings between Mao and Kim and Stalin's response, see *Hangukchon*, pp. 25–27.

10. See Chen, *China's Road to the Korean War*, p.112. At this time Kim apparently did not think much of Mao and disliked those North Korean leaders who praised him. Interview with Yoo Song Chul (who served as director of military operations, Korean People's Army, in 1950), March 30, 1992.

11. See Goncharov, Lewis, and Xue, *Uncertain Partners*, pp. 146–47. Although Khrushchev remembers that Mao did not believe that the United States would intervene in Korea, the Russian diplomatic documents indicate that Mao warned Kim Il Sung in May 1950 about a possible U.S. intervention in Korea. See *Hangukchon*, p. 27.

12. See Harry S. Truman, *Memoirs: Year of Trial and Hope* (Garden City, N.Y.: Doubleday, 1956), pp. 334–37, and Dean Acheson, *Present at the Creation: My Years in the State Department* (New York: W. W. Norton and Co., 1969), pp. 524–28.

13. As quoted inGoncharov, Lewis, and Xue, *Uncertain Partners*, pp. 270–71. For the Chinese text, see Mao Zedong, *Jianguo yilai Mao Zedong wengao* (Mao Zedong's manuscripts after the founding of the republic), vol. 1 (Beijing: Zhongyang wenxian chubanshe, 1987), p. 423 (hereafter cited as *Mao Zedong wengao*).

14. See Chai Chengwen and Zhao Yongtian, *Banmendian tanpan* (Panmunjom Negotiations) (Beijing: Jiefangjun chubanshe, 1989), pp. 35–41. Born in 1915, Chai joined the Eighth Route Army in 1937 and served as director of the Intelligence Agency of the Second Field Army.

15. *Hangukchon*, pp. 31–32, 33.

16. For Mao's views, instructions, and decisions concerning the Korean War, I

relied heavily upon Jian Chen, "China's Changing Aims during the Korean War, 1950–1951," *Journal of American–East Asian Relations*, spring 1992, pp. 8–41; Hao and Zhai, "China's Decision to Enter the Korean War," pp. 94–115; Goncharov, Lewis, and Xue, *Uncertain Partners*; Chen, *China's Road to the Korean War*; and Yao Xu, "Kangmei yuanchaode yingming juece" (Wise decisions for the Resist–America and Aid-Korea war), *Dangshi Yanjiu* (Research on party history), October 28, 1980, pp. 5–14.

The Zhou message was transmitted to Secretary of State Acheson on July 28, 1950. See "Korea," in U.S Department of State, *Foreign Relations of the United States* (herafter cited as *FRUS*) 7 (1950): 488–89. For Panikkar's role in China, see K. M. Panikkar, *In Two Chinas: Memoirs of a Diplomat* (London: George Allen and Unwin Ltd, 1955).

17. As quoted in Chen, *China's Road to the Korean War*, p. 143.
18. As quoted in Goncharov, Lewis, and Xue, *Uncertain Partners*, p. 271.
19. Ibid., p. 272. For the Chinese text, see Mao, *Mao Zedong wengao*, vol. 1, p. 469. See *Hangukchon*, p. 40. On Mao's request, Stalin sent Yudin to China to assist in the compilation of Mao's writings. See Chai and Zhao, *Banmendian tanpan*, p. 67, Hao and Zhai, "China's Decision to Enter the Korean War," p. 101, and Chen, *China's Road to the Korean War*, pp. 147–49. For an example of Mao's advice, see Lim Un, *The Founding of a Dynasty in North Korea* (Tokyo: Jiyusha, 1982), pp. 187–88.
20. Chen, *China's Road to the Korean War*, pp. 150–51. *Hangukchon*, p. 42.
21. See *FRUS* (1950): 742, 793–94.
22. Ibid., p. 852. For the Chinese text, see Zhou Enlai, *Zhou Enlai waijiao wenxuan* (Zhou Enlai's writings on diplomatic issues) (Beijing: Zhongyang wenxuan chubanshe, 1990), pp. 20–24. For example, the warning was reported in the *New York Herald Tribune*, October 1, 1950, and the *New York Times*, October 2, 1950.
23. See the full Korean text of Kim's and Pak's special appeal in *Hanguk Ilbo*, July 21, 1994. *Hangukchon*, p. 55.
24. For the Chinese text of Kim's and Pak's message, see Ye Yumeng, *Chubing chaoxian* (Sending the army to Korea) (Beijing: Shiyue wenyi chubanshe, 1990), pp. 39–40. The contents of this message are almost identical with those of their message to Stalin. Pak Hon Yong, accompanied by Yoo Song Chul, flew to Beijing on October 1 to deliver the message to Mao in person. See Chen, *China's Road to the Korean War*, p. 172; interview with Yoo, March 30, 1992.
25. See Goncharov, Lewis, and Xue, *Uncertain Partners*, pp. 179–83. For an excellent summary of the debates, see Hao and Zhai, "China's Decision to Enter the Korean War," pp. 104–8. Also see Peng Dehuai, *Memoirs of a Chinese General* (Beijing: Foreign Languages Press, 1984), pp. 472–74, and Nie, *Nie Rongzhen huiyilu*, pp. 735–37.
26. As quoted in Goncharov, Lewis, and Xue, *Uncertain Partners*, p. 177.
27. See *FRUS* (1950):839, and Panikkar, *In Two Chinas*, pp. 109–11. The government in Washington immediately sent Zhou's warning to General

MacArthur. See Roy E. Appleman, *South to the Naktong, North to the Yalu: United States Army in the Korean War* (Washington, D.C.: U.S. Government Printing Office, 1961), p. 759. For the Chinese text of Zhou's meeting with Panikkar, see Zhou, *Zhou Enlai waijiao wenxuan*, pp. 25–27. See Acheson, *Present at the Creation*, p. 586. See Thomas J. Christensen, "Threats, Assurances, and the Last Chance for Peace: The Lessons of Mao's Korean War Telegrams," *International Security*, summer 1992, pp. 122–54.

28. Goncharov, Lewis, and Xue,*Uncertain Partners*, pp. 278–79. The text of Mao's message to Kim is on p. 279. Also see Chai and Zhao, *Banmendian tanpan*, pp. 84–85. For Stalin–Zhou meetings, see Goncharov, Lewis, and Xue, *Uncertain Partners*, pp. 188–96, and Shi Zhe, *Zailishi jurenshenbian* (With the great people in history) (Beijing: Zhongyang wenxian chubanshe, 1991), pp. 495–503.
29. *FRUS* (1950): 914.
30. See Goncharov, Lewis, and Xue, *Uncertain Partners*, p. 281.
31. As quoted in ibid., p. 194. For a detailed discussion of this telegram, see Chen, *China's Road to the Korean War*, pp. 202–3.
32. See ibid., p. 204, and Goncharov, Lewis, and Xue, *Uncertain Partners*, pp. 195, 290, and Chen, *China's Road to the Korean War*, p. 208.
33. *Hangukchon*, pp. 57–58.
34. For a similar argument, see Jian Chen, "China's Changing Aims," pp.40–41. See Ki-baik Lee, *New History of Korea*, pp. 209–13.
35. *FRUS* (1950): 953. For MacArthur's own explanation of the Wake Island conference, see Douglas MacArthur, *Reminiscences* (New York: McGraw Hill, 1964), pp. 360–64.
36. *FRUS* (1950): 954.
37. As quoted in Appleman, *South to the Naktong*, pp. 759–60. For the CIA report dated October 12, see *FRUS* (1950): 933–34.
38. See Hong Xuezhi, *Kangmei yuanchao zhanzheng huiyi* (Recollections on the Resist-America and Aid-Korea war) (Beijing: Jiefangjun wenyi chubanshe, 1991), pp. 27–28. It remains controversial whether Lin Biao did not command the CPV because of his illness or because of his fear of the United States (as his critics claimed).
39. For a description of the Peng-Kim meeting, see Chai and Zhao, *Banmendian tanpan*, pp. 95–98.
40. See *Beijing Review*, July 16–22, 1990, p. 25.
41. For the appointments, see Mao, *Mao Zedong wengao*, vol. 1, p. 600. Among the first casualties at the CPV headquarters was one of Mao Zedong's sons—Mao Anying, who was killed by the U.S. bombing attack on November 25, 1950. Educated in Russia, he had served as an assistant to Peng Dehuai. Mao Zedong decided not to bring his son's body to China but to bury him in Korea. The monument for Mao Anying was erected at Hoechang, North Korea. See Hong, *Kangmei*, pp. 79–80.
42. Jian Chen, "China's Changing Aims," p. 24. Hong, *Kangmei*, p. 40. For Mao's order dated October 21, 1950, see Mao Zedong, *Mao Zedong*

junshi wenxuan (Selected military writings of Mao Zedong) (Beijing: Zhongguo renmin jiefangjun zhanshi chubanshe, 1981), p. 653.

43. See Hong, *Kangmei*, pp. 51–52, and *Zhongguo renmin zhiyuanjun kangmei yuanchao zhanshi* (History of the Resist-America and Aid-Korea war by the Chinese People's Volunteers) (Beijing: Zhongyang wenxuan chubanshe, 1990), p. 26.

44. Appleman, *South to the Naktong,* p.673. For the South Korean encounter with the CPV, see Chung Il Kwon, *Chonjaeng kwa hyuchon* (War and armistice) (Seoul: Donga ilbosa, 1986), pp. 205–42.

45. Hong, *Kangmei*, pp. 58, 54–55. See *Zhongguo*, pp.29–30.

46. Mao, *Mao Zedong wengao*, vol. 1, pp. 632, 658. For Mao's telegram to Peng on November 2, see Hong, *Kangmei*, p. 57.

47. As quoted in Appleman, *South to the Naktong,* pp. 762, 755.

48. Ibid., pp. 762–63.

49. Ibid., p. 765.

50. *FRUS* (1950): 1175. Mao, *Mao Zedong wengao,* vol. 1, p. 672. See *Hangukchon pochung munhon*, p. 3.

51. See *Zhongguo*, p.46. *FRUS* (1950): 1237.

52. Ibid., pp. 1320–22, 1253–54.

53. Ibid., pp. 1625, 1323–34, 1279, 1625–26.

54. Acheson, *Present at the Creation*, p. 579.

55. As explained in Alexander L. George, *The Chinese Communist Army in Action: The Korean War and Its Aftermath* (New York: Columbia University Press, 1967), p. 3.

56. For a description of the Mao-Kim meeting, see Ye, *Chubing chaoxian*, pp. 233–38. See Hong, *Kangmei*, p. 76. Kim Ung attended the Whampoa Military Academy and served with the Chinese Eighth Route Army. Appleman, *South to the Naktong* (p. 394), describes him as "a spectacular soldier," "energetic and harsh," and "the ablest" of the North Korean field commanders. Interview with former CPV officer, December 1993.

57. See *Hangukchon*, p. 60. Ye, *Chubing chaoxian,* p. 236.

58. For the full text, see *FRUS* (1950): 1249.

59. Ibid., pp. 1288–90. Austin's astute view was in sharp contrast with Truman's and Acheson's view that China was a complete satellite of the Soviet Union.

60. *FRUS* (1950): 1378–79.

61. For the text of the thirteen-power resolution, see *FRUS* (1950): 1524. The Cease-Fire Group included Nasrollah Entezam of Iran (president of the U.N. General Assembly), Lester B. Pearson of Canada, and Sir Benegal Rau of India. Ibid., pp. 1546–48.

62. For the full text of Zhou's statement, see *FRUS* (1950): 1594–98.

63. See Hong, *Kangmei,* pp. 97–98, and Chen, "China's Changing Aims," pp. 26–27.

64. Hong, *Kangmei*, p. 98. For the text of Mao's telegram, see Mao, *Mao Zedong wengao*, vol. 1, pp. 722–23, and *Zhongguo*, pp.77, 78.

65. For the text of Mao's instruction, see Mao, *Mao Zedong wengao*, vol. 1,

pp. 741–42, and Hong, *Kangmei,* pp. 104–5.

66. Ibid., p. 104. See "China and Korea," part 1, *FRUS* (1951): 50.
67. For Kim Il Sung's anger, see Chen, *China's Road to the Korean War,* p. 212; for the Russian ambassador's complaint, see Hong, *Kangmei,* p. 110, and Yao Xu, "Peng Dehuai dui kangmei yuanchao zhanzheng zhihuishangde gongxian" (Peng Dehuai's contributions in leading the Resist-America and Aid-Korea war), *Dangshi Yanjiu Ziliao* (Documents concerning research on party history), January 20, 1982, pp. 2–12. See Pu Shan's statement in Cohen, "Conversations with Chinese Friends," p.289. Li Shenzhi remembers that the pressure came from North Korea. See Mao's instructions to the CPV on January 19, 1951, in Mao Zedong, *Mao Zedong xuanji* (Selected writings of Mao Zedong), vol. 5, p. 33.
68. See *FRUS,* pt. 1 (1951): 91–93. Zhou proposed that the seven-member conference include China, the United States, the Soviet Union, Britain, France, India, and Egypt. The resolution adopted by the UNGA on February 1 by a vote of forty-four to seven, with nine abstentions, found that the PRC "has itself engaged in aggression in Korea," called upon China "to cease hostilities against the United Nations forces and to withdraw from Korea," and affirmed the determination of the United Nations to continue its action in Korea to meet the aggression. For the text, see ibid., pp. 150–51.
69. *Kangmei yuanchao zhanzheng* (The Resist-America and Aid-Korea war) (Beijing: Zhongguo shehui kexue chubanshe, 1990), pp. 92–93, 100. Hong, *Kangmei,* pp. 117–19. See Chen, "China's Changing Aims," pp. 31–33, 23.
70. Du Ping, *Zai zhiyuanjun zongbu* (At the headquarters of the volunteer army) (Beijing: Jiefangjun chubanshe, 1989), pp. 200–202. Hong, *Kangmei,* pp. 133–34. See *Hangukchon pochung munhon,* p. 4. For the Soviet Union's air support for the CPV, see Anthony Farrar-Hockley, "A Reminiscence of the Chinese People's Volunteers in the Korean War," *China Quarterly,* June 1984, pp. 300–302.
71. Ibid., p.135. Chen, "China's Changing Aims," pp.34–35. For Mao's report, see *Mao Zedong wengao.* vol. 2, pp. 151–53. *Hangukchon,* p. 61.
72. See *FRUS* (1951): 193. For the JCS's assessment and decisions at this time, see *FRUS,* pt. 1 (1951): 174–77.
73. Ibid., pp. 265–66, 267. For the message issued by the JCS, see Truman, *Memoirs,* p. 443. Acheson, *Present at the Creation,* pp. 668–69.
74. For the text of MacArthur's letter written to Congressman Joseph W. Martin Jr. on March 20, see *FRUS ,* pt. 1 (1951): 299. In his speech at the House of Representatives on April 5, 1951, Congressman Martin disclosed the contents of MacArthur's letter. For President Truman's announcement, see *Public Papers of the Presidents of the United States: Harry S. Truman, 1951* (Washington, D.C.: U.S. Government Printing Office, 1965), p. 223. For Panikkar's report and assessment, see *FRUS,* pt. 1 (1951): 369–70.
75. For Mao's decision, see Nie, *Nie Rongzhen,* p. 741, and Hong, *Kangmei,*

pp. 135–36. *FRUS*, pt. 1 (1951): 379. For a vivid report, see Clay Blair, *The Forgotten War: America in Korea, 1950–1953* (New York: Times Books, 1987), pp. 822–23.

76. Ibid., p. 819. *FRUS*, pt. 1 (1951): 386–87, 394–98.
77. Hong, *Kangmei*, pp. 158–59. Nie, *Nie Rongzhen*, p. 741. *Zhongguo*, p. 158.
78 Blair, *Forgotten War*, p. 900. For the Chinese statistics about casualties, see *Zhongguo*, p. 152.
79. Mao, *Mao Zedong wengao*, vol. 2, pp. 331–32, 338. For the limits of Mao's "man-over-weapons" doctrine in Korea, see George, *Chinese Army in Action*. The Soviet Union agreed to deliver to China enough military equipment for sixteen divisions by the end of 1951 and to supply one-third of the remaining equipment each year thereafter.
80. See *FRUS*, pt.1 (1951): 439–42.
81. For the text of the U.N. resolution, see *FRUS*, pt. 2 (1951): 1988–89. See Acheson, *Present at the Creation*, pp. 684–86. For Kennan's reports, see *FRUS*, pt.1 (1951): 460–62, 483–86, 507–11, 493–94.
82. For reports on the Mao-Kim meeting, see Chai and Zhao, *Banmendian tanpan*, p. 123, and Shi, *Zailishi*, p. 506. Also see Mao, *Mao Zedong wengao*, vol. 2, pp. 350–51 and 355–56. *FRUS*, pt.1 (1951): 545.
83. *FRUS*, pt.1 (1951): 546–47.
84. Ibid.
85. Ibid., pp. 586–87.
86. See *Hangukchon*, p. 62. The Kim-Peng message was drafted in Beijing. As alternatives to the Danish ship, the United States had already considered Yodo, an UNC–controlled island near Wonsan, and Kaesong.
87. See Mao, *Mao Zedong wengao* , vol. 2, pp. 379–86.
88. Born in Russia and educated at Smolensk Military School, Nam Il served as captain in the Soviet Red Army during the Second World War. Li Sang Cho served as an officer of the North China Korean Volunteer Army until 1945 and was a leader of the Yanan faction in North Korea. Chang Chun San (Kim Chang Man) was a member of the Yanan faction. A Long March veteran, Deng Hua (1910–80) commanded the Thirteenth Army Corps. Xie Fang (1908–84) graduated from the Japanese Military Academy and served as an aide to Zhang Xueliang in Xian; he joined the Chinese Communist Party in 1936. He served as deputy chief of staff of the Northeast Democratic United Army and as chief of staff of the Fifteenth Army Corps and Thirteenth Army Corps. Li Kenong (1899–1962) took part in the May Fourth Movement and the Long March and assisted Zhou Enlai at the Xian negotiations with Chiang Kai-shek in 1936. Li was also deputy chief of the PLA General Staff. Qiao Guanhua (1912–83) graduated from Qinghua University and studied in Japan and Germany. He was a prominent journalist and a secretary for Zhou Enlai at Chongqing during the Sino-Japanese War. He headed the Xinhua News Agency in Hong Kong. See Rosemary Foot, *A Substitute for Victory: The Politics of Peacemaking at the Korean Armistice Talks* (Ithaca, N.Y.:

Cornell University Press, 1990), pp. 11–12.
89. *FRUS* (1950): 1175. *FRUS*, pt.1 (1951): 650, 652.
90. For the U.S. positions, see C. Turner Joy, *How Communists Negotiate* (New York: Macmillan Company, 1955), and William H. Vatcher Jr., *Panmunjom: The Story of the Korean Military Armistice Negotiations* (New York: Frederick A. Praeger, 1958). Mao, *Mao Zedong wengao*, vol. 2, p. 422.
91. *FRUS*, pt.1 (1951): 652 and 662. See Joy, *How Communists Negotiate*, pp. 12 and 27.
92. Ibid., pp. 12–13, 17. *FRUS*, pt.1 (1951): 673–74. In contrast, Chai Chengwen (a top Chinese liaison officer at Panmunjom) considered Joy a "seasoned and impressive negotiator," but felt that the U.S. interpreters— Kenneth Wu in Chinese and H.G. Underwood and R. F. Underwood in Korean—were "not very good." See Chai and Zhao, *Banmendian tanpan,* pp. 138 and 144. As quoted in Foot, *Substitute for Victory*, p. 11.
93. See Chai and Zhao, *Banmendian tanpan,* pp. 178–79, and Vatcher, *Panmunjom*, p. 54.
94. Interview, December 1993. Foot, *Substitute for Victory*, p.17.
95. See *Renmin Ribao*, August 11, 1951, and Acheson, *Present at the Creation*, p.682. *FRUS*, pt. 1 (1951): 737. *Renmin Ribao*, August 1, 1951.
96. Vatcher, *Panmunjom*, pp. 47–48.
97. Foot, *Substitute for Victory*, pp. 38, 71.
98. *FRUS*, pt. 1 (1951): 1128–30, 1133–34.
99. See Mao's telegram to Li dated November 20, 1951, in Mao, *Mao Zedong wengao*, vol. 2, p. 515. Vatcher,*Panmunjom*, pp. 85–86.
100. *FRUS*, pt. 1 (1951): 1092–93.
101. As quoted in Vatcher, *Panmunjom*, pp. 109–10.
102. Ibid., pp. 104, 107. *FRUS*, pt. 1 (1951): 1173–76.
103. For the debates about the concept of voluntary repatriation in the United States, see Foot, *Substitute for Victory*, pp. 87–92.
104. *FRUS*, pt. 1 (1951): 398. For the mistreatment and indoctrination of POWs on both sides, see Foot, *Substitute for Victory*, pp. 108–29.
105. As quoted in Vatcher, *Panmunjom*, p. 135. Chai and Zhao, *Banmendian tanpan,* p. 227. See "Korea," *FRUS* 15, pt.1 (1952–1954): 35.
106 Vatcher, *Panmunjom*, pp. 125–26, 144.
107. See Mao, *Mao Zedong wengao*, vol. 3, pp.424–25. *FRUS*, pt. 1 (1952–1954): 206–8.
108. Ibid., pp.340–41 and 394–95. Foot, *Substitute for Victory*, p. 137.
109. For Kennan's report dated July 30, 1952, see *FRUS*, pt. 1 (1952–54): 430–35, 438. In response to North Korea's request for 600,000 winter uniforms, for example, Mao agreed to give 300,000 winter uniforms to North Korea without charge. See Mao, *Mao Zedong wengao*, vol. 3, p. 520.
110. For the account of Zhou's Moscow visit, see Shi, *Zailishi*, pp. 509–14 and 516–26.
111. For Mao's instruction, see Mao, *Mao Zedong wengao*, vol. 3, pp. 544–45.

112. For Mao's assessment, see ibid., pp. 632 and 638.
113. For Acheson's speeches and activities in the United Nations, see *Present at the Creation*, pp. 891–98. The eleven members were the Soviet Union, China, the United States, Britain, France, India, Burma, Switzerland, Czechoslovakia, North Korea, and South Korea. Chai and Zhao, *Banmendian tanpan*, p. 246. See the Indian resolution as amended in *FRUS*, pt. 1 (1952–1954): 702–5. For Zhou's arguments, see ibid., p. 712, and Chai and Zhao, *Banmendian tanpan*, p. 248. *FRUS*, pt. 1 (1952–1954): 684, 699–702.
114. As discussed in Chai and Zhao, *Banmendian tanpan*, pp. 254–56.
115. This Red Cross resolution was proposed by India and was adopted in December 1952 over the objections of the Soviet and Chinese delegates. For Zhou's role in the Stalin funeral, see Ulam, *Communists*, p. 106. Zhou also visited Czechoslovakia from March 17 to 20. See *Hangukchon*, p. 64. For Malenkov's "peace offensive," see Gordon Chang, *Friends and Enemies: The United States, China, and the Soviet Union, 1948–1972* (Stanford: Stanford University Press, 1990), p. 98.
116. See Mao, *Mao Zedong wengao*, vol. 4, pp. 148–49. As quoted in Vatcher, *Panmunjom*, pp. 180–81.
117. See the text in ibid., pp. 181–82, and Chai and Zhao, *Banmendian tanpan*, pp. 258, 259.
118. For Chinese awareness of a possible U.S. atomic attack, see *Renmin Ribao*, January 23, 1953, and Zhou Enlai's internal report dated June 5, 1953, in Zhou, *Zhou Enlai*, pp. 58–62. See Dwight D. Eisenhower, *The White House Years: Mandate for Change, 1953–1956* (Garden City, N.Y.: Doubleday, 1963), p. 181, and Chang, *Friends and Enemies*, pp. 88–89. See Foot, *Substitute for Victory*, pp. 180–83. Ulam, *Communists*, p. 106.
119. *FRUS*, pt. 1 (1952–1954): 1109–11, 1133. For the "Terms," see Vatcher, *Panmunjom*, pp. 305–12. Chai and Zhao, *Banmendian tanpan*, p. 266.
120. Ibid.
121. See *FRUS*, pt. 2 (1952–1954): 1197. For the text of General Harrison's assurance given on July 12, see ibid., p.1378. Chai and Zhao, *Banmendian tanpan*, pp. 270, 272. Foot cites fourteen thousand UNC casualties during this campaign in *Substitute for Victory*, pp. 186–87.
122. The UNC wanted the supreme commanders present for the signing of the armistice agreement at Panmunjom, but the Communists changed their mind at the last minute. On July 24 Stalin sent a telegram to Kim and instructed that Peng and a North Korean vice premier (in lieu of Kim) sign the armistice agreement. On the following day the communist side notified the UNC side that Peng and Choe Yong Kun (KPA deputy commander) would sign the armistice agreement. A dispute over the presence of South Korean and Taiwanese reporters at Panmunjom, however, changed the signing procedure. Choe Yong Kun accompanied Peng from Pyongyang to Kaesong. See *Hangukchon*, p. 64, and *FRUS*, pt. 2 (1952–1954): 1439. In the Chinese text of the agreement Harrison transliterated his name as "Hailisheng" (victory on the sea) rather than

"Helisun." See Chai and Zhao, *Banmendian tanpan*, p. 281. For the statistics, see Foot, *Substitute for Victory*, pp. 190–191, and David Rees, *Korea: The Limited War* (New York: St. Martin's Press, 1964), p. 436.

123. For Zhou's reaction and Dulles's assessment, see *FRUS*, pt. 2 (1952–1954): 1725, 1730.

124. See Mao's speech on September 12, 1953, in Mao, *Mao Zedong xuanji*, pp.101–6. Joy, *How Communists Negotiate*, p. 178. Philip West, "Confronting the West," *Journal of American–East Asian Relations*, spring 1993, pp. 5–28.

125. Philip West, "The Korean War and the Criteria of Significance in Chinese Popular Culture," *Journal of American–East Asian Relations*, winter 1992, pp. 383–408. Nie, *Nie Rongzhen*, p. 746.

CHAPTER THREE

1. Interview with Chinese scholars, December 1993.

2. See the text of the treaty between China and North Korea in *Documents on International Affairs 1961* (London: Oxford University Press, 1965), pp. 258–59. For the comparison of the treaties, see Byung Chul Koh, *The Foreign Policy of North Korea* (New York: Praeger, 1969), pp. 61–63.

3. See the text of the joint statement in *Peking Review*, June 28, 1963, pp. 8–12.

4. See the text of his speech in *Peking Review*, September 27, 1963, p. 9.

5. *Peking Review*, October 23, 1964, pp. 7–8.

6. For Mao's and Zhou's meetings with Choe Yong Kun, see *Renmin Ribao*, October 1–4, 1969.

7. For Chinese positions on the *Pueblo* and the EC–121 cases, see *Peking Review*, February 2, 1968, p.7, and May 1, 1969, pp. 48–49.

8. For the Nixon-Sato joint communiqué, see Chae–Jin Lee and Hideo Sato, *U.S. Policy toward Japan and Korea*, p. 40.

9. *Peking Review*, December 5, 1969, pp. 10–12. *Renmin Ribao* editorial, November 28, 1969.

10. For the text of Zhou's speech, see *Peking Review*, April 10, 1970, pp. 13–14.

11. See the joint communiqué in *Peking Review*, April 10, 1970, pp. 3–5.

12. Interview with Chinese scholars, December 1993. General O Chin U (chief of the General Staff of the Korean People's Army) visited China in July–August 1970. See *Peking Review*, July 31, 1970, pp. 16–19.

13. The Chinese delegation visited Pyongyang to celebrate the tenth anniversary of the Sino–North Korean security treaty. See *Peking Review*, July 16, 1971, pp. 8–11. See the joint message in *Peking Review*, July 16, 1971, p. 4.

14. See the Shanghai communiqué in the Department of State, *U.S. Policy*

toward China, Selected documents no. 9 (Washington, D.C.: U.S. Government Printing Office n.d.), pp. 6–8. Henry A. Kissinger, *White House Years* (Boston: Little, Brown, 1979), pp. 1061–89.

15. For inter-Korean negotiations, see Chae-Jin Lee, "The Development of Sino-Japanese Competition over Korea," in Y. C. Kim, ed., *Foreign Policies of Korea* (Wasington, D.C.: Institute for Asian Studies, 1973), pp. 37–53.

16. *Korea Herald,* October 18, 1972.

17. For North Korea's constitutional change, see Chong-Sik Lee, "The 1972 Constitution and Top Communist Leaders," in Dae-Sook Suh and Chae-Jin Lee, eds., *Political Leadership in Korea* (Seattle: University of Washington Press, 1976), pp. 192–219.

18. *Renmin Ribao* editorial, July 9, 1972.

19. For information on Kim's proposal, see Parris H. Chang, "Beijing's Policy toward Korea and PRC-ROK Normalization of Relations," in *The Changing Order in Northeast Asia and the Korean Peninsula* (Seoul: Institute for Far Eastern Studies, 1993), p. 163. See the joint communiqué signed by Kim Il Sung and Deng Xiaoping in *Peking Review,* May 2, 1975, pp. 8–11.

20. For Hua's activities and speeches in China, see *Peking Review,* May 12, 1978, pp. 6–8.

21. See Kim Il Sung's remarks in *Tokyo Shimbun,* September 15, 1980. See the text of the joint message in *Renmin Ribao,* July 11, 1981, which also carried Kim Il Sung's message.

22. The visit was publicly acknowledged by Hu Yaobang for the first time in September 1982, when he spoke at the banquet welcoming Kim Il Sung's state visit to China. See *Renmin Ribao,* September 17, 1982. A forty-minute special program on Deng's and Hu's visit to North Korea was shown on Chinese television; it highlighted their meetings with Kim Il Sung and Kim Jong Il. Hu made this characterization in his banquet speech at Pyongyang. See *Renmin Ribao,* May 5, 1984. Wang's interview was reported in *Asahi Shimbun,* October 8, 1982.

23. *Renmin Ribao,* June 20 and 22, 1982. *Asahi Shimbun,* October 12, 1982.

24. See the text of Hu's speech in *Renmin Ribao,* September 25, 1982, or *Pyongyang Times,* September 29, 1982.

25. See Kim's Chengdu speech in *Pyongyang Times,* September 25, 1982, or in *The Great Leader Comrade Kim Il Sung's Official State Visit to the People's Republic of China* (Pyongyang: Foreign Languages Publishing House, 1982), p. 13.

26. For this important information, see *Hachijunendai no nitchu kankei* (Japan-China relations during the 1980s)(Tokyo), November 1982, p. 14. It was further reported that, during their secret meeting at Dalian in August 1983, Deng Xiaoping and Kim Il Sung discussed possible Chinese assistance for North Korea's nuclear program. See ibid., December 1983, p. 14.

27. This information is given in Hu's speech, *Renmin Ribao,* May 5, 1984.

Hu Qili, born in Shanxi Province in 1929, was active in China's youth movements. He was Beijing University branch secretary of the China New Democratic Youth League, chairman of the All-China Students Federation, vice chairman of the Communist Youth League, and chairman of the All-China Youth Federation. He also served as vice president of Qinghua University and mayor of Tianjin. He was a regular member of the CCP Central Committee.

For the Deng-Kim meeting in Dalian, see *Nihon Keizai Shimbun,* October 7, 1983.

28. See Hu's speeches in North Korea in *Renmin Ribao,* May 5, 7, and 11, 1984. For Hu's North Korea visit, see *Great Lasting Friendship: Comrade Hu Yaobang's Visit to the DPRK* (Pyongyang: Foreign Languages Publishing House, 1984).

29. *Beijing Review,* November 3, 1980, p. 8. *Renmin Ribao,* October 25, 1980.

30. *Renmin Ribao,* July 29, 1983. In May 1984, Xu Xin accompanied Hu Yaobang to North Korea. Hong was accompanied by another Korean War veteran—Fu Chongbi, first deputy commander of the Beijing Military Region. See *Renmin Ribao,* July 27, 1983. The decision was to extend the tower's height from 20 to 30 meters and to enlarge its area from 20,000 to 50,000 square meters; this project was to be completed by October 25, 1984. See *Renmin Ribao,* December 2, 1983, and April 2, 1984.

31. *Chugoku Nenkan* (China yearbook)(Tokyo: Ishisaki shoten, 1955), p. 130. See *Peng Dehuai* (Peng Dehuai) (Hong Kong: Zilian chubanshe, 1969), p. 130, and Hong Xuezhi's memoir, *Kangmei yuanchao zhanzheng huiyi* (Recollections on the Resist-America and Aid-Korea war) (Beijing: Jiefangjun wenyi chubanshe, 1991).

32. The information is compiled from Tan Zheng, *Zhongguo renmin zhiyuanjun renwulu* (Biographical directory of the Chinese People's Volunteers) (Beijing: Zhonggong dangshi chubanshe, 1992).

33. For samples of such personal reminiscences, see *Renmin Ribao,* December 20, 1981; September 24, December 8, 1982; October 10, November 23, 1983.

34. See the text of Kim's message in *Pyongyang Times,* January 15, 1983. See *Renmin Ribao,* November 10, 1994. Michael D. Swaine, *The Military and Political Succession in China* (Santa Monica, Calif.: RAND, 1992), p. 203.

35. Especially in the aftermath of President Park's assassination, the Chinese often spoke of the "power vacuum" and "political uncertainty" in South Korea. See *Beijing Review,* November 9, 1979, pp. 14–15 and December 21, 1979, p. 24. In the summer of 1980, Chinese ambassador Cai Zemin asked the United States to stabilize the South Korean domestic situation. See Lee, "China's Policy toward South Korea."

36. For example, see Hu Yaobang's assurances given to Prime Minister Nakasone in *Nihon Keizai Shimbun,* November 25, 1983. *Tokyo Shimbun,* May 4, 1981, November 26, 1983. *Beijing Review,* April 2,

1984, p. 11; May 7, 1984, p. 8. In his interview with a *Nodong Shimbun* delegation, Hu Yaobang emphasized that the only correct policy for Korea was to seek a "peaceful reunification in a confederation." He made it clear that "should any country invade the northern part of Korea, we will, as we have stated, go all out to help you defeat the invaders." See *Beijing Review*, April 9, 1984, p. 9. See the UPI report from Beijing as quoted in *Korea Herald*, June 6, 1987.

37. *Asahi Shimbun*, May 2, 1984. *Pyongyang Times*, May 11, November 26, 1983.

38. Interview with a senior American diplomat, July 25, 1984, Beijing.

39. *Sankei Shimbun*, October 23, 1986. *Asahi Shimbun*, November 20, 1986.

40. Interview with Chon Myong Su, August 4, 1981, Beijing.

41. Henry Kissinger, *White House Years* (Boston: Little, Brown, 1979), p. 1090.

42. Premier Zhao Ziyang and Defense Minister Geng Biao referred to "complete withdrawal" in their speeches in North Korea. See *Renmin Ribao*, December 24, 1981 and June 16, 1982. As to the Chinese usage of "immediate withdrawal," see *Renmin Ribao* editorial, September 16, 1982, which welcomed Kim Il Sung's visit to China.

43. See An Ding's commentary in *Beijing Review*, March 17, 1980, pp. 12–13. Italics added.

44. *Beijing Review*, May 7, 1984, p. 8; May 14, 1984, p. 17–18. See Hu's press interview following his North Korean trip in *Beijing Review*, May 21, 1984, pp. 20–22.

45. See the Chinese statements in *Renmin Ribao*, February 8, 1983, and February 9, 1984. See *Beijing Review*, May 18, 1981, p. 10, *Renmin Ribao*, May 4, 1981, and *Beijing Review*, January 18, 1982, p. 13.

46. This statement was reprinted in *Beijing Review* (August 22, 1983, pp. 15–16) with a large picture showing Deng Xiaoping and Kim Il Sung together at Chengdu; the picture suggests that Deng's remarks were directed to the North Korean case. For the original text, see *Deng Xiaoping Wenxuan* (Selected works of Deng Xiaoping)(Beijing: Renmin chubanshe, 1983), pp. 278–79.

47. *Renmin Ribao*, April 25 and 27, 1989.

48. See the text of the Sino-Soviet joint communiqué (May 18, 1989) in *Beijing Review*, May 29–June 4, 1989, pp. 11–13.

49. *Beijing Review*, September 17–23, 1990, pp. 12–13.

50. As reported by the Korean Central News Agency, January 26, 1991. Interview with a leader of the Korean Association of Social Scientists in June 1991.

51. For the Qin-Kim meeting, see *Renmin Ribao*, August 27, 1990. *Renmin Ribao*, October 25, 1990.

52. *Beijing Review*, November 5–11, 1990, p. 9. Other delegations included a group of CPV martyrs' families headed by General Hu Guiyou and a Chinese People's Friendship mission led by Huang Huang (CCP secretary of the Ningxia Hui Autonomous Region). For Kim Il Sung's meeting with

Li Tieying and other Chinese visitors, see *Renmin Ribao*, October 27, 1990.

53. See the text in *Renmin Ribao*, May 20, 1991, or *Beijing Review*, May 27–June 2, 1991, pp. 17–19.
54. For the contents of the Deng-Kim meeting, see *Zhengming*, November 1, 1991, p.18, and *Asahi Shimbun*, November 1, 1991.
55. *Beijing Review*, October 14–20, 1991, p. 7.
56. *Renmin Ribao*, October 18, 1991. *Sankei Shimbun*, November 17, 1991, and *Zhengming*, November 1, 1991, p. 18.
57. *Renmin Ribao*, January 2, 1992.
58. Zhang Jinfang, "Koreans Move Closer towards Reconciliation," *Beijing Review*, March 9–15, 1992, p. 16.
59. *Renmin Ribao*, April 15, 1992. According to *Renmin Ribao* (April 7, 1992), the Chinese donated 400 tons of pork to North Korea for Kim's birthday celebration, but *Nodong Sinmun* (April 5, 1992) failed to mention "pork" in its report on China's "gift" to Kim Il Sung.
60. For Yang's activities and meetings in Pyongyang, see *Renmin Ribao*, April 14–18, 1992, and *Nodong Sinmun*, April 13–18, 1992. Interview, May 1992.
61. *Dongxiang*, October 15, 1991, as quoted in *Hanguk Ilbo*, October 17, 1991.
62. *Renmin Ribao*, July 11, 1991.
63. *Renmin Ribao*, October 18, December 13, 1991; April 27, June 6, 1992.
64. *Los Angeles Times*, November 15, 1991. See the statement of James Lilley (former U.S. ambassador to China) in *Hanguk Ilbo*, August 29, 1991.
65. *China Daily*, March 13, 1992.
66. *New York Times*, March 4, 1993.
67. The verbatim record of the U.N. Security Council, May 11, 1993 (S/PV.3212), pp. 42–43. See the text of the U.N. Security Council Resolution 825 adopted on May 11, 1993, in *U.S. Department of State Dispatch*, May 24, 1993, p. 383.
68. For Qian's and Han's visits, see *Hanguk Ilbo*, May 27 and October 29, 1993, and *Renmin Ribao*, October 30, 1993. For President Kim's China visit, see *Hanguk Ilbo*, March 28–30, 1994, and *Renmin Ribao*, March 29, 1994.
69. See the text in *Korea Herald*, April 2, 1994. *New York Times*, April 5, 1994.
70. See the list in *China Daily*, June 17, 1994. For the text of Clinton's statement, made on May 26, 1994, see *U.S. Department of State Dispatch*, May 30, 1994, pp. 345–46. For Choe Kwang (Korean People's Army chief of staff), see *Renmin Ribao*, June 8 and 14, 1994. This bilateral discussion probably continued when Kim Il Sung met with Wang Ke (commander of the Shenyang Military Region) on June 28, 1994, in Pyongyang. See *Renmin Ribao*, July 1, 1994. For Foreign Minister Han's China visit, see *China Daily*, June 10, 1994, and *Hanguk Ilbo*, June 10, 1994. Interview with a high-level South Korean diplomat, September

1994. See the statement by a spokesman of the Ministry of Foreign Affairs in *Renmin Ribao*, June 16, 1994, and *Los Angeles Times*, June 13 and 29, 1994.

71. *China Daily*, October 24, 1994. The North Koreans did not closely consult with the Chinese regarding the progress of the Geneva negotiations, but the United States had a regular consultation about the progress with all permanent member-states of the U.N. Security Council. Interviews, March and April 1995.

72. *Washington Post*, November 4, 1994.

73. For the meeting between Tang and North Korean vice minister of foreign affairs Song Ho Kyong, see *Renmin Ribao*, September 2, 1994, and *New York Times*, September 3, 1994. See Foreign Minister Qian's remarks in *China Daily*, September 2, 1994. For Premier Li's news conference on November 4, 1994, see *Hanguk Ilbo*, September 5, 1994.

74. See *Hanguk Ilbo*, May 11, 1995. In February 1995 a South Korean military delegation led by Lieutenant General Cho Sung Tae (assistant minister of national defense) had visited Beijing and had met with Chinese military leaders. See *Korea Herald,* February 24, 1995.

CHAPTER FOUR

1. For the Geneva conference on Korea (April 26–June 15, 1954), see *Foreign Relations of the United States 1952–1954* (hereafter, *FRUS*). Vol. 16 (1981) *The Geneva Conference*, pp. 1–394; *The Korean Problem at the Geneva Conference*; and *Documents Relating to the Discussion of Korea and Indo-China at the Geneva Conference*.

2. Interview with Chinese scholars, December 1993.

3. For example, see the text of a boundary agreement between China and Pakistan in *Peking Review*, March 15, 1963, pp. 67–70.

4. For a succinct review of this relationship, see Dae-Sook Suh, *Kim Il Sung: The North Korean Leader* (New York: Columbia University Press, 1988), pp. 188–208.

5. As quoted in Robert A. Scalapino and Chong-Sik Lee, *Communism in Korea: The Movement* (Berkeley: University of California Press, 1972), p. 641.

6. Ibid., p. 642. For the persecution of Zhu Dehai and other Korean leaders in China, see Chae-Jin Lee, *China's Korean Minority* (Boulder, Colo.: Westview Press, 1986), pp. 88–95. See *New York Times*, November 23, 1970.

7. *Foreign Broadcast Information Service: Daily Report-Far East*, January 26, 1967.

8. See Seung-Hwan Kim, *The Soviet Union and North Korea* (Seoul: Research Center for Peace and Unification of Korea, 1988), pp. 111–12.

9. Interview, December 1993.
10. For China's earlier statements, see *Peking Review*, December 3, 1965, pp. 10–11; January 1, 1966, pp. 13–16; January 1, 1967, p. 28; December 1, 1967, pp. 33–34; and December 8, 1967, pp. 20–21.
11. For the text of Qiao's speech, see *Peking Review*, November 19, 1971, pp. 5–9.
12. See the text of Qiao's speech in *Peking Review*, October 13, 1972, pp. 4–10. For a discussion of U.N. debates on the Korean question, see Chae-Jin Lee, "The Direction of South Korea's Foreign Policy," *Korean Studies* (1978): 124–28.
13. For Huang's speech, see *Peking Review*, November 23, 1973, pp. 14–15. The "Stevenson" formula proposed to invite both South Korea and North Korea to the U.N. debates on Korea without the right to vote if North Korea "first unequivocally accepts the competence and authority of the U.N. within the terms of the Charter to take action on the Korean question, as has already been done by the Republic of Korea"; North Korea rejected this formula.
14. For China's constructive role in the United Nations, see Samuel S. Kim, *China, the United Nations, and World Order* (Princeton: Princeton University Press, 1979), pp. 135–36. See *Renmin Ribao* editorial, November 24, 1973.
15. Lee, "Direction of South Korea's Foreign Policy," pp. 27–28.
16. See the text of Qiao's speech in *Peking Review*, October 3, 1975, pp. 10–15.
17. *New York Times*, November 19, 1975.
18. For Park's image of China, see Byung Chul Koh, *The Foreign Policy Systems of North and South Korea* (Berkeley: University of California Press, 1984), pp. 100–101, and the joint communiqué Park signed with President Lyndon B. Johnson on November 2, 1966. *Korea Herald*, January 12, 1971. *Korea Herald*, August 7, 1971. See Kim Yong Shik, *Huimang kwa tojon* (Hope and challenge) (Seoul: Donga ilbosa, 1987), pp. 219–20.
19. For the text of Park's speech, see Se-Jin Kim, ed., *Korean Unification: Source Materials with an Introduction* (Seoul: Research Center for Peace and Unification, 1976), pp. 338–40.
20. For examples of Chinese statements, see *Peking Review*, June 18, 1976, p. 4; June 17, 1977, pp. 16–17; and June 30, 1978, p. 25. See *Yomiuri Shimbun*, March 30, 1980.
21. See Chae-Jin Lee, "South Korea in 1983: Crisis Management and Political Legitimacy," *Asian Survey*, January 1984, pp. 113–14. Interview, July 10, 1983, Seoul.
22. See the memorandum in *Korea Herald*, May 11, 1983. *Renmin Ribao*, May 12, 1983. See Wu's speeches and activities in North Korea in *Renmin Ribao*, May 21, 22, 24, 25, and 26, 1983.
23. For China's position on the KAL incident, see *Beijing Review*, September 12, 1983, p.12, and September 26, 1983, pp. 8–10. China, however,

abstained in the Security Council's vote on the anti-Moscow resolution. For North Korea's position, see *Pyongyang Times,* September 28, 1983. See *Tokyo Shimbun,* October 11, 1983. For example, see Premier Zhao Ziyang's discussions with Japanese prime minister Nakasone Yasuhiro and President Ronald Reagan in *Beijing Review,* April 2, 1984, p. 11 and May 7, 1984, p. 8.

24. *Asahi Shimbun,* April 14, 1984. The North Koreans also complained that an interpreter at the Chinese Ministry of Foreign Affairs used "North Korea" instead of the "DPRK" at a press conference in April 1984. *Korea Herald,* September 27, 1984.

25. See *Korea Herald,* March 27–29, 1985. See *Donga Ilbo,* March 28, 1985.

26. *Tokyo Shimbun,* October 27, 1985.

27. See *Asahi Shimbun,* January 12, 1984, and Lee, "China's Policy toward North Korea," pp. 203–4. For Tao Bingwei's assessment of North Korea's policy change, see *Mainichi Shimbun,* February 6, 1984. Tao is a Korea-educated director of the Asian and Pacific Research Department of the Institute of International Studies—a research organization under the Chinese Ministry of Foreign Affairs. He admitted that China played a role in changing North Korea's position on the tripartite talks. See *Sankei Shimbun,* June 29, 1984.

28. *Renmin Ribao,* January 12, 1984. For Chinese reports on the Zhao-Reagan meeting, see *Renmin Ribao,* January 11 and 12, 1984. For Reagan's counterproposal, see *Asahi Shimbun,* January 12, 1984. *Beijing Review,* May 7, 1984, p. 8.

29. The text was widely distributed in a press release by the North Korean Permanent Observer Mission to the United Nations in New York (special issue, April 11, 1984).

30. For the contents of both letters, see *Renmin Ribao,* December 30, 1985.

31. See *Donga Ilbo,* December 11, 22, and 25, 1987. *Mainichi Shimbun,* May 15, 1988. For the text of his speech, see Roh Tae Woo, *Korea: A Nation Transformed* (New York: Pergamon Press, 1990), pp. 3–17.

32. *Renmin Ribao,* July 4, 1988. For Yang Shangkun's visit to North Korea, see *Renmin Ribao,* September 8, 9, and 10, 1988. See the spokesman's press conference, *Renmin Ribao,* September 9, 1988.

33. See *Renmin Ribao,* April 6, 1989, or *Beijing Review,* April 17–23, 1989, p. xxii. For the Zhao-Kim meetings, see *Renmin Ribao,* April 26 and 27, 1989.

34. Ruo Yu, "Eastern Powers Thaw Lines to S. Korea," *Beijing Review,* January 9–15, 1989, pp. 15–16.

35. *Renmin Ribao,* December 6, 1988. For example, see China's evenhanded reports on the Hungary–South Korea agreements and North Korea's angry reactions in *Renmin Ribao,* October 29 and December 7, 1988. Interview, October 24 and 25, 1988, Beijing.

36. *Renmin Ribao,* March 12 and 20, 1987.

37. *Renmin Ribao,* April 27, 1989. For a report on Japan's decision, see *Renmin Ribao,* September 14, 1988. For Takeshita's visit to China, see

Renmin Ribao, August 26, 27, and 30, 1988. For Li Peng's Japan visit, see *Beijing Review*, May 1–7, 1989, pp. 10–11.

38. *Renmin Ribao*, September 9, 1988.
39. See the text in *Beijing Review*, May 29–June 4, 1989, pp. 12–13.
40. See Vasily V. Mikheev, "Soviet Policy toward the Korean Peninsula in the 1990s," *Korean Studies* 15 (1991): 31–49. *Nodong Sinmun*, April 6, 1990.
41. For negotiations, see *Los Angeles Times*, June 6, 1990. Interview with Alexander Panov (who accompanied Shevardnadze to Pyongyang in September 1990), April 1992.
42. *Minju Choson*, September 19, 1991. See *The Roh-Gorbachev Summit on Cheju* (Seoul: Korean Overseas Information Service, 1991).
43. *Nodong Sinmun*, October 5, 1990.
44. Korean Central News Agency (KCNA), February 1, 1991.
45. *Renmin Ribao*, November 13, 1989. For reports on Jiang Zemin's visit to North Korea, see *Renmin Ribao*, March 15 and 16, 1990, and *Nodong Sinmun*, March 14–18, 1990.
46. Interview with a Chinese official, July 1990, Beijing.
47. For Song Ping, Qin Jiwei, and Li Tieying's visits, see *Renmin Ribao*, October 8 and 10, August 27, and October 29, 1990.
48. For the texts of Li and Yon's banquet speeches, see *Nodong Sinmun*, May 4, 1991, and *Beijing Review*, May 20–26, 1991, pp. 8–9.
49. For the Li-Kim meeting, see *Renmin Ribao*, May 6, 1991, and *Nodong Sinmun*, May 5, 1991. The North Korean formula is different from China's formula of "one state and two systems."
50. *China Daily*, May 10, 1991.
51. See *Los Angeles Times*, October 21, 1990, and *Hanguk Ilbo*, October 21, 1990.
52. See *Hanguk Ilbo*, October 3, November 14, 1991. Interview with Lee Sang Ock, November 22, 1992, Seoul. *Chungang Ilbo*, April 14, 1992.
53. Interview with Roh Jae Won, August 22, 1992, Beijing.
54. Interview with Chinese scholars, December 1993. See Parris H. Chang, "Beijing's Policy toward Korea and PRC-ROK Normalization of Relations," in *The Changing Order in Northeast Asia and the Korean Peninsula* (Seoul: Institute for Far Eastern Studies, 1993), pp. 155–72.
55. Interviews with Chinese scholars, August 1992 and December 1993. The two events were reported on the front page of *Renmin Ribao*, April 14, 1992. On his visit to Pyongyang, Yang Shangkun was accompanied by relatively low-level Chinese officials, including Xu Xin (deputy chief of the PLA's General Staff). Interview with Chinese scholars, December 1993. For Kim Il Sung's meetings with Ding Guangen and Yang Baibing, see *Renmin Ribao*, May 28 and June 6, 1992.
56. Interview with Kim Sok Wu (director-general of the Bureau of Asian Affairs, South Korean Ministry of Foreign Affairs), November 4, 1992, Seoul.
57. For Qian-Lee meetings and the joint communiqué, see *Los Angeles Times*, August 24, 1992, *Korea Herald*, August 25, 1992, and *Renmin Ribao*,

August 25, 1992.

58. See *China Daily*, August 25, 1992, and *Hanguk Ilbo*, August 25, 1992. Interview with Kim Sok Wu. A few members of the South Korean National Assembly criticized Foreign Minister Lee Sang Ock for failing to obtain a formal apology from China for its aggression in Korea. It is interesting to note that at the time of the Seoul-Hanoi diplomatic normalization in December 1992, South Korea did not apologize for its large-scale participation in the Vietnam War.

59. See *Free China Journal*, September 1, 1992. Interview with Lee Sang Ock. Interview with Roh Jae Won. After a series of high-level discussions between Seoul and Taipei, the two sides agreed in July 1993 to exchange "the Korean Mission in Taipei" and "the Taipei Mission in Korea." Each mission is a nongovernmental agency, but its members fulfill consular responsibilities and enjoy semidiplomatic privileges.

60. For the significance of the Sino–South Korean diplomatic normalization, see Doo-Bok Park, *Hanchung sukyowa chunggukui taehanbando chongchaek* (Sino–South Korean diplomatic normalization and China's policy toward the Korean Peninsula)(1992, unpublished manuscript). Interview with Chinese scholars, December 1993.

61. For President Roh's visit to China and the text of a joint press communiqué, see *Korea Herald*, September 29 and 30 and October 1, 1992, and *Renmin Ribao*, September 29 and 30 and October 1, 1992.

62. Interview with Chinese scholars, December 1993.

63. Hu Jintao was born in Anhui Province in 1942 and graduated from Qinghua University in hydraulic engineering. He served as CCP secretary in Gansu Province and Tibet. For his activities in Dandong and Pyongyang, see *Renmin Ribao*, July 27–31, 1993.

64. See the text of Deng's message in *Renmin Ribao*, July 11, 1994. Evidently Deng was notified of Kim Il Sung's death before it was publicly announced. *China Daily*, July 11, 1994.

65. Interview, March 1995.

66. For Li's meetings with Jiang Zemin and Li Peng, see *Renmin Ribao*, September 30 and October 1, 1994. See *The People's Korea*, October 8, 1994.

67. Interview, March 1995.

68. *Beijing Review*, November 14–20, 1994, p. 4. *Hanguk Ilbo*, November 1, 1994. For China's positive assessment of the democratically elected civilian government of President Kim, see Tao Bingwei and Wu Jingjing, "Jin Yongsan jiuren hanguo zongtong yu chaoxian bandaode jushi" (The inauguration of President Kim Young Sam and the situation of the Korean Peninsula), *Guojiwenti Yanjiu* (International studies), April 1993, pp. 15–20.

69. For Qiao's visit, see *Renmin Ribao*, April 20, 21, and 24, 1995. For Lee's visit, see Renmin Ribao, May 11, 1995, *China Daily*, May 11, 1995, and *Hanguk Ilbo*, May 11, 1995.

CHAPTER FIVE

1. For example, see *Peking Review*, June 12, 1964, pp. 9–10, May 7, 1971, pp. 18–19, July 16, 1976, p. 32, and February 10, 1978, p. 29.
2. See Chin O. Chung, *Pyongyang between Peking and Moscow* (University: University of Alabama Press, 1978), pp. 18–19, and *China's Foreign Relations: A Chronology of Events (1949–1988)* (Beijing: Foreign Languages Press, 1988), p. 157. Dae-Sook Suh, *Kim Il Sung: The North Korean Leader* (New York: Columbia University Press, 1988), p. 140. See *Pukhan Kaeyo* (An outline of North Korea) (Seoul: Pyonghwa tongil yonguso, 1986), p. 209.
3. See Chae-Jin Lee, "Economic Aspects of Life in North Korea," in C. I. Eugene Kim and B. C. Koh, eds., *Journey to North Korea: Personal Perceptions* (Berkeley: Institute of East Asian Studies, University of California, 1993), pp. 55–61. *Renmin Ribao*, October 28 and 29, 1982. *China's Foreign Relations*, p. 171.
4. See Chung, *Pyongyang between Peking and Moscow*, pp. 32-33.
5. For the completion of the Taipingwan project, see *Renmin Ribao*, November 16, December 29, 1987. See Chae-Jin Lee, "China's Policy toward North Korea," in Robert A. Scalapino and Hongkoo Lee, eds., *North Korea in a Regional and Global Context* (Berkeley: Institute of East Asian Studies, University of California, 1986), pp. 201–2.
6. Vasily V. Mikheev, "Soviet Policy toward the Korean Peninsula in the 1990s," *Korean Studies*, 1991, pp. 31–49. In contrast, see a positive Chinese report on North Korea's "rapid economic development" in *Beijing Review*, May 6–12, 1991, pp. 16–17.
7. As reported in *Hanguk Ilbo*, December 15, 1990.
8. *Renmin Ribao*, November 27, 28, 1990. Given their intensely nationalistic tendencies, the North Koreans resent the suggestion that they should follow the Chinese model of economic development. Discussion with a North Korean diplomat, May 1995.
9. See Chong-Sik Lee, *The Political Economy of North Korea, 1994* (Seattle, Wash.: National Bureau of Asian Research, 1994), and Yong-Sup Han, "China's Leverages over North Korea."
10. See Harry Harding, *China's Second Revolution: Reform after Mao* (Washington, D.C.: Brookings Institution, 1987). For a discussion of China's open-door economic policy and its impact on Korea, see Chae-Jin Lee, "China and South Korea's Northern Diplomacy," *Asia Pacific Review*, spring 1990, pp. 31–32. For China's participation in international financial organizations, see Nicholas R. Lardy, *Foreign Trade and Economic Reform in China, 1978–1990* (New York: Cambridge University Press, 1992). *Beijing Review*, March 6–12, 1989, pp. 22–23.
11. *Beijing Review*, January 20–February 5, 1989, p. 20.

12. Ibid., November 17, 1980, p. 13. Lee, "China and South Korea's Northern Diplomacy," *Asia Pacific Review*, spring 1990, p. 34, and Chae-Jin Lee, "China's Pragmatic Policy Orientation and Its Implications for Korean Unification," in *Perspectives on the Peaceful Reunification of Korea* (Seoul: Institute of Korean Studies, 1988), pp. 1–27. See Qian Jiajun's two chapters, "The South Korean Government's Intervention in Economy" and "How Did South Korea's Economy Develop So Fast?" in *Waiguo jingji jiegou wenji* (Collected articles on foreign economic structures) (Beijing: Zhongguo shehuikexue chubanshe, 1980), pp. 320–42. Zhang Wen's article in *Shijie Jingji Daobao* (World economic journal), May 9, 1983, p. 7, as translated in *Foreign Broadcast Information Service, Daily Report, China*, May 27, 1983, pp. D3–D5.

13. For Sino–South Korean trade in the 1980s, see Jae Ho Chung, "South Korea–China Economic Relations: The Current Situation and Its Implications," *Asian Survey*, October 1988. Quoted from Dan C. Sanford, *South Korea and the Socialist Countries: The Politics of Trade* (New York: St. Martin's Press, 1990), p. 9.

14. *Beijing Review*, March 23, 1981, p. 9, April 13, 1981, and *Renmin Ribao* commentary, March 12, 1981. An English translation was widely distributed by the Chinese embassy in Washington in a press release, March 18, 1981. See the text of Zhao's speech at Pyongyang in *Renmin Ribao*, December 24, 1981. Ding Min (deputy director of the First Department of Asian Affairs, Ministry of Foreign Affairs) said that China wanted to stop importing commodities even indirectly if they were made in South Korea. Interview with Ding, June 16, 1982, Beijing.

15. As reported in *Sankei Shimbun*, October 2, 1986. For example, see Wu Linggeng, "Yazhou sexiaolong jingji qiji pouxi" (Analysis of the economic miracle in Asia's four dragons), *Hongqi* (Red flag), April 1, 1987, pp. 29–32)

16. Li You, "Hancheng xinbu" (Aimless stroll in Seoul), *Renmin Wenxue* (People's Literature), November 1986, pp. 62–74.

17. Sanford, *South Korea and the Socialist Countries*, p. 13.

18. See ibid., p. 32, and Chung, "South Korea–China Economic Relations."

19. *Beijing Review*, April 28, 1986, p. xvii.

20. *Los Angeles Times*, January 19, 1987. *Beijing Review*, April 20, 1987, p. xiv.

21. Lee, "China and South Korea's Northern Policy," pp. 33–34.

22. *Los Angeles Times*, September 21, 1990.

23. See *Korea Herald*, August 27, 1992.

24. Ibid., February 14, 1995.

25. *Hanguk Ilbo*, February 18, 1994.

26. See *Korea Newsreview*, April 2, 1994, p. 4. *Beijing Review*, November 14–20, 1994, p. 4. Interview, March 1995.

27. See *Chiyok Kyongjae* (Journal of area studies), May 1993, pp. 37–58.

28. See *Renmin Ribao*, May 12, 1992.

29. *Korea Herald*, May 12, 1993. See An Chong Sok, *Hanguk kiup daechung*

tuja siltae wa hyanghu kwajae, p. 29.

30. Ibid., pp. 53–56.
31. Ibid., p. 57.
32. Ibid., pp. 62–63. See *China Focus*, October 1, 1994, p. 2.
33. *Korea Herald*, September 17, 1993. See Nicholas R. Lardy, *China in the World Economy* (Washington, D.C.: Institute for International Economics, 1994), p. 72.
34. *Beijing Review*, June 28–July 4, 1993, p. 19.
35. See Chae-Jin Lee, *China's Korean Minority* (Boulder, Colo.:Westview Press, 1986).
36. For Lee's meetings with Jiang Zemin and Li Peng in Beijing, see *Renmin Ribao*, April 13, 1995, and *Korea Times*, April 14, 1995. See *Korea Herald*, February 12 and 14, 1995.
37. *Beijing Review*, June 21–27, 1993, p. 25. *Korea Herald*, September 10, 1993. *Hanguk Ilbo*, October 13, 1994.
38. For negotiations, see *Korea Herald*, March 16, May 23, 1993.
39. *Hanguk Ilbo*, September 20, 1994. See *Los Angeles Times*, December 6, 1994.
40. *Beijing Review*, April 20–26, 1992, p. 5.
41. See *Korea Newsreview*, October 15, 1994, p. 7.

Chapter Six

1. The Chinese pronunciation of the Democratic People's Republic of Korea is *Chaoxian minzhu zhuyi renmin gongheguo* and of the Republic of Korea, *Dahan minguo*.
2. For this argument, see Chae-Jin Lee, "The Role of China in the Korean Unification Process," *Asian Perspective*, spring–summer 1986, pp. 96–112.
3. James A. Winnefeld et al., *A New Strategy and Fewer Forces: The Pacific Dimension* (Santa Monica, Calif.: RAND, 1992), p. 13.
4. Interview with Chinese officials, March 1995.
5. Discussions with North Korean diplomats, May 1995.

BIBLIOGRAPHY

● ●

Acheson, Dean. *Present at the Creation: My Years in the State Department.* New York: W. W. Norton and Co., 1969.

An Chong Sok. *Hanguk kiupui daechung tuja siltae wa hyanghu kwajae* (The situation of South Korean industries' investment in China and its future tasks). Seoul: Center for Area Studies, June 1993.

Appleman, Roy E. *South to the Naktong, North to the Yalu: United States Army in the Korean War.* Washington, D.C.: U.S. Government Printing Office, 1961.

Bailey, Sydney D. *The Korean Armistice.* New York: St. Martin's Press, 1992.

Blair, Clay. *The Forgotten War: America in Korea, 1950–1953.* New York: Times Books, 1987.

Chai Chengwen and Zhao Yongtian. *Banmendian tanpan* (Panmunjom negotiations). Beijing: Jiefangjun chubanshe, 1989.

Chang, Parris H. "Beijing's Policy toward Korea and PRC-ROK Normalization of Relations." In Manwoo Lee and Richard W. Mansback, eds., *The Changing Order in Northeast Asia and the Korean Peninsula.* Seoul: Institute for Far Eastern Studies, 1993, pp. 155–72.

Chang, Gordon H. *Friends and Enemies: The United States, China, and the Soviet Union, 1948–1972.* Stanford: Stanford University Press, 1990.

Jian Chen. "China's Changing Aims during the Korean War, 1950–1951." *Journal of American–East Asian Relations*, spring 1992, pp. 8–41.

Chen, Jian. *China's Road to the Korean War: The Making of the Sino–American Confrontation.* New York: Columbia University Press, 1994.

China's Foreign Relations: A Chronology of Events (1949–1988). Beijing: Foreign Languages Press, 1989.

Christensen, Thomas J. "Threats, Assurances, and the Last Chance for Peace: The Lessons of Mao's Korean War Telegrams." *International Security*, summer 1992, pp. 122–54.

Chugoku Nenkan (China yearbook). Tokyo: Ishizaki shoten, 1955.

Chun Hae-jong. *Hanchung kwankye yongu* (A study of Korean-Chinese relations). Seoul: Ilchokak, 1970.

Chun, Hae-jong. "Sino–Korean Tributary Relations in the Ch'ing Period." In John K. Fairbank, ed., *The Chinese World Order.* Cambridge: Harvard University Press, 1968, pp. 90–111.

Chung, Chin O. *Pyongyang between Peking and Moscow: North Korea's Involvement in the Sino–Soviet Dispute, 1958–1975.* University: University of Alabama Press, 1978.

Chung Il Kwon. *Chonjaeng kwa hyuchon* (War and armistice). Seoul: Donga ilbosa, 1986.

Chung, Jae Ho. "South Korea–China Economic Relations: The Current Situation and Its Implications." *Asian Survey*, October 1988, pp. 1031–48.

Chungguk Pyonram (China almanac). Seoul: Center for Area Studies, 1994.

Cohen, Warren I. "Conversations with Chinese Friends: Zhou Enlai's Associates Reflect on Chinese-American Relations in the 1940s and the Korean War." *Diplomatic History*, summer 1987, pp. 283–89.

Cumings, Bruce. *The Origins of the Korean War: Liberation and the Emergence of Separate Regimes, 1945–1947.* Princeton: Princeton University Press, 1981.

———. *The Origins of the Korean War: The Roaring of the Cataract, 1947–1950.* Princeton: Princeton University Press, 1990.

Deng Xiaoping. *Deng Xiaoping wenxuan* (Selected works of Deng Xiaoping). Beijing: Renmin chubanshe, 1983.

Denny, O. N. *China and Korea.* Shanghai: Kelly and Walsh, 1888.

The Diplomacy of Japan, 1894–1922, vol. 1. Tokyo: Kajima Institute of International Peace, 1976.

Documents Relating to the Discussion of Korea and Indo-China at the Geneva Conference. London: Her Majesty's Stationary Office, 1954.

Du Ping. *Zai zhiyuanjun zongbu* (At the headquarters of the volunteer army). Beijing: Jiefangjun chubanshe, 1989.

Eckert, Carter J., Ki-baik Lee, Young Ick Lew, Michael Robinson, and Edward W. Wagner. *Korea Old and New: A History.* Seoul: Ilchokak, 1990.

Eisenhower, Dwight D. *The White House Years: Mandate for Change, 1953–1956.* Garden City, N.Y.: Doubleday, 1963.

Fairbank, John K., ed. *The Chinese World Order.* Cambridge: Harvard University Press, 1968.

Fairbank, John K., and Ssu-yu Teng. *Ch'ing Administration: Three Studies.* Cambridge: Harvard University Press, 1960.

Farrar-Hockley, Anthony. "A Reminiscence of the Chinese People's Volunteers in the Korean War." *China Quarterly,* June 1984, pp. 287–304.

Foot, Rosemary. *A Substitute for Victory: The Politics of Peacemaking at the Korean Armistice Talks.* Ithaca, N.Y.: Cornell University Press, 1990.

George, Alexander L. *The Chinese Army in Action: The Korean War and Its Aftermath.* New York: Columbia University Press, 1967.

Goncharov, Sergei N., John W. Lewis, and Xue Litai. *Uncertain Partners: Stalin, Mao, and the Korean War.* Stanford: Stanford University Press, 1993.

Goodman, Allan E., ed. *Negotiating while Fighting: The Diary of Admiral C. Turner Joy at the Korean Armistice Conference.* Stanford: Hoover Institution Press, 1978.

Great Lasting Friendship: Comrade Hu Yaobang's Visit to the DPRK. Pyongyang: Foreign Languages Publishing House, 1984.

The Great Leader Comrade Kim Il Sung's Official State Visit to the People's Republic of China. Pyongyang: Foreign Languages Publishing House, 1982.

Halliday, Jon, and Bruce Cumings. *Korea: The Unknown War.* New York: Pantheon, 1988.

Han, Yong-Sup. "China's Leverages over North Korea." *Korea and World Affairs,* summer 1994, pp. 233–49.

Hangukchon munso yoyak (The summary of documents concerning the

Korean War). Seoul: Ministry of Foreign Affairs, 1994.

Hangukchon pochung munhon (The supplementary documents concerning the Korean War). Seoul: Ministry of Foreign Affairs, 1994.

Hao Yufan. "China and the Korean Peninsula: A Chinese View." *Asian Survey*, August 1987, pp. 862–84.

Hao Yufan and Zhai Zhihai. "China's Decision to Enter the Korean War: History Revisited." *China Quarterly*, March 1990, pp. 94–115.

Harding, Harry. *China's Second Revolution: Reform After Mao.* Washington, D.C.: Brookings Institution, 1987.

He Di. "The Most Respected Enemy: Mao Zedong's Perception of the United States." *China Quarterly*, March 1994, pp. 144–58.

Hiramatsu Shigeo. *Chugoku to Chosen senso* (China and the Korean War). Tokyo: Keiso shobo, 1988.

Hong Xuezhi. *Kangmei yuanchao zhanzheng huiyi* (Recollections on the Resist-America and Aid-Korea war). Beijing: Jiefangjun wenyi chubanshe, 1991.

Hwang, Eui-Gak. *The Korean Economies.* New York: Oxford University Press, 1993.

Jia Hao and Zhuang Qubing. "China's Policy toward the Korean Peninsula." *Asian Survey*, December 1992, pp. 1137–56.

Jiang Yonghui. *Sanshibajun zai chaoxian* (The 38th army in Korea). Shenyang: Liaoning renmin chubanshe, 1988.

Joy, C. Turner. *How Communists Negotiate.* New York: Macmillan Company, 1955.

Kangmei yuanchao zhanzheng (The Resist-America and Aid-Korea war). Beijing : Zhongguo shehuikexue chubanshe, 1990.

Khrushchev, Nikita. *Khrushchev Remembers.* Translated by Strobe Talbott. Boston: Little, Brown, 1970.

——. *Khrushchev Remembers: Last Testament.* Translated by Strobe Talbot. Boston: Little, Brown, 1974.

Kihl, Young Whan, ed. *Korea and the World: Beyond the Cold War.* Boulder, Colo.: Westview Press, 1994.

Kim, C. I. Eugene, and B. C. Koh, eds. *Journey to North Korea: Personal Perceptions.* Berkeley: Institute of East Asian Studies, University of California, 1983.

Kim, H. N. et al., eds. *Perspectives on the Peaceful Reunification of Korea.* Seoul: Institute of Korean Studies, 1988.

Kim, Hakjoon. *Korea's Relations with Her Neighbors in a Changing World.* Seoul: Hollym, 1993.

Kim, Ilpyong. "The Korean Question in Sino-American Relations." *In Depth,* fall 1993, pp. 51–66.

Kim, Samuel S. *China, the United Nations, and World Order.* Princeton: Princeton University Press, 1979.

Kim, Se-Jin, ed. *Korean Unification: Source Materials with an Introduction.* Seoul: Research Center for Peace and Unification, 1976.

Kim, Seung-Hwan. *The Soviet Union and North Korea: Soviet Asian Strategy and Its Implications for the Korean Peninsula, 1964–1968.* Seoul: Research Center for Peace and Unification, 1988.

Kim Yong Shik. *Huimang kwa tojon* (Hope and challenge). Seoul: Donga ilbosa, 1987.

Kim, Young C., ed. *Foreign Policies of Korea.* Washington, D.C.: Institute for Asian Studies, 1973.

Kissinger, Henry. *White House Years.* Boston: Little, Brown, 1979.

Byung Chul Koh. "China and the Korean Peninsula." *Korea and World Affairs,* summer 1985, pp. 254–79.

———. *The Foreign Policy of North Korea.* New York: Frederick A. Praeger, 1969.

———. *The Foreign Policy Systems of North and South Korea.* Berkeley: University of California Press, 1984.

Lardy, Nicholas R. *China's Entry into the World Economy.* New York: Asia Society, 1987.

———. *China in the World Economy.* Washington, D.C.: Institute for International Economics, 1994.

———. *Foreign Trade and Economic Reform in China, 1978–1990.* New York: Cambridge University Press, 1992.

Lee, Chae-Jin. "China and South Korea's Northern Policy." *Asia Pacific Review,* spring 1990, pp. 29–41.

———. *China's Korean Minority.* Boulder, Colo.: Westview Press, 1986.

———. "China's Policy toward North Korea: Changing Relations in the 1980s." In Robert A. Scalapino and Hong Koo Lee, eds., *North Korea in a Regional and Global Context.* Berkeley: Institute of East Asian Studies, University of California, 1986, pp. 190–225.

———. "China's Pragmatic Policy Orientation and Its Implications for Korean Unification," In H. N. Kim et al., eds., *Perspectives on the Peaceful Reunification of Korea.* Seoul: Institute of Korean Studies, 1988, pp. 1–27.

———. "The Development of Sino-Japanese Competition over Korea." In Young C. Kim, ed., *Foreign Policies of Korea.* Washington, D.C.: Institute for Asian Studies, 1973, pp. 37–53.

———. "The Direction of South Korea's Foreign Policy," *Korean Studies,* 1978, pp. 95–137.

———. "Economic Aspects of life." In C. I. Eugene Kim and B. C. Koh, eds., *Journey to North Korea.* Berkeley: Institute of East Asian Studies, University of California, 1983, pp. 55–61.

———. "The Role of China in the Korean Unification Process." *Asian Perspective,* spring–summer 1986, pp. 96–112.

Lee, Chae-Jin, and Hideo Sato. *U.S. Policy toward Japan and Korea: A Changing Influence Relationship.* New York: Praeger Publishers, 1982.

Lee, Chong-Sik. "The 1972 Constitution and Top Communist Leaders." In Dae-Sook Suh and Chae-Jin Lee, eds., *Political Leadership in Korea.* Seattle: University of Washington Press, 1976, pp. 192–219.

———. *The Political Economy of North Korea, 1994.* Seattle, Wash.: National Bureau of Asian Research, 1994.

———. *The Politics of Korean Nationalism.* Berkeley: University of California Press, 1963.

Lee, Hong Yung. "China and the Two Koreas: New Emerging Triangle." In Young Whan Kihl, ed., *Korea and the World.* Boulder, Colo: Westview Press, 1994, pp. 97–110.

———. "Future Dynamics in Sino-Korean Relations." *Journal of Northeast Asian Studies,* fall 1990, pp. 34–49.

Lee, Ki-baik. *A New History of Korea.* Translated by Edward W. Wagner and Edward J. Schultz. Seoul: Ilchokak, 1984.

Lee, Manwoo, and Richard W. Mansback, eds. *The Changing Order in Northeast Asia and the Korean Peninsula.* Seoul: Institute for Far Eastern Studies, 1993.

Li You. "Hancheng xinbu" (Aimless stroll in Seoul). *Renmin Wenxue*

(People's literature), November 1986, pp. 62-74.

Lim Un. *The Founding of a Dynasty in North Korea*. Tokyo: Jiyusha, 1982.

Liu, Hong. "The Sino–South Korean Normalization: A Triangular Explanation." *Asian Survey*, November 1993, pp. 1083–94.

MacArthur, Douglas. *Reminiscences*. New York: McGraw-Hill, 1964.

Mao Zedong. *Jianguo yilai Mao Zedong wengao* (Mao Zedong's manuscripts after the founding of the republic), vols. 1–4. Beijing: Zhongyang wenxian chubanshe, 1987–1990.

———. *Mao Zedong junshi wenxuan* (Selected military writings of Mao Zedong). Beijing: Zhongguo renmin jiefangjun zhanshi chubanshe, 1981.

———. *Mao Zedong xuanji* (Selected writings of Mao Zedong), vol. 5. Beijing: Renmin chubanshe, 1977.

Merrill, John. *Korea: The Peninsular Origins of the War*. Newark: University of Delaware Press, 1989.

Mikheev, Vasily V. "Soviet Policy toward the Korean Peninsula in the 1990s." *Korean Studies*, 1991, pp. 31–49.

Nie Rongzhen. *Nie Rongzhen huiyilu* (Memoirs of Nie Rongzhen). Beijing: Jiefangjun chubanshe, 1984.

Noh, Hee Mock. "The Development of Korean Trade and Investment in the PRC." *Korea and World Affairs*, fall 1989, pp. 421–39.

Panikkar, K. M. *In Two Chinas: Memoirs of a Diplomat*. London: George Allen and Unwin Ltd., 1955.

Park, Doo-Bok. *Zhonggong canjia hanzhan yuanyinzhi yanjiu* (A study on the causes of communist China's participation in the Korean War). Taipei: Liming wenhuashiye gufen youxiangongsi, 1975.

Peng Dehuai. *Memoirs of a Chinese General*. Beijing: Foreign Languages Press, 1984.

Peng Dehuai (Peng Dehuai). Hong Kong: Zilian chubanhshe, 1969.

Peng Dehuai. *Peng Dehuai zishu* (Peng Dehuai's memoirs). Beijing: Renmin chubanshe, 1981.

Pollack, Jonathan D. *The Sino-Soviet Summit: Implications for East Asia and U.S. Foreign Policy*. New York: Asia Society, 1989.

———. "U.S.-Korea Relations: The China Factor." *Journal of Northeast Asian Studies*, fall 1985, pp. 12–28.

Pukhan Kaeyo (An outline of North Korea). Seoul: Pyonghwa tongil yonguso, 1986.

Qian Jiajun. "Nanchaoxian jingji shi zenyang xunsu fazhande" (How did South Korea's economy develop so fast?). In *Waiguo jingji jiegou wenji* (Collected articles on foreign economic structures). Beijing: Zhongguo shehuikexue chubanshe, 1980, pp. 328–42.

———. "Nanchaoxian zhengfu dui jingjide ganyu" (The South Korean government's intervention in the economy). In *Waiguo jingji jiegou wenji*, pp. 320–27.

Rees, David. *Korea: The Limited War*. New York: St. Martin's Press, 1964.

Roh Tae Woo. *Korea: A Nation Transformed*. New York: Pergamon Press, 1990.

The Roh-Gorbachev Summit on Cheju. Seoul: Korean Overseas Information Service, 1991.

Ruo Yu. "Eastern Powers Thaw Lines to South Korea." *Beijing Review*, January 9–15, 1989, pp. 15–16.

Sanford, Dan C. *South Korea and the Socialist Countries: The Politics of Trade*. New York: St. Martin's Press, 1990.

Scalapino, Robert A., and Chong-Sik Lee. *Communism in Korea, Parts 1–2*. Berkeley: University of California Press, 1972.

Scalapino, Robert A., and Hong Koo Lee, eds. *North Korea in a Regional and Global Context*. Berkeley: Institute of East Asian Studies, University of California, 1986.

Shi Zhe. *Zailishi jurenshenbian* (With the great people in history). Beijing: Zhongyang wenxian chubanshe, 1991.

Shulman, Marshall. *Stalin's Foreign Policy Reappraised*. Cambridge: Harvard University Press, 1963.

Simmons, Robert R. *The Strained Alliance: Peking, P'yongyang, Moscow and the Politics of the Korean Civil War*. New York: Free Press, 1975.

Song Yong Woo, ed. *Hanchung kwankyeron* (Studies on Korea-China relations). Seoul: Jiyongsa, 1993.

Suh, Dae-Sook. *Kim Il Sung: The North Korean Leader*. New York: Columbia University Press, 1988.

———. *The Korean Communist Movement, 1918–1948*. Princeton: Princeton University press, 1967.

Suh, Dae-Sook, and Chae-Jin Lee, eds. *Political Leadership in Korea*.

Seattle: University of Washington Press, 1976.

Swaine, Michael D. *The Military and Political Succession in China.* Santa Monica, Calif.: RAND, 1992.

Tan Zheng. *Zhongguo renmin zhiyuanjun renwulu* (Biographical directory of the Chinese People's Volunteers). Beijing. Zhonggong dangshi chubanshe, 1992.

Tao Bingwei. "A Historical Review of China–North Korea Relations." Paper delivered at a conference on "Sino-Korean Relations and Their Policy Implications," George Washington University, December 1993.

Tao Bingwei and Wu Jingjing. "Jin Yongsan jiuren hanguo zongtong yu chaoxian bandao jushi" (The inauguration of President Kim Young Sam and the situation of the Korean Peninsula). *Guojiwenti Yanjiu* (International studies), April 1993, pp. 15–20.

Truman, Harry S. *Memoirs: Years of Trial and Hope.* Garden City, N.Y.: Doubleday, 1956.

Ulam, Adam. *The Communists: The Story of Power and Lost Illusions, 1948–1991.* New York: Charles Scribner's Sons, 1992.

U.S. Department of State. *Foreign Relations of the United States 1950.* Vol. 7, *Korea.* Washington, D.C.: U.S. Government Printing Office, 1976.

———. *Foreign Relations of the United States 1951.* Vol. 7, *Korea and China,* Part 1. Washington, D.C.: U.S. Government Printing Office, 1983.

———. *Foreign Relations of the United States 1952–1954.* Vol. 15, *Korea,* Part 1. Washington, D.C.: U.S. Government Printing Office, 1984.

———. *Foreign Relations of the United States 1952–1954.* Vol. 16, *The Geneva Conference.* Washington, D.C.: U.S. Government Printing Office, 1981.

———. *The Korean Problem at the Geneva Conference.* Washington, D.C.: U.S. Government Printing Office, 1954.

Vatcher, William H., Jr. *Panmunjom: The Story of the Korean Military Armistice Negotiations.* New York: Frederick A. Praeger, 1958.

Waiguo jingji jiegou wenji (Collected articles on foreign economic structures). Beijing: Zhongguo shehuikexue chubanshe, 1980.

Weathersby, Kathryn. *Soviet Aims in Korea and the Origins of the Korean War, 1945–1950: New Evidence from Russian Archives.* Washington, D.C.: Woodrow Wilson International Center for Scholars, 1993.

West, Philip. "Confronting the West: China as David and Goliath in the Korean War." *Journal of American–East Asian Relations*, spring 1993, pp. 5–28.

———. "The Korean War and the Criteria of Significance in Chinese Popular Culture." *Journal of American–East Asian Relations*, winter 1992, pp. 383–408.

Whiting, Allen S. *China Crosses the Yalu: The Decision to Enter the Korean War*. Stanford: Stanford University Press, 1960.

Winnefeld, James A., et al. *A New Strategy and Fewer Forces: The Pacific Dimension, Executive Summary*. Santa Monica, Calif.: RAND, 1992.

Wu Linggeng. "Yazhou sexiaolong jingji qiji pouxi" (Analysis of the economic miracle in Asia's four little dragons). *Hongqi* (Red flag), April 1, 1987, pp. 29–32.

Xie Lifu. *Chaoxian zhanzheng shilu* (The true record of the Korean War). Beijing: Shijie zhishi chubanshe, 1993.

Xie Yixian. "China's Foreign Policy." *Beijing Review*, February 13–26, 1989, pp. 12–17.

Yao Xu. "Kangmei yuanchaode yingming juece" (Wise decisions for the Resist-America and Aid-Korea war). *Dangshi Yanjiu* (Research on party history), October 28, 1980, pp. 5–14.

———. "Peng Dehuai dui kangmei yuanchao zhanzheng zhihuishangde gongxian" (Peng Dehuai's contributions in leading the Resist-America and Aid-Korea war). *Dangshi Yanjiu Ziliao* (Documents concerning research on party history), January 20, 1982, pp. 2–12.

Ye Yumeng. *Chubing chaoxian* (Sending the army to Korea). Beijing: Shiyue wenyi chubanshe, 1990.

Zhongguo renmin zhiyuanjun kangmei yuanchao zhanshi (History of the Resist-America and Aid-Korea war by the Chinese People's Volunteers). Beijing: Junshi kexue chubanshe, 1988.

Zhou Enlai. *Zhou Enlai waijiao wenxuan* (Zhou Enlai's writings on diplomatic issues). Beijing: Zhongyang wenxuan chubanshe, 1990.

INDEX

Acheson, Dean, 18, 27, 34, 37–38, 47, 50
Agreement on the Encouragement and
  Reciprocal Protection of Investments
  (China–South Korea, 1992), 155
"Agreement on Reconciliation, Nonaggression and Exchanges and Cooperation," 123, 170, 174
air control boundary, 164–65
Almond, General Edward N., 24
Appleman, Roy B., 24
armistice negotiations (Korean War):
  agreed terms of, 41; conclusion of, 55;
  de facto cease-fire during, 45; Indian
  proposal during, 50–52; Mao/Stalin
  communication on, 39–40, 42–43;
  NSC 48/5 on, 37; over military demarcation line, 43–45; parties agree to, 38–
  39; POW issue of, 46–56
Article 118 (Geneva Convention), 46–47
Article One (Sino-Soviet treaty), 60
Article One (Soviet–North Korean treaty),
  60
Article Two (Sino–North Korean treaty),
  60
Asia-Pacific Economic Cooperation
  (APEC), 96, 123

Asia-Pacific Economic Cooperation meet-
  ing (1991), 151
Asian Games (1990), 150
Austin, Warren R., 29, 182n.59

Ba Jin, 57
Baker, James, 93
Beijing. See People's Republic of China
  (PRC)
Bohlen, Charles E., 53
Bowles, Chester B., 51
Bradley, Omar, 35, 43
Bush, George, 5, 115

Castro, Fidel, 59
Cease-Fire Group, 29–30, 32
Central Military Commission (CMC,
  China): initial decisions by, 13–14;
  Korean War veterans within, 74–78;
  troops commissioned by, 15
chaebol, 151, 154, 163
Chai Chengwen, 15, 19, 47, 179n.14
Chang Chun San, 40, 184n.88
Chen Muhua, 69, 129, 135
Chen Yun, 18, 49
Chi Haotian, 74, 87, 88, 129

Chiang Kai-shek, 4, 8–9, 30, 55
Chiang Yen-shih, 127
China Chamber of International Commerce (CCOIC), 122, 150
China. See People's Republic of China (PRC)
China-Korea Friendship Pipeline, 134
China-Korea Joint Committee on Science and Technology, 168
Chinese Ministry of Foreign Affairs, 19–20
Chinese People's Volunteers (CPV): casualties of, 36; counterattack by, 33–34; decorated by North Korea, 74; follows MacArthur's retreat, 27–28; occupies Onjong, 25; Ridgway's offensive against, 32–33; sent to Korea, 19
Chinese torpedo boat incident (1985), 109–10
Choe Kwang, 93, 95
Choe Yong Kun, 61–62, 100, 102, 186n.122
Chollima Undong (1958, North Korea), 135
Christensen, Thomas, 18
Chu Chang Jun, 87, 93
chuche ideology (Kim Il Sung), 79, 136, 139
Chun Doo Hwan, 109
civil aviation agreement (China–South Korea), 165–66
Clark, General Mark W., 51–52, 55
Clinton, Bill, 95–96, 125
cold war, 89–97
Collins, General J. Lawton, 27
Cultural Revolution (China), 100–101

Daewoo Group, 163
Davis Tennis Cup's preliminary games (1984), 109
Dean, Arthur, 56
Democratic People's Republic of Korea: begins reconciliation with South Korea, 91–97; boundary negotiations with China (1963), 99–100; China renews pledge to, 65–66; China's two-Korea policy and, 122–31; conflicting policies of China and, 78–84; creation of, 4; current relationship with China, 171;

denounces U.S.-Soviet treaty, 61–62; economic agreement with China (1990), 138–39; economic performance of (1985–94), 137; economic ties to China, 134–42; impact of cold war end on, 89–97; joins United Nations, 89, 91, 103–5; nuclear program (1991–92) of, 93–94; reaction to Soviet/S. Korea relations, 86–89, 117–18, 128; renewed ties with China, 120–21; Sino-Soviet competition over, 70–78; trade balance (1970–94), 140–41; trade debt to Soviets, 138; treaty between China and, 59–61
Deng Hua, 13, 15, 28, 40–41, 184n.88
Deng Xiaoping: condolences on Kim Il Sung's death, 129; economic progression of, 142; joint communiqué with Kim, 68; meeting with Gorbachev (1989), 84–85; pledges to N. Korea by, 119; pragmatic policies of, 4–5, 79, 83; secret visit to North Korea, 71; supports relations with S. Korea, 106, 124–25
Deng Zhifang, 123
Denny, O. N., 2
Ding Guoyu, 52
Ding Min, 40
Dobrynin, Anatoly, 117
Du Ping, 33
Dulles, Allen, 56

EC-121 plane, 62
eight-point plan for peaceful national reunification (1971), 103
Eisenhower, Dwight D., 50, 52
Eveready plan, 55

Fairbank, John K., 1
First Committee, 50–51
Five Principles of Peaceful Coexistence, 117, 126
four modernizations program (China), 68–69

"gang of four," 68
Gao Gang, 13, 14, 18, 28, 31

Geneva Conference on Korea (1954), 56
Geneva Convention (1947), 46–47
Geng Biao, 68, 71
Gong Ro Myong, 107
Gorbachev, Mikhail, 81, 88–89, 116, 136
Gorbachev-Deng summit meeting (1989), 5, 84–85, 134, 149
Graves, Hubert, 16
Great Leap Forward Movement (China), 135
"Greater East Asia Co-prosperity Sphere," 3, 63

Han Bong Su, 147, 151
Han Sung Ju, 95
Han Xianchu, 24
Hans Toy Company, 155
Hao Yufan, 8
Harrison, William K., Jr., 42, 55
"hijack diplomacy," 106–7, 110
Hong Xuezhi, 24–25, 33, 36, 73–74, 129
Hu Jintao, 129, 196n.63
Hu Qili, 72, 84, 129, 188–89n.27
Hu Yaobang, 71, 73, 81, 82, 143, 188n.22, 190n.36
Hua Guofeng, 68–70, 135
Huang Hua, 56, 69, 73, 103–4
Huang Yongsheng, 74

Inchon landing, 15–16
Indian armistice proposal, 50–51
International Atomic Energy Agency (IAEA), 94, 95, 171
International Private Economic Council of Korea (IPECK), 147
Ito Hirobumi, 3

Japan: Chinese/North Korea policies on, 79–83; Kim's attack against, 64; normalization with South Korea, 62–63; threatened by China-Seoul trade, 154; treaty with China (1978), 68
Jiang Qing, 68, 104
Jiang Zemin, 74, 88–90, 95, 131, 154
"Joint Declaration on the Denuclearization of the Korean Peninsula," 91, 123, 128, 171, 174

Jones, Lt Glen C., 25
Joy, Vice Admiral C. Turner, 40–44

Kaesong, 39, 45
Kang Sheng, 101
Kang Song San, 138
Kennan, George F., 37–38, 48
Kennedy, John F., 59
Khrushchev, Nikita, 9, 101
Kim Il, 9, 10
Kim Il Sung: appeals to Stalin, 16–17; attacks Japan, 64; Beijing December meeting of, 28; birthday celebration (1982) of, 71; birthday celebration (1992) of, 91–92; *chuche* ideology of, 136, 139; death of, 129–30; economic grants requested by, 134; impact of Korean War on, 58; initiates invasion of South Korea, 7–11; meets with Peng and Pak, 23–24; public praise of Soviets by, 111; reaction to Sino-Seoul relations, 125, 128; reaction to Sino-U.S. détente by, 65–70; Red Guard attacks on, 101–2; urged to support reunification, 68; visit to China (1991), 90–91; visits to China (1982), 72–73; visits to Soviet Union (1984), 81
Kim Jong Il: Chinese recognition of, 130; Chinese support of, 83–84; meets Hu Yaobang, 71; response to two-Korea policy, 131; visit to China (1983) by, 72–73
Kim Kwang Hyop, 10
Kim Sang Ha, 151
Kim Tal Hyon, 138
Kim Ung, 28, 182n.56
Kim Yong Nam, 117–20, 138
Kim Yong Sik, 105
Kim Young Sam, 95, 117, 154
Kirk, Alan G., 38
Kissinger, Henry A., 65, 66, 82
Kong Chin Tae, 135
Korea Electric Power Corporation (KEPCO), 163
Korea Exchange Bank, 164
Korea Trade Promotion Corporation (KOTRA), 150–51
Korea-China Economic Council, 151
Korean Air Line plane incident (1983), 108

Korean armistice agreement anniversary (1993), 129
Korean Peninsula: armistice set up in, 56–57; Chinese vested interest in stability of, 171–72, 174–76; current political status of, 171–72; historical links between China and, 1–2; impact of China's détente policy on, 65–70; Japanese control over, 3; relations with modern China, 5–6; Sino-Soviet consensus on, 86; 38th parallel division of, 3–4; U.N. consensus statement (1973) on, 104; U.N. statements (1975) on, 105; underground fortifications in, 49; unification debate and, 172–74; U.S. military presence in, 81–83
Korean War: armistice negotiations, 37–58; China and outbreak of, 7–10; China/North Korea linked through, 73–74, 119; 41st anniversary of China's entrance to, 93; Inchon landing, 15–16; international impact of, 56–58; Stalin's response to, 8–9; Unsan-Onjong engagement, 24–25; Yalu river bombing, 26
Kwon Byong Hyon, 123

Lazarev, G. R., 32
League of Red Cross Societies, 51
Lee Hong Koo, 97, 131
Lee Kyu Sung, 115–16, 147
Lee Sang Ock, 122, 125–27, 196n.58
Lee Teng-hui, 127
Lee Won Kyung, 80
Lee Yong Duk, 130
Lho Shin Young, 110
Li Desheng, 65, 74
Li Hung-chang, 3
Li Jong Ok, 120, 130, 145
Li Kenong, 40, 42, 45, 48, 54, 184n.88
Li Lanqing, 122, 151
Li Peng, 73, 88, 90–91, 113, 121, 130–31
Li Rusong, 21
Li Sang Cho, 40, 47, 184n.88
Li Tieying, 87, 120
Li Xiannian, 65, 73
Li You, 145–46
Li Zhaoxing, 94–95
Liang Biye, 71

Lie, Trygve, 29
Limited Nuclear Test Ban Treaty (1963), 61–62
Lin Biao, 10, 18, 19, 23, 65
Liu Huaqing, 93
Liu Shaoqi, 60–61, 100
Lucky-Goldstar Group, 163

MacArthur, General Douglas: arrogant posturing by, 21–23; dismissal of, 34–35; Inchon landing by, 15–16; issues ultimatum for surrender, 17; misjudges CPV, 25–26; withdraws U.N. forces to Pusan area, 27–28
Malenkov, Premier Georgy, 51, 186n.115
Malik, Jacob, 37–38, 43
Mao Anying, 181n.41
Mao Zedong: accepts armistice, 56; armistice advice by, 52; armistice communication with Stalin, 39–40, 42–43; as Chinese civil war victor, 4; commits to military support, 17–18, 20–21; concerns over U.S. involvement, 14–15; considers cease-fire, 36; death of, 68; meets with Kim (December 3), 28; orders counterattack, 33; on proposed cease-fire, 30–31; response to Korean War by, 8–12; warning on U.S. intervention, 179n.11
Marshall, General George, 27, 30
Martin, Joseph, Jr., 35
Menon, Krishna, 50
Merchant, Livingston T., 16
Middle Kingdom. See China
Mikheev, Vasily V., 136
Military Armistice Commission (Panmunjom), 96
military demarcation line, 43–45
Molotov, Vyacheslav, 51
Mu Chong, 3
Muccio, John, 26, 40

Nakasone Yasuhiro, 79, 80
Nam II, General, 40–42, 55, 184n.88
Nehru, Jawaharlal, 16, 51
Neutral Nations Inspection Teams (NNIT), 46
Neutral Nations Supervisory Commission

(NNSC), 45
Ni Zhiliang, 8, 19
Nie Rongzhen, 10, 14, 36, 57
"Nine Measures Adopted by South Korea to Promote Exports" (Zhang Wen), 143
Nixon, Richard M., 44, 62, 65–66
NNRC, 54, 55–56
North Korea. *See* Democratic People's Republic of Korea
Northeast Frontier Force (NFF), establishment of, 13–14
northern policy (South Korea), 5, 112–22
NSC 48/5 document, 37
Nuclear Nonproliferation Treaty (NPT), 94
nuclear weapons: current Chinese policy on, 171; North Korea's (1991–92) program on, 93–94; U.S./N. Korean agreement on, 96

O Chin U, 72, 93
open-door policy (China), 68–69, 143, 169, 197n.10
Operation Big Switch, 55
Operation Little Switch, 53

Paek Hak Rim, 73
Paek Sun Yop, 40
Pak Hon Yong, 10, 16–17, 19, 23, 50, 180n.24
Pak Il U, 19, 24
Pandit, Madam, 48
Panikkar, K. M., 14–16, 18. 30, 48
Park Chung Hee, 64, 67, 105–6, 189n.35
Park Tong Jin, 112
Peng Dehuai, 18, 19, 23–25, 31–33, 74
Peng Zhen, 84
People's Liberation Army (PLA): demobilization of, 8; military options of, 23–24; ready to enter Korea, 13; sent into Korea, 23–24
People's Republic of China (PRC): accedes to NPT, 94; air boundary of, 164–65; attends Seoul Asian Games (1986) and Olympic Games (1988), 112; boundary negotiations with N. Korea (1963), 99–100; changing politics of, 4–5; competition between Soviets and, 70–78; conflicting policies of North Korea and, 78–84; creation of, 4; Cultural Revolution of, 100–101; current relationship with North Korea, 171; current trade/investments with Seoul, 151–68; denounces U.S.-Soviet treaty, 61 62, détente policy of, 65–70; economic agreement with North Korea (1990), 138–39; economic basis of Korean policy by, 169–71; economic ties to North Korea, 134–41; economic ties to South Korea, 142–51; geographic distribution of investment in, 160–62; historical links between Korea and, 1–2; Kim Jong Il's visit to, 72–73; Korean Peninsula and modern, 5–6; Korean unification and, 172–75; Korean War impact on, 56–57; Korean War veteran impact within, 74–78; mediator role (1983) of, 110–11; most favored nation status given to, 95–96; problems with investment in, 159; recognizes Korean independence, 3; reconciliation with Soviets, 84–89; relations with S. Korea (1983–86), 105–12; renewed ties with N. Korea, 120–21; response to Korean conflict by, 16; Seventh Five-Year Plan (1986–90), 147–48; on S./N. Korea U.N. membership, 116; South Korean investment in (1988–93), 156; Soviet military threat to, 80; summary of five-year plans, 148; trade with South Korea (1979–94), 146; treaty between North Korea and, 59–61; two-Korea policy of, 122–31, 170; vested interest in Korean stability, 171–72, 174–76; visits between South Korea and (1985–94), 166
Persian Gulf war, 88
Pidan Island, 100
Pohang Iron and Steel Corporation (POSCO), 153
Political Bureau (China), 17–18
Political Conference (1953), 55–56
POW repatriation terms, 54
"The Price of Peace" program (radio), 38
prisoner of war (POW) issue, 46–56
Pu Shan, 8, 32, 40
Pyongyang. *See* Democratic People's Republic of Korea

Pyongyang-Wonsan line, 43–44

Qian Jiajun, 143
Qian Qichen, 86, 90, 122-23, 125
Qiao Guanhua, 40, 42, 103, 105, 184n.88
Qiao Shi, 129, 131
Qiao Zonghuai, 129
Qin Jiwei, 74, 87, 92, 120
Qingdao, 160, 162

Rangoon bombing incident (1983), 108, 110–11
Reagan, Ronald, 79, 80, 82, 110–11
Red Guards (China), 101–2
Republic of Korea: brings reconciliation with North Korea, 91–97; China's two-Korea policy and, 122–31; constitutional referendum (1972) in, 67; creation of, 4; current trade/investments with China, 151–68; diplomatic relations with Soviets, 86, 114–15, 117–19; economic performance of (1985–94), 137; economic ties with China, 142–51; geographic distribution of investment by, 160–62; investment in China (1988–93), 156; normalization with Japan, 62–63; northern policy of, 112–22; problems with investment in China, 159; relations with China (1983–86), 105–12; resistance to Cultural Revolution by, 101–2; severs diplomatic ties with Taiwan, 126–27; trade with China (1979–94), 146; U.N. resolution supporting, 12; U.S. military presence in, 81–83; visitors between China and (1985–94), 166
Resist-America and Aid-Korea movement, 57
Rhee, Syngman, 3–4, 18, 38, 54–55, 58, 177n.8
Ridgway, General Matthew, 31, 32, 38–39, 44
Roh Jae Won, 122, 155
Roh Tae Woo, 112–14, 125–28, 151
Roosevelt, Theodore, 3
Roshchin, N.V., 10, 13
Ruo Yu, 114
Russo-Japanese War (1904–5), 3

Samsung Group, 163
Sanford, Dan C., 147
Sasaki Ryosaku, 79
Sato Eisaku, prime minister, 62–63
Scali, John, 104
Sebald, William J., 40
Second Seven-Year Plan (1978–84, North Korea), 69
Seoul Asian Games (1986) and Olympic Games (1988), 111–12, 114, 134, 145
Seoul. See Republic of Korea
Seventh Five-Year Plan (China, 1986–90), 147–48
Shen Tu, 106
Shen-Gong memorandum (1983), 107–8
Shevardnadze, Eduard, 86, 117–18, 138
Shtykov, Terentii, 9
Shulman, Marshall, 8
Shultz, George, 80
Sino-Japanese War (1894–95), 2–3
Sino-Japanese War (1937–45), 3
Sino-Seoul communiqué (1992), 126
Sino–South Korean economic cooperation (1994), 168
Sino-Soviet alliance: developments of, 4; Korean War impact on, 57–58
Sino-Soviet conflict: competition adds to, 70–78; development of, 59
Sino-Soviet reconciliation, 84–89
Sino-Soviet Treaty of Friendship, Alliance and Mutual Assistance (1950), 7
Sino-U.S. détente, 65–70
Six-Year Plan (1971–76, North Korea), 64
Song Ping, 120
Song Shilun, 25, 87
South Korea. See Republic of Korea
South Korean Export and Import Bank, 164
Soviet Union: armistice negotiation role of, 39–40, 42–43, 53; competition between China and, 70–78; diplomatic relations with South Korea, 86, 114–15, 117–19; Kim Il Sung's visits (1984) to, 81; Korean division by, 3–4; limited nuclear test ban treaty with U.S., 61–62; as military threat to China, 80; North Korea's trade debt to, 138; reaction to Sino-Seoul economic ties, 144–

45; reconciliation with China, 84–89; rejected as NNSC member, 45; sends consular corps to Olympics, 114; Zhou's meeting in (1952), 49–50
Ssu-yu Teng, 1
Stalin, Joseph: armistice advice by, 49–50; decides to support Chinese forces, 20–21; Kim/Pak's appeal to, 16–17; Korean invasion supported by, 8–9, 13; military advice by, 28; reneges on Korean support, 19
"Stevenson" formula, 103, 193n.13
Su Yu, 13, 49
Swaine, Michael D., 78

Taekam Korea-China Friendship Cooperative Farm, 135
Taft, Robert A., 44
Taft-Katsura agreement (1905), 3
Taiwan: boycotts over China's athletes, 109; Chinese/North Korean policy conflict over, 78; South Korea severs relations with, 126–27
Takeshita Noboru, 115
Tang Jiaxuan, 96
"Team Spirit" exercises (U.S./South Korea), 83, 86–87
"Terms of Reference for Neutral Nations Repatriation Commission," 54
Thimayya, Chairman K. S., 55
Third Seven-Year Economic Plan (1987–93, North Korea), 135, 136
37th parallel, 31–32
38th parallel: as military demarcation line, 43; proposed cease-fire at, 29–31; South Korean army crosses, 16; UNC forces approach, 34
"three worlds" theory, 4
"three-joint" (*santong*) principle, 100
Tiananmen Square (1976), 68
Tiananmen Square (1989), 119, 120, 124, 149–50
Tianchi (Chonji) Lake, 100
Tianming (heavenly mandate), 1
"torpedo diplomacy," 109–10
Treaty of Friendship, Cooperation and Mutual Assistance (1961), 59–61, 92, 99
Treaty of Peace and Friendship (1978,

Sino-Japan), 68, 80
Treaty of Portsmouth (1905), 3
Trident airplane hijacking (1983), 106–8
Trigubenko, Mariana, 138
Truman, Harry: approves armistice negotiations, 38; dismisses MacArthur, 34–35, South Korean support by, 12; voluntary repatriation belief of, 47
Tumen River Project (North Korea), 91, 135–36, 139, 167
"two-camp" outlook, 4
two-Korea policy, 122–31, 170

Ulam, Adam, 8, 53
U.N. General Assembly: consensus statement on Korea (1973) by, 104; embargo resolution by, 37; passes Indian armistice proposal, 51; pro-Seoul statement (1974) by, 104; pro-Seoul/pro-Pyongyang resolutions (1975) by, 105
U.N. Security Council: Korean resolution by, 12; rejects Chinese resolution, 29; urges North Korean NPT compliance, 94
UNCURK, 66, 103-4
"underground great walls," 49
unification issues, 172–75
United Nations: admission of both Koreas to, 121; Chinese diplomacy with, 28–29; North Korea joins, 89, 91, 103–5; PRC membership in, 102–3
United Nations Command (UNC): approach to 38th parallel, 34; on armistice negotiation, 41–42; counterattack by, 35–36; establishment of, 13; proposed termination of, 104–5
United Nations Development Project, 167
United States: agrees to armistice negotiations, 38–39; Chinese/North Korea policies on, 79–83; crosses the parallel, 18–19; division of Korea by, 3–4; Korean War impact on, 56–58; Mao's concerns over, 14–15; as military presence in South Korea, 81–83; NSC 48/5 document by, 37; proposes U.N. sanctions against N. Korea, 95–96; regarding military demarcation line, 44; response to Korean War by, 11–12; threatened

United States (contintued)
   by China-Seoul trade, 154; voluntary
   repatriation policy of, 47–56
USS *Pueblo,* 62
Utsunomiya Tokuma, 79

Van Fleet, General, 35
Vatcher, William H., 46
Vyshinsky, Andrey, 50, 51

Walker, General Walton H., 24, 27–28
Wang Bingnan, 71
Wang Jiaxiang, 38
Wang Ping, 73
Watanabe Michio, 90
Weathersby, Kathryn, 8
Weihai, 160
Weinberger, Caspar, 110
West, Philip, 56
Whiting, Allen, 8
Willoughby, General Charles A., 22
World Trade Organization (WTO), 167
Wu Xiuquan, 29, 42
Wu Xueqian, 87, 91, 107–8
Wu Yi, 154

Xi Zhongxun, 73
Xie Fang, 24, 40, 42, 184n.88
Xu Dayu, 122
Xu Shiyu, 74
Xu Xiangqian, 36
Xu Xin, 73, 91

Yalu River, 100, 135–36
Yalu River bombing, 26
Yang Baibing, 87, 93, 125

Yang Chengwu, 87
Yang Dezhi, 74, 76, 87
Yang Shangkun, 73, 90, 92, 125, 128
Yang Xingchao, 25
Yang Yong, 76
Yano Junya, 79
Yao Xian, 87
Ye Jianying, 71
Yellow Sea Development Project (South
   Korea), 149
Yeltsin, Boris, 89
Yon Hyong Muk, 92, 120, 138
Yudin, P. F., 14

Zhai Zhihai, 8
Zhang Baifa, 109
Zhang Hanfu, 54
Zhang Ruijie, 123
Zhang Tingfa, 74
Zhang Wen, 143
Zhang Zhen, 74, 87
Zhao Nanqi, 74, 87
Zhao Ziyang, 71, 79, 84, 110, 113, 115,
   143, 145
Zhenbao (Damansky) Island, 62
Zheng Hongye, 122, 155
Zhou Enlai: attends Moscow meeting
   (1952), 49–50; cease-fire counterpro-
   posal by, 32; death of, 68; denounces
   Cease-Fire Group, 29–30; meets with
   Panikkar, 18; on Nixon-Sato
   communiqué, 63; plans initial Korean
   War movements, 13–16; POW conun-
   drum proposal by, 52–53; rejects Indian
   proposal, 51; summit meetings with
   Nixon, 66
Zhu De, 68
Zhu Dehai, 101
Zhu Liang, 112